Sleeping Through the Night

SLEEPING THROUGH THE NIGHT

How Infants, Toddlers, And Their Parents Can Get A Good Night's Sleep

Jodi A. Mindell, Ph.D.

St. Joseph's University
Allegheny University of the Health Sciences
MCP-Hahnemann School of Medicine

HarperPerennial
A Division of HarperCollinsPublishers

HarperCollins books may be purchased for educational, business, or sales promotional use. For information, please write to: Special Markets Department, HarperCollins Publishers, Inc., 10 East 53rd Street, New York, New York 10022.

FIRST EDITION

Designed by Elina D. Nudelman

Library of Congress Cataloging-in-Publication Data

Mindell, Jodi A.
   Sleeping through the night : how infants, toddlers, and their parents can get a good night's sleep / Jodi A. Mindell.
     p. cm.
   Includes index.
   ISBN 0-06-273409-1
   1. Infants—Sleep. 2. Children—Sleep. 3. Sleep disorders in children—Popular works.   I. Title.
RJ506.S55M54   1997
618.92'8498—dc21   96-39372

99 00 01 ❖/RRD 10

To my husband, Scott

Contents

Acknowledgments   ix

Part One: Introduction

1   "Help, My Baby Won't Sleep!": An Introduction
to Sleep and Sleep Problems   1

2   What Is Sleep?: Basics of Sleep   11

3   "Please Be Good": Managing Behavior   27

Part Two: Establishing Good Sleep Habits

4   "To Sleep, Perchance to Dream": Getting
Through the First Few Months   47

5   Bedrooms, Bedtimes, and Bedtime Routines   63

6   Bedtime Struggles and Night Wakings   79

7 "What Do I Do If . . . ?": Coping with Difficult
   Situations   111

8 "Am I Doing the Right Thing?": How to Cope   136

9 It's Off to Grandma's House We Go: Obstacles
   to Continued Good Sleep   158

Part Three: Other Common Sleep Problems

10 Snoring and Snorting: Sleep Apnea   183

11 Babies Who Go Bump in the Night:
   Parasomnias   202

12 Mumbling and Grumbling: More Common
   Sleep Problems   220

**Part Four: "What About Me?": Adult Sleep
and Sleep Problems**

13 "Now, I Can't Sleep!": Adult Sleep   235

14 "I'm So Tired": Common Adult
   Sleep Disorders   251

Appendices

A Baby Bedtime Books   277

B Resources for Parents   281

Index   287

Acknowledgments

I wish to thank all the families and friends who shared their stories with me, and all of the babies who are now sleeping through the night.

Special thanks are extended to Dr. V. Mark Durand for sparking my interest in children's sleep; Dr. Mary A. Carskadon, who has been a great supporter of my work in pediatric sleep disorders and who has taught me so much; and to the staff at the Sleep Disorders Center at Allegheny University of the Health Sciences, especially Dr. June M. Fry and Dr. Rochelle Goldberg for their wisdom and endless knowledge about sleep and sleep disorders.

Finally, my deepest appreciation to those who have supported this project from the very beginning: Dr. Irwin W. Mindell, who started me on the path to writing this book; my agent, Carol Mann, and my editor, Robert Kaplan, for their enthusiasm for this project; and, most important, to my husband and best friend, Dr. Scott P. McRobert, for his unwavering support and humor, as well as endless hours of advice and editing. I couldn't have done this book without him.

This book contains advice and information regarding the use of various prescription drugs that are used to help both children and adults sleep. This information, however, is not intended to replace medical advice from your pediatrician or physician, and it is recommended that you consult a physician before taking any such medications.

Part One

Introduction

✳

Chapter 1

"HELP, MY BABY WON'T SLEEP!"
An Introduction to Sleep and Sleep Problems

--------- ⌐ ---------

Susan's daughter, Elisa, has never slept through the night. She falls asleep sometime between 7:30 and 10:00, sleeps for a few hours, then wakes up and begins crying. In order to fall back asleep, Elisa needs Susan to rock her. This pattern has been repeated every single night at least twice a night since Elisa came home, nineteen months ago. One Tuesday night a few weeks ago Elisa slept from 10:00 P.M. until 5:30 A.M. According to Susan, "It was a miracle." Susan and her husband are both at their wit's end. They have fought frequently about this problem, and at this point they are both too tired to function, let alone enjoy being parents.

--------- ✳ ---------

Right after "Is it a boy or a girl?" and "What is her name?" the next question that veteran parents ask is "Is she sleeping through the night?" The above scenario describes the situation faced by many parents of infants and toddlers. Study after

1

study has shown that approximately 25 percent of all young children experience some type of sleep problem. Most of the time these problems are related to getting to sleep and then sleeping through the night.

Sleep, or the lack thereof, is a critical aspect of childrearing. Good babies sleep. Most babies don't. As long as you get enough sleep, a parent can deal with just about anything during the day. However, when it is 4:00 in the morning and you have just been awakened for the third time and are facing a screaming baby, all sanity goes out the window. It would try anybody's patience. What parents resort to is even more incredible. Many parents, as they are circling the block in their car at 3:30 in the morning wearing only their pajamas and mismatching socks, with their baby sleeping peacefully in the car seat, try to imagine how they are going to explain this behavior if pulled over by a police officer.

Sleep—What Is It?

Everyone sleeps. Humans sleep, toads sleep, monkeys sleep, dogs sleep, and whales sleep. Perhaps all species sleep. But, surprisingly, we know very little about sleep. Although sleep researchers understand the mechanisms of sleep and what happens to the brain and body when we do sleep, we still do not know why we sleep. What is sleep's function? No one knows. Some believe it is a restorative function. Others believe that it is for energy conservation. And even others believe that it is adaptive, that it enhances survival. We do know that everyone has to sleep. People cannot function without it. The body craves sleep if too much time has gone by without it. People also don't feel like themselves if they haven't gotten enough sleep. So while we are not exactly sure what it is, we know that we all need to sleep.

One aspect of sleep that is well understood is that many people have sleep disorders. Approximately 25 percent to 30 percent of adults have some type of sleep problem, whether it is insomnia, sleepwalking, or just too little sleep. Babies and toddlers also have sleep problems. Some are quite serious, such as sleep apnea, whereas most are just difficult to deal with, such as bedtime problems or frequent night wakings.

Since sleep is a natural process, we must all know how to sleep. However, good sleeping habits must be developed. And sleep, especially falling asleep, involves a number of behaviors. These behaviors are what become problematic for many babies and toddlers. Babies learn to fall asleep in specific circumstances, such as being rocked, lying in a crib, or being pushed in a carriage. It is these specific circumstances that may or may not lead to a baby's sleep problems; that is, many babies develop good sleep habits, whereas other babies develop poor sleep habits. These issues will be addressed more thoroughly throughout this book.

Why Doesn't My Baby Sleep?

As discussed above, sleep problems in young children are much more common than you may think. Every study has consistently shown that between 25 percent and 30 percent of infants and toddlers have some type of sleep disturbance. That is a large number of children. If you put ten infants in a room, three or four of them will have some difficulty sleeping, which means that you are certainly not alone if you have problems with your baby's sleep.

Of course, if the other six or seven babies in the room sleep fine, then you may ask yourself, Why does my child have a problem? First of all, and most important, it seems there is a biological predisposition to having sleep problems. This means that some babies are more susceptible to sleep problems. Some babies start sleeping through the night within weeks of coming home from the hospital and never have a sleep problem. Others never seem to get a good night's sleep. Thus, some babies seem to be "sleepers" and some babies are not. Some babies have more difficulty learning to fall asleep, are more easily aroused from sleep, and are more sensitive to changes in routines that affect their sleep patterns. I once heard a parent joke that when she ordered her next baby, she was going to check the "sleeper" box. Many parents feel that way.

Some parents blame themselves for their child's sleep problems. Some believe that if they just hadn't rocked him to sleep as an infant, he would be fine. Others feel that they let their child sleep in bed with them for too long, and that is what caused all their baby's problems. And, unfortunately, the truth is that parents often do play a role in their child's sleep problems. They may have inadvertently maintained the poor sleep habits that contributed to their child's sleep problems. But a baby's sleep problems are not entirely the parents' fault. The baby also contributes. Many babies are rocked or nursed to sleep, and sleep fine. They go to sleep quickly and don't wake during the night. It is apparent, then, that the same parenting behavior can lead to sleep problems in some babies and not in others. Parents therefore need to change their behavior only if their baby has a problem sleeping through the night.

Predictors of Sleep Problems

In addition to a biological predisposition, there are certain things that make a child at risk for sleep problems. Being "at risk" means that a higher percent of these children will develop a sleep problem. Below are a number of things that can contribute to a baby having a sleep problem.

Firstborn. Firstborns are more at risk for sleep problems. Why? Probably because parents are more anxious with their first child. This is their first time at parenting, and they are usually more concerned about whether they are doing it right or wrong. They tend to be much less tolerant of their child's cries and have more time to devote to their first child. They also find it easier to take the time to get up and rock the baby back to sleep in the middle of the night. Later, when the family is larger, it seems more important to set a definitive bedtime. When it is bedtime, everyone goes to bed. There are no ifs, ands, or buts about it. And it is rare to have the luxury of rocking later-born children to sleep or nursing them to sleep when you are trying to get everyone into pajamas with teeth brushed and so on.

Sex. Boys are more likely to develop a sleep problem than girls. We do not know exactly why that is, but overall boys are more at risk for many things. For example, boys are more at risk to die of SIDS (sudden infant death syndrome), are more at risk to be hyperactive, and are more likely to develop some illnesses. It also seems that parents treat boys differently. Studies show that parents are less likely to be consistent in the way they treat boys. While parents are likely to respond to a girl baby the same way every time, they are more likely to change their responses to a boy baby. For example, when Mark's baby, Adam, cries after falling down, sometimes he picks him up but other times he ignores him and lets him try to stand up again on his own. If Adam was a girl, studies show that Mark would be more likely to always pick her up or to always ignore her. No one knows why parents differ in their behavior in this way, but this type of inconsistency can lead to sleep problems.

Colic or ear infections. Children with colic or frequent ear infections are much more likely to have sleep problems. These babies have sleep problems primarily because they get into the bad habit of waking during the night when they aren't feeling well. Then, even when they are feeling better, they may still wake during the night and have difficulty returning to sleep without parental intervention. For the parents, it is difficult to determine whether their baby is still in pain from an ear infection or is just having problems sleeping.

Same bed or room. Studies have shown that almost all children who sleep in the same bed or in the same room as their parents wake during the night. Chapter 5 explains why this happens.

Breast-feeding. Breast-fed babies are also more likely to take longer to sleep through the night. One study found that 52 percent of breast-fed infants, but only 20 percent of bottle-fed infants, wake during the night. A complete discussion on breast-feeding and sleep can be found in Chapter 7.

Foods. In rare instances foods may be related to sleep problems. For example, milk intolerance may be related to persistent sleeplessness. Some infants with milk intolerance take longer to fall asleep at bedtime, sleep fewer hours, and have more night wakings. Since milk intolerance happens in so few children, it should be suspected only when all the usual causes of sleeplessness have been excluded. Many people believe, however, that the eating of solid foods by infants affects sleep. This is not true. Infants who eat solid foods do not sleep any better than those who do not eat solid foods. Sleeping for longer periods at a stretch is caused by maturation, not changes in diet.

Major changes. Major changes, such as going on a trip, a death in the family, a parent returning to work, an illness, or even a major developmental change, can bring on sleep problems even in babies who were always good sleepers.

Awake or asleep? Studies show that infants who fall asleep in their cribs are much less likely to wake during the night than infants who are put in their cribs already asleep. If your baby is falling asleep before you put her in her crib, she is much less likely to sleep through the night.

Is It a Sleep Problem or Is It a Sleep Disorder?

One question that parents need to ask themselves when faced with a baby who is not sleeping well is whether the problem is a behavioral problem or an indication of a more serious sleep disorder that has an underlying physiological basis. The likelihood is that it is simply a sleep problem that can be behaviorally managed. But in rare cases an underlying sleep disorder may be the cause of your child's not sleeping through the night. But even if there is an underlying sleep disrupter, there is often an additional behavioral component. For example, if your child is waking at night because of sleep apnea, she should still be able to put herself back to sleep with no help from you. If she needs

Does Your Child Have a Sleep Disorder?

How do you know if your child has a sleep disorder? Answer true or false to the following statements:

1. My child snores.
2. My child is a noisy breather.
3. My child breathes through his/her mouth when sleeping.
4. My child often chokes or coughs during the night.
5. My child sweats a lot during the night.
6. My child appears extremely confused when s/he awakens during the night.
7. My child rocks to sleep or bangs his/her head when falling asleep.
8. My child looks terrified when s/he awakens during the night.
9. My child seems to kick his/her legs in a rhythmic fashion when s/he sleeps.
10. My child is a very restless sleeper.

If you answered yes to any of these questions, be sure to read about the different sleep disorders that are described in Chapters 10, 11, and 12. If your child seems to have the signs and symptoms of any of these sleep disorders, be sure to discuss the problem with your pediatrician.

you in the middle of the night, she probably also has a sleep problem in addition to the sleep disorder of sleep apnea.

Is It an Environmental Problem?

Another factor that you should consider is whether your child's sleep problems are caused by something in your child's environment. Is your child too cold or too hot during the night? Are loud noises disturbing your child's sleep? Are there spooky shadows on the wall caused by the night-light? Try to clear away the things in your child's bedroom environment that may be causing her problems sleeping. If the sleep problems persist, then it is time to look into alternative explanations, namely behavioral issues.

Sleep Problems Persist

You will often hear, "Oh, it is just a stage," or, "He'll grow out of it." This is usually not true for sleep problems. Babies and young children simply do not grow out of most sleep problems. Several studies have found that babies who don't sleep become toddlers who don't sleep and then young children who don't sleep. One study found that 84 percent of children who had sleep problems at a young age continued to have problems three years later. Not only do sleep problems continue, but they seem to be one of the most persistent behavioral problems. Studies that looked at many different behavioral problems found that sleep issues were much more likely to persist than other issues, such as temper tantrums or problems with eating. This means that if your child has a sleep problem, you should not ignore it. Do something about it now rather than have to deal with it later. It is much easier to deal with sleep problems when your child is an infant and in a crib than later when she is big enough to jump out of a crib or is in a bed. The younger your child is, the easier it will be to teach her to sleep through the night because the bad sleep habits are less ingrained. But if your child is a bit older, do not despair. She can be taught to sleep through the night; it will just take a bit more effort.

The Benefits of Sleeping Through the Night

Sleeping through the night helps babies. Babies who sleep through the night are more rested, happier, and less cranky during the day than babies who don't sleep. There aren't any definitive studies that support these conclusions, but many parents comment on the changes they have seen when their baby began to sleep through the night.

Sleeping through the night also helps families. Several studies have observed the impact of children's sleep problems on families and the subsequent improvements after the baby is sleeping through the night. More than one marriage has been saved with the onset of a sleeping baby. Parents feel better; they feel better about themselves as parents and are able to function better once the baby is sleeping. In addition, parents enjoy their children more. After a night of pleading, arguing, and power struggles to get a child to sleep, it is difficult to be enthusiastic about seeing the child in the morning. Having a child who sleeps through the night makes for happier and better parents.

What Will Be Covered in This Book

This book provides practical techniques and tips on how to get infants and toddlers to sleep through the night. The book is geared toward parents of young children, from infancy through 3½ years. Included are steps on how to get babies to fall asleep and sleep through the night, as well as answers to commonly asked questions.

This book, designed for parents who need a user-friendly method to get their child to sleep through the night, addresses the practicalities of life. For instance, this method takes into account parental guilt and the everyday problems that can undo sleep training, such as illness, travel, breast-feeding, toilet training, and baby-sitters—anything outside the normal routine. This book will help you adjust to and cope with the unexpected, and it will help you succeed in teaching your baby to sleep through the night. The book is organized into four sections:

Part one (Chapters 1 through 3) includes an introduction to sleep and sleep problems in babies, a basic overview of sleep, and a general review of basic parenting skills and behavior management strategies to be used with infants and toddlers.

Part two (Chapters 4 through 9) helps parents deal with those first few newborn months and prescribes ways for parents to get their infant or toddler to sleep through the night. Implementing the suggestions provided, sleep problems will quickly resolve and your baby will be sleeping through the night within one to two weeks. Common problems that parents encounter are addressed, and coping strategies on how to deal with these issues are recommended.

Part three (Chapters 10 through 12) introduces other common sleep problems of which parents should be aware, such as sleep apnea, parasomnias, and nightmares.

Part four (Chapters 13 and 14) includes a brief discussion regarding adult sleep and ways in which parents can sleep better themselves.

Chapter 2

WHAT IS SLEEP?
Basics of Sleep

───────────────── ☾ ───

"Is my baby getting enough sleep?"

☾

"When should my one-year-old stop taking morning naps?"

───────────── ✳ ─────

Information about the basics of sleep will help you understand your child's sleep and will be useful when implementing the procedures outlined later for helping your baby sleep through the night.

Stages of Sleep

Sleep is primarily two major states, non-REM and REM. REM stands for rapid-eye-movement sleep. The stages of sleep, as described here, are typical of the sleep of adults. How sleep is different in young children will be discussed later.

Non-REM Sleep

Non-REM sleep is comprised of four stages, each with its own distinct features.

Stage one. Stage one sleep occurs when you feel drowsy and start to fall asleep. If the phone rings or something else wakes you, you may not even realize that you have been asleep. Stage one lasts for the first thirty seconds to five minutes of sleep.

Stage two. During stage two sleep, your body moves into a deeper state of sleep. You can still be easily wakened, but you are clearly asleep. The stage two period lasts from ten to forty-five minutes.

Sometimes during stage two sleep a person will awaken with a sudden jerk. This is quite normal. This startling event is actually the result of REM intrusion, meaning that your body has entered REM sleep at the wrong time. The sudden muscle paralysis and onset of dreaming, which are key features of REM sleep, cause you to feel as if you are falling. People who suddenly awaken like this often remember dreaming that they were falling off a cliff or out of an airplane.

Stages three and four. Stages three and four, known as "deep sleep," are the deepest stages of sleep and a time during which your body experiences the most positive and restorative effects of sleep. A person in either of these two stages has regular, steady breathing and heart rate. For some people, sweating is common during these stages of sleep. You may find that your baby sweats so much that she is soaking wet. This is normal. It is also difficult to be awakened from deep sleep. You may not hear a phone ringing or someone calling your name. When people sleep through earthquakes or major storms, it is because they are in deep sleep. If you do get awakened from deep sleep, you will often be confused, and it will take you a few minutes to respond. Following the first deep sleep period of anywhere from a few minutes to an hour, there is a return to stage two sleep prior to the first REM period.

REM Sleep

REM sleep is distinctly different from non-REM sleep. REM sleep is when you dream. REM sleep is also a very active type of sleep. Both your breathing and heart rate become irregular, although no sweating occurs. The majority of your body, other than the normal functioning of your organs, becomes paralyzed, and all of your muscles become extremely relaxed. Your eyes dart back and forth under your eyelids, hence the term rapid-eye-movement sleep. Some people also experience minor twitching of their hands, legs, or face during REM sleep. (This is sometimes very obvious; you can observe it by watching your dog or cat during REM sleep.) And men sometimes get erections during REM sleep.

Sleep Cycles

Sleep in adults typically occurs in ninety-minute cycles. The first ninety minutes is all non-REM sleep. After ninety minutes, a period of REM sleep will occur, followed by a return to non-REM sleep. After that, about every ninety minutes a REM period will occur. The first REM periods of the night are quite short, lasting just a few minutes. As the night goes on, REM periods increase in length. By early morning much of sleep is REM. This is the reason you are likely to be dreaming when you awaken in the morning. This is also the reason that men may wake with an erection. If you are sleep deprived, the first REM period will be earlier in the night, after only thirty or forty minutes, and more REM sleep will occur. This is the reason your dreams may be much more vivid the first night that you get a good night's sleep after losing sleep. People who are sleep deprived will also have more stages three and four sleep on nights they are catching up on their sleep.

It is not true that sleep is logical and that one stage of sleep always follows the next. During sleep, the body will move from one stage to another, not necessarily in any particular order or in any logical fashion. In general, your body will cycle sequentially through all the stages of sleep, but not always. Some nights you may never have any stage three or four sleep. Other nights you will have a great deal.

Structure of Sleep in Infants and Young Children

Like everything else that changes as you grow, sleep changes too. Sleep in infants is dramatically different from sleep in adults. In fact, sleep in infants is quite different from sleep in children and adolescents. Infant sleep patterns begin to develop in the uterus, before birth. A fetus of six or seven months' gestation experiences REM sleep, with non-REM sleep beginning shortly afterward. By the end of the eighth month of gestation, sleep patterns are well established.

The Early Months

Active versus quiet sleep. Instead of discussing REM and non-REM sleep, as is done with adults, researchers classify the sleep of a newborn infant as either active or quiet. During active (REM) sleep, infants are quite mobile. They may move their arms or legs, cry or whimper, and their eyes may be partly open. Their breathing is irregular, and their eyes may dart back and forth under their eyelids. During quiet (non-REM) sleep, infants are behaviorally quiescent. Their breathing is regular, and they lie very still. They may, however, have an occasional startle response or make sucking movements with their mouths. The quiet (non-REM) sleep in infants does not have the four stages of non-REM sleep seen in adults. It is not until about six months that babies develop the four distinct stages of non-REM sleep.

In addition, an infant's sleep is different in structure from that of adults. For example, about 50 percent of the sleep of newborns is active (REM) sleep, whereas REM constitutes only about 20–25 percent of adult sleep. As in adults, active (REM) sleep is cyclical, but in comparison to the ninety-minute cycle of adults, infant cycles are sixty minutes. Also, infants may immediately have an active (REM) period upon falling asleep, which is unusual for adults to experience.

Quiet (non-REM) sleep in infants is also different from non-REM sleep in adults. First, as mentioned above, infants do not have the characteristic four stages experienced by adults. Also, quiet (non-REM) sleep accounts for a smaller proportion of total sleep time—50 percent in infants but almost 75 percent in adults. These differences in infants' and adults' sleep patterns, as to both type and structure, quickly dissipate. By three months of age the sleep stages of infants begin to resemble those of adults. For example, short bursts of rapid brain activity, known as "stage two spindle activity," occurs by three or four months. Also, another aspect of sleep, "spontaneous K complexes," which are characterized by large, slow brain waves during sleep, develops at six months. Other changes include a decrease in REM sleep and an increase in non-REM sleep so that by six months of age REM sleep accounts for 30 percent of the time sleeping and non-REM for 70 percent of the time—more like adult sleep.

Babies are not quiet sleepers. As anyone who has watched a baby sleep knows, babies are not quiet sleepers. Babies' sleep is not as quiet as you would expect. Many babies sigh in their sleep. Babies will smile, sigh, squeak, coo, moan, groan, and whimper in their sleep. Toddlers and young children will do similar things while sleeping. They will sigh, talk, mumble, and grumble. It is all perfectly normal. Do not worry that your child is not getting good solid sleep if he seems to be active during sleep.

Later Months

By six months of age the full spectrum of non-REM and REM sleep occurs. However, the percentage of time spent in each stage is still different from that in adults, as is the length of the sleep cycle. Not until your child is three or four years old will her sleep resemble an adult's sleep. Young children continue to spend more time in REM sleep, and during non-REM sleep they go into deep, stage four sleep faster. For example, if your child falls asleep in the car, she may be in deep sleep within ten minutes. Upon arriving home you can bring her in the house, change her, and put her to bed without her ever stirring.

After about an hour of deep sleep, your child will typically have a brief arousal. Most children will simply move or grimace briefly. Other children will have a more pronounced arousal, even to the point of sleepwalking or having a sleep terror (see Chapter 11 for a full description). After this arousal, your child will return to deep sleep. An arousal may also happen after a period of REM sleep, but it will be very different. During this type of arousal your child will be awake and alert, as always occurs after waking from REM sleep. This will be the time of night when your child may call out to you because he needs you to help him go back to sleep. These are normal night wakings. They are only problematic if your baby can't go back to sleep on his own. You may then need to rock or nurse him back to sleep. Dealing with these types of night wakings is covered in Chapter 6.

Sleep Patterns

Another difference between infants' sleep and adults' sleep is how their sleep patterns are organized. Infants have polyphasic sleep periods, meaning that they have many sleep periods throughout the day. This pattern is unlike adults who typically have only one sleep period lasting about eight hours (although there are many adults who continue to nap). In the beginning, your baby will be sleeping in two- to four-hour blocks throughout the day. By six weeks of age your baby will begin to have a clear diurnal/nocturnal sleep pattern; that is, your baby will begin to be awake more during the day and sleep more at night.

As she gets older, your baby's sleep will begin to consolidate—she will begin to sleep fewer times throughout the day but for longer periods.

Finally, it is important to understand that every infant displays a unique sleeping pattern. The information presented here provides broad generalizations drawn from the behavior of hundreds of infants. However, your child's sleep pattern may very well be different. Some newborns sleep through the night immediately, whereas the sleep of others does not consolidate for several months. In all ways, the sleep patterns of infants are as different and varied as those seen in adults.

Napping

Although almost all babies nap, it may take a number of months before your baby establishes a napping schedule. By four months of age most children are taking either two or three naps per day. By six months most children (nearly 90 percent) are taking only two naps per day, a morning nap and an afternoon nap, usually at set times. By about fifteen months some babies are beginning to give up their morning nap, and almost all children take only one nap per day by the age of two years. Most toddlers continue to nap until they are three years old, with many children starting to give up naps after their third birthday. Not until a child is between three and five years old will all sleep occur at one time: during the night. Remember, though, every child is different. Some children will stop napping as young as two, while others continue to need a nap until they are six.

Surprisingly, the time of day in which the nap occurs affects the type of sleep involved in the nap. Early naps, occurring mid-morning, have more active (REM) sleep, and afternoon naps have more quiet (non-REM) sleep. Thus, naps at different times of day are actually different. What's more, naps are very beneficial. Children who nap have longer attention spans and are less fussy than their non-napping counterparts. Some parents, concerned about their child's nighttime sleeping habits, try to get their child to sleep more at night by depriving their child of a daytime nap. This is not effective and may in fact be detrimental since children need naps. Also, evidence shows that keeping children up during the day does not help them sleep more at night. Rather, nap sleep and nighttime sleep are independent of each other, and restricting daytime sleep does not lead to better sleep at night. And for younger children, eliminating naps can backfire because the more overtired a child becomes, the more difficulty he will have going to sleep at night.

Also, research has shown that children who sleep well during naptimes also sleep well at night. Both are necessary for babies to function at their best. After age five, though, eliminating afternoon naps can help get your child to bed earlier in the evening.

It is best to have your child nap in the same place that she sleeps at night, that is on days that she is napping at home. In this way sleep will be strongly associated with her crib or bed, which is important to help your child sleep through the night. Napping on the couch or in the car may also cause naps to be shorter because your child will be awakened by the activities of others or when the car stops. A set naptime in a set place will ensure that your child gets the proper sleep that she needs. The best times for naps are mid to late morning for morning naps and early afternoon for afternoon naps. Don't let your child sleep past 3:00 or 4:00 in the afternoon, or else he will have a difficult time falling asleep at bedtime. At least four hours should elapse between the end of an afternoon nap and bedtime.

If your child is watched by a caregiver during the day, whether at home or in another setting, make naptimes consistent. Try to have your child nap at the same time every day, no matter who is caring for her. Also, discuss with your caregiver the latest time for your child to sleep in the afternoon so that your child can fall asleep easily at an appropriate time at night.

How can you tell if your child is ready to give up naps? Your child still needs to nap if he is slow to wake in the morning, seems tired during the day, or gets cranky in the afternoon. Your child is likely ready to give up naps if he often doesn't fall asleep at naptime or takes a long time to fall asleep at bedtime. On days that your child does not nap, if he does not appear tired and does not become cranky or irritable, it is likely that he is ready to give up naps.

Naps are good not only for your baby but also for you if you are at home with her. They are often the way to maintain your sanity: You can have a few minutes of peace and quiet to play with your other children, do some household chores, call a friend, watch your favorite soap opera, or take a nap yourself. Therefore, when your child is ready to give up naps, they can be replaced with "quiet time"—watching a video, playing a quiet game. One way that Katie's mother dealt with this change is by having her daughter have quiet time in a playpen in the living room rather than putting her in her crib in the bedroom. Katie had lots of toys to play with and learned that this was quiet time. To help with the transition to quiet time, Katie was put in her playpen for progressively longer times, beginning with five minutes and working up to forty-five minutes. Katie's mother enjoyed the peace and quiet, and Katie learned to play by herself. This concept of learning to play alone is an important skill that your child needs to acquire. Your child needs to learn how to entertain herself and be on her own. This will be important as she gets older, especially when she starts school and is required to work on her own.

Waking During the Night

An important aspect of sleep is waking during the night. Everyone does it—babies wake, children wake, adolescents wake, and adults wake. The important thing to know is that waking during the night is a normal part of sleep, and it always happens. Many people, though, don't even know that they do it. They may wake for anywhere from a few seconds to a couple of minutes, and return immediately to sleep. The human body is programmed to do this. In fact, studies show that a person has to be awake for at least five minutes to be aware of waking. So if you remember waking up last night, then you know that you must have been up for at least five minutes.

What causes problems is when you don't fall instantly back to sleep after waking during the night. And for most infants this isn't a problem. They fall back asleep on their own after waking at night. These infants are called "self-soothers." Most parents of self-soothers never even know their baby was awake several times during the night. On the other hand, infants known as "signalers" cannot return to sleep on their own after waking during the night. Parents of "signalers" know when their baby is awake at night. These babies need help falling back to sleep—and they signal this need by crying.

At one month of age about two-thirds of babies are waking more than once per night and signaling their parents. By six months of age most infants have "settled"; that is, they are sleeping through most of the night (to the relief of many parents), having normal wakings but returning to sleep on their own. Only about 15 percent of infants wake more than once per night. However, for some reason that at this time is unclear, this problem becomes more prevalent (up to 40 percent) in babies between the ages of six and nine months.

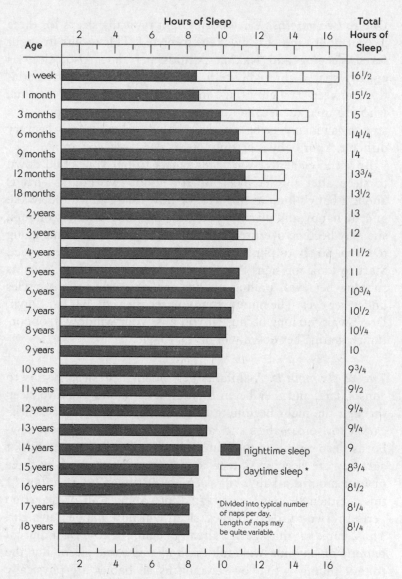

Typical Sleep Requirements in Childhood

Age	Hours of Sleep	Total Hours of Sleep
1 week		16½
1 month		15½
3 months		15
6 months		14¼
9 months		14
12 months		13¾
18 months		13½
2 years		13
3 years		12
4 years		11½
5 years		11
6 years		10¾
7 years		10½
8 years		10¼
9 years		10
10 years		9¾
11 years		9½
12 years		9¼
13 years		9¼
14 years		9
15 years		8¾
16 years		8½
17 years		8¼
18 years		8¼

■ nighttime sleep
☐ daytime sleep *

*Divided into typical number of naps per day. Length of naps may be quite variable.

Pulling It All Together—by Age

One to two months. A newborn infant typically sleeps for three to four hours and only awakens to be fed. This results in about seven sleeping and waking periods per day. Also, sleep is equally spaced throughout the day, with no clear differentiation between daylight hours and nighttime hours. For parents, who are used to sleeping anywhere from six to ten hours at a stretch, suddenly being on their baby's schedule can be very difficult. Your baby is getting lots of sleep, but you aren't.

By six to eight weeks of age, expect to put your child down to sleep after she has been up for about two hours. That is about a baby's limit at this age for how long she will be awake and be happy and alert. If you wait too long after two hours, she may become overtired and have a more difficult time going to sleep. So try to put her down to sleep before she gets upset. Start to look for signs that your baby is getting tired, such as rubbing her eyes, pulling on her ear, or getting slight circles under her eyes. The minute that you see the sign, put her down. Don't wait too long because if you miss your window of opportunity, getting her down will be a struggle.

Two to six months. As infants get older, their sleep begins to consolidate, and they begin to sleep less. Babies begin to sleep through the night beginning around eight weeks. This will be earlier for some babies and later for others. While typical newborns sleep seventeen to eighteen hours a day, by one month of age they are sleeping sixteen to seventeen hours, and by three or four months a baby will sleep about fifteen hours a day. At this age their sleep is consolidated into about four or five sleep periods. Two-thirds of babies' sleep will now happen at night. Thus, babies at this age are already beginning to have a diurnal pattern of daytime wakefulness and nighttime sleep. But the rule of thumb is that by six months all babies are physically capable of sleeping through the night, with most being able to do so at a younger age.

Six to nine months. At six months infants have fewer daytime sleep periods, and they sleep progressively longer at night. Whereas newborn infants sleep almost three-fourths of the time, six-month-olds sleep a little over one-half of the time, for about fourteen hours per day. At this age the longest sustained daily sleep period is about seven hours. Many of these children wake for brief periods during the night but can put themselves back to sleep. Thus, many parents who assume their child is sleeping for periods of ten to twelve hours continuously may be inaccurate in their assessment. Their child may actually be waking for brief periods of time without disrupting anyone.

When your baby is between six and nine months, she may begin to have sleep problems even if she has never had them before. These sleep problems usually coincide with cognitive and motor development, not with a growth spurt. Parents who think their baby is going through a growth spurt often decide their baby is waking during the night because she is hungry. This is not true. You should not start feeding her during the night. You will just prolong the sleep problem and make it worse. Your baby can get all the nutrition she needs during the day. If your baby is going to bed between 8:00 and 9:00 P.M. and all of a sudden she begins to waken during the night, you'll find that, surprisingly, she's much more likely to sleep through the night if you move her bedtime earlier by a half-hour. It really works. Try it.

Nine to twelve months. By now your baby is getting ten to twelve hours of sleep at night and napping twice a day. Be sure to keep to a regular nap schedule. Once naps start slipping, a common event with children this age, nighttime sleep can become problematic. You may begin to have more problems getting your baby to sleep at night, and she may start waking again. When a routine nap schedule is regained, nighttime sleep problems often disappear. And babies this age definitely need two naps a day.

Twelve to eighteen months. At one year your baby is probably still taking two naps per day. By eighteen months, however, most babies have given up their morning nap and are napping only once a day for one and a half to two hours. Some babies do continue morning naps until the age of two, so don't force your baby into a once-a-day nap schedule because you think that she is too old for it. There will probably be a period of time when one nap is too little and two naps are too much. There are different ways to deal with this transition time. One choice is to alternate one-nap and two-nap days, depending on the prior night's sleep. Another alternative is to put your child to bed earlier in the evening on one-nap days.

Pillows

"When should I give my baby a pillow? She always likes to use one when she is on my bed or the couch. I just don't know whether to put one in her crib."

There are no hard-and-fast rules as to when to give your child a pillow. Pillows are not recommended for children under two years of age because they can easily smother. If you give your child a pillow while he is still in his crib, give him one that is small, the size of an airline pillow. Make sure that it is not too soft and squishy. A feather pillow is not recommended, again because of concerns about smothering. Many parents give their child their first pillow when they move them from a crib to a bed. It just seems that a bed should have a pillow. You should remember, however, that your child doesn't need to have a pillow at this time. Use your own judgment and give him a pillow when you are both ready.

Eighteen months to two years. Most eighteen-month-olds are sleeping ten to twelve hours at night and taking one afternoon nap. Some holdouts continue to take two naps per day, and don't worry if your child is one of them. Relish your continued peace and quiet.

Two to three years. By two years the sleep of toddlers has decreased to a total of about twelve hours in a twenty-four-hour period, with most children continuing to take a nap in the afternoon. Most toddlers are going to bed between 7:00 and 9:00 P.M. and waking between 6:30 and 8:00 A.M. During this age span, most children move from a crib to a bed. Two- to three-year-olds often start developing other sleep issues. Many start to have fears—of the dark, of monsters, or of being separated from you. These fears are common and are part of normal development. Ways to deal with these common fears are discussed in Chapter 12. Some children also start to resist bedtime at this age, while others get out of their crib or bed at night. These issues are discussed in Chapters 5 and 6.

Three to six years. Older children are not a focus of this book but will be discussed here so you know what to expect. At these ages most children are still going to sleep between 7:00 and 9:00 at night and waking between 6:30 and 8:00 in the morning. These children are therefore sleeping about ten to twelve hours per day, with most sleep occurring at nighttime. Some three- and four-year-olds are still taking afternoon naps, but most children give up their naps by the age of five. Don't force your child to give up naps too early because of nursery school schedules or other planned activities. Some children need their naps, and you will pay the price if you ignore this need. If your child was a good sleeper, he probably still is, and it is rare for new sleep problems to develop after age three. Children of this age are excellent at stalling bedtime, however, and have learned to ask for another drink of water, to tell you just one more time that they love you, or to need to go potty incessantly.

Getting Enough Sleep

Make sure that your baby gets plenty of sleep! Even if it is not a priority for you, sleep should be a priority for your baby. Babies need lots of sleep. Although we don't know the exact purpose of sleep, we know that it is important. We also know that it is vital for babies. Development is dependent on sleep. Without it, your baby will not develop as he should.

As part of the plan to ensure that your baby gets plenty of sleep, a reasonable bedtime is essential. Most babies and children, from the age of three months until at least ten years, need at least ten to twelve hours of uninterrupted sleep at night. Your baby should therefore be in bed by 8:00 or 8:30. Most children can even go to bed by 7:30. If you are keeping your baby up late at night because you work during the day and you are also waking him early to get him to day care, he is not going to get enough sleep. Don't deny your baby what he needs based on your needs or your schedule. Part of being a good parent is ensuring your child's well-being. Getting adequate sleep is part of that well-being.

Reminders

- Sleep is comprised of two major states, non-REM and REM sleep.

- Infant sleep patterns, which are different from the patterns of adults, begin to develop before birth.

- Newborns sleep many times throughout the day, but by six months most babies have a predictable sleep pattern consisting of a long night's sleep plus a morning and afternoon nap.

- Naps are important and are independent of nighttime sleep.

- All babies wake during the night. By the age of six months, however, self-soothers can return to sleep on their own while signalers need help to fall back to sleep.

- Babies need lots of sleep for proper development.

Chapter 3

"PLEASE BE GOOD"
Managing Behavior

———————————— ☾ ————————————

Theresa often gets frustrated with her son, Andrew. Everyone tells her that it is just the "terrible twos," but this doesn't make her feel better. She can't get Andrew to stay still for anything, he is always hitting and biting the other children at day care, and she can't leave him alone for a moment because he inevitably breaks something. She feels that she spends all her time with Andrew pleading with him to "please be good."

———————————— ✳ ————————————

Before you can begin to implement the suggestions made in this book, you need to understand the basic principles of behavior management. The concepts discussed in this chapter are universal to all behavior problems, whether it is refusing to lie down for diaper changes, throwing food, or having temper tantrums in grocery stores. These concepts are also applicable to sleep issues. Sleep problems and the behaviors surrounding sleep are not uniquely different from other behavioral problems with which parents must deal. Sleep issues are just a bit more complex. This chapter addresses the ways to get babies and toddlers to do what you want and how to stop them from doing what you don't want.

When you think about modifying your child's behavior, you want to focus on increasing good behavior and decreasing bad behavior. If you think of it this way, you will keep in mind your ultimate goal: having a well-behaved child. Your role is to be a parent, not a disciplinarian or a judge and jury. Parenting means teaching your child right from wrong, teaching him how to be good and how not to be bad.

Get Your Child to Do What You Want

There are many ways to get your child to do what you want. A number of tried-and-true methods are provided here:

Reinforcement

Reinforcement, otherwise known as rewards, is the best way to get your child to do what you want. Reinforcement increases good behavior. Praise your child for doing the right thing, whether that is eating properly with a fork or being quiet in the library. Don't feel awkward or embarrassed to do this, even in public places. Reinforcement will help your child to know right from wrong. Reinforcement works.

What does your child like? It may sound easy to reward a child, but every child likes something different. You need to figure out what it is that your child likes and what he doesn't like. What is fun and exciting for one child can be scary and upsetting for another. Does your child like her feet tickled, or would she rather play peekaboo? Your child may have a favorite toy or favorite sound that you make that always makes her laugh. Some children love to roughhouse and be thrown up in the air.

Others will become scared and will instantly cry. Some children love to cuddle. You'll need to spend some time simply observing your child. What does she like? What gets her excited?

You will have noticed differences between babies, beginning at a very young age, in terms of what they like. Some parents find that a swing is their savior. Their child blissfully zones out the moment he is put in the swing. Other parents find that a swing is a waste of money. Their child just cries every time he is put in it. When your child is young, it can be easier to distinguish what he likes and what he doesn't like. As a newborn, he will have basically two states. One involves crying when he doesn't like something, and the other involves being calm when he does like something.

As your child gets older, his responses to things become more complex, and whether he likes or dislikes something will be more difficult to distinguish. You must spend time with your child in order to learn what he does and does not enjoy.

Praise. There is a lot to be said for praise. Praise is a highly effective behavior management tool. We don't spend nearly enough time giving praise. Think about how happy it makes you when someone tells you that you look good or appreciates something you have done. And people often complain that their partners don't say nearly enough nice things about them. So don't short shrift your child. Take the time to tell him he is good. Mention his good points. Tell him how proud you are of him.

Some argue that you are spoiling your child if you praise him too much. Others say not to praise a child or give him a treat for doing something that he should be doing anyway, such as cleaning up his room or behaving at the dinner table. There is no such thing as too much praise or too much love. Your child will prosper when encouraged to do the right thing.

Spend time. Another excellent way to teach your child how to behave is to spend time with him to demonstrate appropriate behavior. For example, coloring together will show him an acceptable behavior. Also, during your time together, comment on what he is doing. While playing with blocks together say, "Wow! You put the blue block on top of the yellow block." Again, this is a way of showing him that you approve of what he is doing.

Treats (otherwise known as bribery). Bribery gets bad press. But at times it can be worthwhile to bribe your child. "If you clean up your toys, we can play outside." "If you are quiet in the store, we'll go get pizza." Now, the important thing about using bribery is to give your child the treat only if he really did what he was supposed to do. Going to get pizza even if he misbehaved in the store will teach him that no matter what he does, he gets what he wants. That is not the way it works in the real world, and it shouldn't be the way it works in your child's world.

When establishing positive consequences for behavior, your child's appropriate behavior must be clearly spelled out. "Be good" doesn't mean much to a child. Rather, "stay with Daddy," "be quiet," or "don't touch anything" is much clearer. "Get ready for school" is not specific enough. It is better to tell your child the specific things that need to be done, such as, "get dressed," "eat breakfast," "get your book bag," or "put on your coat."

The consequences should also fit the behavior. In the work world, you would never get paid $10,000 for walking down the hall to mail some letters. On the other hand, you wouldn't get $5 for working forty hours. The same should be true for your child. Small behaviors should get small rewards, and big behaviors should get big rewards. You can also establish short-term goals and long-term goals. The general rule is the younger the child, the shorter the goal; that is, for young children, little time should pass between the good behavior and getting rewarded. For using the potty each time, give your child a treat. After a week of using the potty consistently, get her that toy she wants.

Do the same thing for other behaviors. Establish daily and weekly goals.

Give Acceptable Choices

Young children have little control over their lives. They eat when they are told to eat, sleep when they are told to sleep, and go for a ride when they are told to get in the car. But young children, like most people, also like to have some control over their lives. So whenever possible, give your child choices. Of course, only give him choices that are acceptable to you. Rather than asking, "Do you want to go to bed now?" ask, "Do you want to go to bed now or in five minutes?" This way your child feels that he has some control, and you get your child to bed. "Do you want carrots or peas?" ensures that your child eats some type of vegetable.

Don't Ask Questions When You Don't Mean It

Don't ask a question when you really mean to give a command. Questions allow your child to say no. Think about it. "Do you want to put your toys away?" "Do you want to take a nap?" If you are a child, the obvious answer is no. You then have no choice but to give in to your child's response or give a command. When your child really doesn't have a choice, don't provide him with one. Give requests as requests, not as questions.

Make Reasonable Rules and Requests

Another downfall for parents is setting unreasonable rules. Unreasonable rules are difficult or impossible to follow. Reasonable rules take an appropriate amount of time and are doable. A reasonable rule for a one-year-old would be to put his teddy bear on a chair. It takes little time and can be done by a child of that age. A reasonable rule for a two-and-a-half-year-old would be to get his shoes. An unreasonable rule for a two-year-old is to go upstairs, pick out clothes, get dressed, and brush his teeth. This request is likely to be beyond the capabilities of a child that age. It also has too many imbedded requests. By the time your child gets upstairs, he may not be able to remember all the other things that need to be done. Overwhelmed, he will sit down to play. You will be angry when, ten minutes later, you find him playing contentedly with his trucks. He is not being disobedient; it was just that the request was too much for him.

Your rules should also be absolutely clear, as mentioned earlier. "Clean up your room" is not clear. Does this mean put all the toys away, or does it mean to dust all the furniture? Also, what you think is clean and what your child thinks is clean are probably two very different things. A better rule is to "put all your toys in the toy box." It is clear, and everyone will know if it has been done. Being told to "be good" when walking in a store is not clear. What in the world does "being good" mean? Rather, tell your child, "I want you to be quiet, hold on to my hand, and not touch anything while we are in the store." Your child will now know what is expected of him, and it is clear what he is supposed to do.

Have Few Rules

Expect to be tested. Children will test most requests made of them. They will make sure that this is a real rule about which you will be consistent. There are many ways that children test rules. They will break the rule, break part of the rule, argue, plead, cry, scream, or have a temper tantrum. They are not doing this to be belligerent. They are doing this to make sure that the rule stands. Once you expect a child to test you, you will be much better prepared for it and will not feel that it is a personal attack.

It is therefore best to have few rules. If you were to keep count in a day how many times you gave your child commands, you would be astounded. Between your child testing the rules and your not having enough energy to follow through on every command, it is impossible to expect your child to be perfectly behaved all the time. Thus, the answer is to give as few commands as possible. The best place to start is with one rule for yourself: Don't have rules for every single problem. It just won't work.

Stop Your Child from Doing What You Don't Want

Much of the time you will be focusing on how to get your child to stop doing something that you don't like, whether that is getting out of his car seat or hitting another child. This section talks about how to change your child from behaving badly to being well-behaved. First, though, a discussion on punishment is important because this is often the first choice made by many parents when faced with a misbehaving child.

Punishment

The first reaction of most parents is to punish their children when they do something wrong. This punishment can be yelling, taking away privileges, spanking, or sending the child to his room. At that particular moment, punishment seems like the right solution to the problem, but it typically doesn't work in the long run.

Punishment rarely works. Punishment is not very effective in changing children's behavior—or anyone's behavior for that matter. Think about yourself and punishment. Imagine yourself driving down the highway. The speed limit is fifty-five miles per hour. All the cars around you seem to be going sixty-five miles per hour or more. Why do they do this? Everyone knows that there is a strong likelihood of getting a ticket and being fined large amounts. That doesn't seem to deter speeding. Imagine yourself now driving sixty-five miles per hour. You just passed Exit 11, and you get pulled over by a police officer and are given a ticket for $120. After much grumbling, you pay it. Will you speed again? Sure you will, but likely not right at Exit 11 again. That is how people behave. If they do change their behavior following punishment, it is usually specific to those particular circumstances.

Punishment doesn't teach appropriate behavior. You may have come to the startling realization that your child doesn't know anything, and you are the one who has to teach him everything. You have to teach him to dress himself, how to make a phone call, how to behave in a library, and so on. It can be quite daunting. Punishment will only teach him what not to do; it doesn't teach what to do. Randy realized this when he was dealing with his daughter, Melissa, who was coloring on the furniture. The first time he caught her coloring on the table, he yelled at her. The next time, Melissa colored on the kitchen counter. He took her crayons away for the afternoon. Later, when Melissa then colored on the wall, he sent her to sit in the "naughty chair." Obviously, Melissa wasn't getting the message. Punishment wasn't working. Melissa needed to be taught that coloring should be done only on paper. As obvious as that may be to an adult, it may not be that obvious to a three-year-old. Melissa needed to be taught exactly what was the right thing to do.

Spanking doesn't usually work. Punishment that involves spanking or hitting is even less effective. Often spanking or hitting is done in response to your child doing something truly bad, such as biting or hitting. By spanking your child for this behavior, you have taught him that hitting is sometimes okay and that hitting is an effective way to stop someone from doing something you don't like. You are simply modeling a behavior that you don't want your child to do. Imagine the confusion: You are spanking your child and saying that he shouldn't hit anyone else. Your child will learn more by your actions than by your words.

Punishment rarely lasts. Another disadvantage to punishment is that it only works in the short run. Punishment is not a long-term solution. It may be effective for a few minutes or for the afternoon, but it won't change your child's behavior the next day or the next week. This is because punishment doesn't teach your child a correct replacement behavior.

Don't use your child's crib, bed, or bedroom for punishment. A mistake that many parents make is to put a child in his crib or room as a consequence of bad behavior. This is not good because you don't want your child to associate his crib or bed with punishment. Your child's crib is obviously an easy place to put him when he is being bad. It puts him in time-out, gets him away from you, and ensures that he will be safe. Unfortunately, it can lead to more sleep problems. Your child will think that he is being punished when you put him to bed at night.

Instead, you should have a special place, such as a "naughty chair" or a certain room, when he is acting up. Some parents have found it effective to set up a playpen in another room. This way they have a safe place to put a misbehaving child that is not his crib.

Saying No

Saying no can be hard for parents to do, but it is something they must do often. Some ways to say no are better than others. First of all, when you say no, mean it. Say it in a firm voice and follow through. Second, be calm. The calmer you are, the more your child will know that you mean it. If you lose control, your child will lose control. And, lastly, as mentioned several times, be consistent. If you say no the first and second time, be sure to say no the ninth time.

When telling your child she did something wrong, always be sure to comment on your child's behavior, not on her character. Be sure you make clear that you are upset that your daughter threw her cup, not that you think she is a bad person. Don't tell her, "You are bad." Tell her, "Don't throw your cup." Be sure to tell her that what she did was bad, not that she is bad. Telling your child that she is bad, lazy, worthless, or stupid can have many negative consequences. First of all, and most important, it affects a child's self-esteem. A child's evaluation of himself depends in large part on what his parents think: If Mom or Dad thinks I am bad, then I must be bad (or lazy or stupid). Children need as much confidence as they can get to do well in life. Another reason that this tactic doesn't work is that it will become a self-fulfilling prophecy. If you tell your child that she is lazy, why should she bother to put her toys away? In her mind it is not going to change your opinion of her. Also, a child will feel that she can't change something that is part of who she is, but she can change her behavior. So let your child know that you are frustrated because she gets dressed so slowly, not that she is slow.

Ignoring

Ignoring bad behavior is a powerful tool. Much bad behavior is done to get your attention. If the end result is to get your attention, then change the consequences. Ignore the behavior instead.

Think about what frequently happens when a parent is on the phone. The parent is talking to someone else and not paying any attention to the child. This is a time when many children act up. Why do they act up? To get the parent's attention. Imagine yourself in that situation. The phone rings. You go to answer it, leaving your child playing quietly with her building blocks. It is your close friend whom you haven't spoken to in days. You settle in to hear her latest story when you hear a huge crash from the next room. You tell your friend to hold on and go to see what happened. Your daughter has pulled all the videotapes off the shelf. You put her back near her blocks and tell her that you are on the phone and that she needs to play quietly. You go back to the phone, and your friend continues her story. Within a minute you hear another crash and a thunk. You tell your friend that you'd better go and save your belongings, and you'll call her back later. Upon entering the living room again you see that your daughter has pulled all the books off the shelf, too. You yell at her and sit down on the floor to help pick up the books and videos.

What has your child just learned from this situation? She has learned that if she misbehaves, you will get off the phone. If she had continued to be good, sitting quietly and playing with blocks, you would have remained on the phone, ignoring her. She got what she wanted: your attention. And you had to stop doing what you were doing.

In many situations the correct response is to ignore your child's bad behavior. Ignoring the bad behavior will make it go away. In psychological terms this is called extinction. It works. Obviously, you cannot ignore your child's behavior if she is putting herself in danger or is about to destroy something. In those cases you must get her or your belongings out of harm's way and then go back to ignoring her. She'll get the message.

You must also understand, however, that when you start to ignore a behavior, the behavior will often get worse before it gets better. This is your child's way of saying "I mean it. Pay attention to me!" If you persist, your efforts will be rewarded. So if your child is singing loudly to get your attention while you are talking to someone else, ignore it. You can take a moment and tell him that it would make you happy if he stopped, but go right back to your conversation. When the singing doesn't work, your child will stop. Then praise him for stopping the singing. Ignoring bad behavior can be difficult to do, but it will pay off in the long run.

Time-out

Time-out is a highly effective method for managing your child's behavior. Time-out involves placing your child someplace where he must sit quietly for a few moments after he has misbehaved. This can be a very good way to deal with your child's bad behavior while remaining calm yourself. A child's being sent to his room or being made to sit on the stairs or being put in a chair are all forms of time-out. And though it may seem to be a type of punishment, it is not the same as being yelled at or being spanked. Plus, it can be done almost anywhere.

Time-out sounds a bit easier than it actually is. With a little practice, however, you will become very good at it. Here are some useful tips for implementing time-out and making it work:

How long? The general rule of thumb is that a child should be in time-out one minute for every year of age. So a two-year-old should be in time-out for two minutes, a three-year-old for three minutes, and so forth.

Where? One of the biggest problems for parents is finding a place to put their child for time-out. The best place is a time-out chair or "naughty chair" that is not an enjoyable place to be. This chair shouldn't be placed in front of the television or in a place where your child can play with toys. Don't put your child into her bedroom for time-out. There are too many fun things to do in there, and you don't want her associating her bedroom with being punished. Having your child sit on the stairs is okay if your child will stay there. Some parents put their child in the bathroom. Bad idea. I have heard horror stories about children stuffing things down the toilet or causing the sink to overflow while in time-out. Many children have also locked themselves in the bathroom, either intentionally or by accident. Also, don't put your child anyplace where she can cause major destruction, such as next to the bookcase where she can pull every book off the shelves. And don't put your child anywhere that is dangerous. For example, don't put her in the laundry room if there is a possibility that she can drink any caustic fluid. It is best to put your child in a chair someplace where you can keep an eye on her.

Set a timer. Another mistake that parents sometimes make is forgetting that their child is in time-out. Set a timer. This will remind you and also helps your child know when time-out is over. When the bell goes off, she knows that she can get up. It may even be best to use a digital timer, like the one on a microwave, so your child can see the time counting down.

Pick your battles. You will drive yourself crazy if you try to put your child in time-out for every single thing she does wrong. You cannot expect your child to be perfect. She can't be perfect—no one can. She doesn't know all the rules, and she can't follow every one of them all the time. So pick your battles and decide what is really important to you. Your list should include only a few major issues. Follow through on those and ignore the rest. What you will want to put on your list is any behavior that leads to your child being in danger, hurting himself or someone else, or destroying property. Once you choose bad behaviors that lead to time-out, be consistent in your efforts and always follow through.

Staying in time-out. One of the most difficult aspects of time-out is making your child stay. It is important that she stays there the entire time. Having a child struggle against time-out and then giving up and letting her go will defeat the entire purpose, and the next time that you warn her that she will be put in time-out, she will not take you seriously. It will become an idle threat. But how do you keep your child there? It is easiest if your time-out is in a naughty chair. If she gets out, put her right back in. Be consistent and keep your cool. The calmer you are, the more likely that your child will calm down. If she sees you getting out of control, she will become more upset. If your child is persistent, there are two simple ways to keep her sitting. One way is to stand behind her and push down on her shoulders. You only need to do this when she tries to get up. When she is sitting calmly, you can keep your hands resting lightly on her shoulders. The other way to do it also involves standing behind her. Cross her arms over her chest and hold her hands lightly. She will not be able to stand up.

Don't engage in prolonged conversation. Many parents spend too much time explaining to their child why their behavior was wrong. Many children find this reinforcing, and they may misbehave to get your attention. So be careful about giving your child too much attention for doing something wrong by engaging in a prolonged conversation.

Don't let time-out be fun. Children can have fun and make a game of things almost anywhere. Time-out shouldn't be fun. Your child shouldn't be allowed to bring any toys with her into time-out. She shouldn't be allowed to watch television. One parent talked about having to take her child's shoes and socks off while in time-out because she would take them off, swing them around, and basically have fun. After a few times of losing her shoes and socks, she stopped playing and sat quietly.

She is still screaming and crying. Don't let your child out of time-out if she is screaming and crying. Let your child out of time-out only when she is quiet, and only after the timer goes off. If she is screaming, inform her in a calm tone that she can get up when she is quiet. If you let her up while she is screaming, you will be reinforcing your child's screaming behavior.

Don't reset the timer; just let her know that the moment she is quiet, she can get up. This doesn't mean that if she is quiet from the start she can get up right away. She has to wait for the timer to go off first.

Your child still has to follow directions. If you are putting your child in time-out because you asked her to do something and she didn't, such as putting away toys or getting dressed, make sure she does what you originally asked after time-out is over. This will ensure that time-out is not being used as a means of escape. If she never has to do what you requested, your child will be saying to herself, "I don't want to put my toys away, so I'll just go into time-out for three minutes." Time-out should not be a way for your child to escape doing what she is told to do.

Other Basics of Managing Behavior

Be Consistent

The key to changing behavior is being consistent. Once you decide to focus on a behavior that you want to change, you need to follow through each and every time. The reason for being consistent can be explained using two psychological terms, consistent reinforcement and partial reinforcement. Consistent reinforcement involves getting something every time that you perform a certain behavior. On the other hand, partial reinforcement is getting something only sometimes. Surprisingly, partial reinforcement makes bad behaviors persist much longer. Think of playing a slot machine. If you win every time you put a quarter in a slot machine, you will continue to play. Now imagine that you won five times in a row. On the sixth, seventh, and eighth try, however, nothing happened. You would realize that the machine has stopped paying out when you play. You would leave or at least move to another machine. Now think of the slot machine that has a partial reinforcement schedule. The first time you get nothing. The second time you win two quarters. The third, fourth, and fifth time you win nothing. The seventh time you win seven quarters. The eighth time nothing. The ninth time twenty quarters. The tenth nothing. Are you going to keep playing? You sure are! This is because you hope and expect that if you keep persisting, you will win again. Not winning on this machine every time doesn't mean anything. There is always hope. You didn't have any hope with the first machine because not winning anything meant something. (And don't think that casinos don't understand these principles and use them! Unfortunately, in the long run you will lose money at the slot machines, but by using a partial reinforcement schedule, they will have you playing for a longer time.)

The same principles are true for parenting. You can be a slot machine that is consistent, or you can be a slot machine that provides partial reinforcement. The parent who uses partial reinforcement, or partial punishment, is going to have a child who may be a behavioral problem. The child knows that his parent may or may not follow through. It is worth nagging or throwing a temper tantrum because it could pay off. The parent who uses consistent reinforcement, or consistent punishment, will have a child who is better behaved. In this case, the child knows the consequences for his behavior and knows that his parent is going to follow through. That is why being consistent is so important. It doesn't mean that your child can never have a special unexpected treat or won't get away with something once in a while. It just lets everyone know what is expected and what will happen if misbehavior occurs.

The grocery store syndrome is an excellent example of the trap of partial reinforcement that parents fall into and why bad behavior often persists. Imagine the following scenario. It is one that we have all seen, and one that we all dread.

A mother is wheeling a grocery cart through a grocery store with her three-year-old seated in the front of the cart. She is hoping that she will be able to make it through the grocery store without mishap. She has a smile pasted on her face and is trying to engage her child in light banter, trying to distract him from all the junk food on the aisle shelves. She has successfully made it to the front of the grocery store and is now on line for the cashier. Her child spots the candy bars near the cash register. (Do they put them there to torture parents?) He points to the M&Ms and asks for them. She says no. He points again. She says no. He starts whining. She says no. He starts crying. She says no. He starts crying as if his life depends on it. She says no. He starts screaming as if he is getting beaten. She looks around at everyone staring at her. She hands him the M&Ms. He smiles, wipes his eyes, and happily starts munching on his candy.

———————— ✳ ————————

What has happened in this scenario, and why is it so easy for us to imagine it and cringe? Everyone has seen this happen again and again, possibly with our own children. And it is likely that this same scene has happened with this same mother and child before. This is just another example of the powers of partial reinforcement. By giving in when he got really cranked up, the mother has just taught him to scream. The more persistent he is, the more likely it is that he is going to get that candy bar.

The same is true when it involves sleep. If you decide to put your child in his crib at bedtime and rescue him a half-hour later because he is crying, you will simply teach him to cry. The next time he will cry even more. The message is to follow through and be consistent. Remember the issue of partial reinforcement, and remember that it leads to increased persistence of bad behavior.

The Soggy Potato Chip Theory

There is another theory that has been nicknamed the soggy potato chip theory. This theory states that a soggy potato chip is better than no potato chip at all. How does this relate to managing your child's behavior? Well, the corollary to this theory is that bad attention is better than no attention at all. To your child, attention from you is often the most important thing in her world. The best attention is obviously good attention (praise, spending time together, going for a walk), but the next best thing is bad attention. Bad attention is getting yelled at or being told not to do something. In your child's mind, if she has been playing quietly for the past hour and being ignored, she may choose to misbehave. Why? Because staying quiet means that you will continue to ignore her, but spilling her juice is likely to get your attention. She may get scolded and have to clean it up, but it still will get your attention.

Rather than putting your child into this bind—"Would I rather get no attention or bad attention?"—do the opposite, which means that you should "catch 'em being good." Catch 'em being good means paying attention to your child when she is being good. If she gets your attention for playing quietly, putting her toys away, or eating without spilling, there will be no reason for her to misbehave. If you respond to her positively for being good, she won't need to have you respond to her negatively for being bad.

Some parents respond to this advice by saying, "But when I respond to her when she is playing quietly, she inevitably acts up." Patricia noticed that this happened when her son, Joseph, was playing by himself with his toy cars. If she went in and talked to him about how well he was playing, he became aware of her presence and demanded that she play with him. If she didn't disturb him, he would continue to play quietly on his own, and she could get things done around the house. She had gotten to the point where she hated to disturb him because it would make him more demanding.

At first this may be a problem, with your child becoming more demanding of you. To deal with this, be calm and firm. Tell him you must do something else, but continue to praise him for being good. In time he will realize that your praise doesn't always mean you can stay and play. He will keep playing on his own, and the praise will reinforce his good behavior.

Reminders

- Focus on increasing good behavior and decreasing bad behavior.

- Reinforcement is the best way to get your child to do what you want.

- Provide acceptable choices.

- Don't ask questions when you intend to give commands.

- Make reasonable rules.

- Punishment is not a very effective way to change your child's behavior.

- Ignoring bad behavior and implementing time-out are excellent ways to stop your child from doing what you don't want.

- The key to changing behavior is being consistent.

- Sleep is similar to any other behavior; you can manage it just like any other behavior.

✳

Part Two

Chapter **4**

"TO SLEEP, PERCHANCE TO DREAM"
Getting Through the First Few Months

———— ❊ ————

Jill and David brought their new baby, Craig, home when he was six days old. Craig had stayed in the hospital after Jill was released because he was jaundiced. Jill and David were thrilled to finally have him home. In the hospital Craig had been an easygoing baby, seeming to cry less than the other babies in the nursery. The first few days at home went well. Jill's mother helped during the day, and David helped at night. But then everything changed. Craig got fussy. He seemed to cry all the time, and Jill had no idea what to do. When he wasn't crying, he was sleeping. He slept for much of the afternoon, which was a relief to Jill, but then he was up and crying from the moment David got home until everyone collapsed at 11:00 at night. At 2:00 in the morning it all started again, with Craig up and crying. Jill and David were at their wit's end. Was being a parent always going to be like this?

———— ✳ ————

The first days and weeks at home with a newborn can be overwhelming. All babies cry, and it always seem to be at the worst times, whether it is early evening or the middle of the night. And although everyone claims that newborns sleep for sixteen to eighteen hours a day, no one seems to get any sleep. How can that be? Although your baby is sleeping so many hours, it is only in two-to-four-hour chunks of time. So your desire for an uninterrupted block of six to eight hours of sleep simply won't happen. In the meantime, try to get *some* sleep and remember: "This too will pass."

Getting Through the First Six Weeks

The first six weeks with a new baby can be extremely difficult. This is especially true with your first baby because everything is new and different, and you will have a great deal to learn about the day-to-day basics of taking care of a baby. It is also true with later children because you have to deal with balancing the needs of your newborn with the demands of your other children. It is all relative. Many parents with a firstborn are overwhelmed by the demands of a newborn. On the other hand, parents who have more than one child often comment on how they didn't realize how easy they had had it when they had only one child.

The difficulties of dealing with a newborn are compounded by the parents' lack of sleep. Mothers often comment that the small amount of sleep they got during their last weeks of pregnancy, when they were waking on an hourly basis, seemed like heaven compared to the demands of a round-the-clock newborn.

The best thing you can do is nap when your baby naps, if possible. If the baby naps for an hour at 11:00 in the morning, you should, too. Another idea is to hire a baby-sitter for your older child or children. Or you might treat your other children to a day away with their favorite person. And forget about returning all those phone calls that you have never gotten to. You should sleep. It will make you a happier person and a better parent. Other suggestions include screening your calls with an answering machine and discouraging drop-in visitors. Your friends and family will eventually have plenty of time with the baby. Make arrangements to get help. Getting a reprieve for even a half-hour will make a large difference in your sanity.

While it is important to simply get through those first few weeks with a newborn, be sure to savor the moments. Babies grow so fast, and your baby will never be this small again. The time goes by quickly, and the next thing you know, your newborn has become a toddler and is no longer a tiny baby. As much as time may feel as if it is dragging during those first few weeks when you're pacing the floor with a crying newborn, you will realize later when you look back how fast the time really went.

Dealing with a Nighttime Baby

Some babies are night owls. They just don't seem to understand that they are supposed to be active during the day and quiet at night. In fact, during the day, things seem so easy. Your baby sleeps much of the time, wakes to feed, plays a little, and goes back to sleep. During the night, however, she seems to turn into a monster. She's awake and fussy, and nothing seems to calm her down.

What can you do? In the beginning, during the newborn stage, not much. You may have to become a night owl yourself, knowing that eventually things will get better. Then, when your baby is a few weeks old, there are some things that you can do to help get her clock on track. During the day, play with her as much as you can. Even if she seems to be sleeeping soundly, wake her for feedings. Keep the shades open in her room and don't try to stay quiet all the time. Be your usual noisy self. Don't turn the ringer off the phone or avoid turning on the dishwasher. This will also help ensure that your baby doesn't become the lightest sleeper in the world and force you to spend the next ten years of your life tiptoeing around the house when she is sleeping. During the night, play very little with her. Keep her room dark. Put on only a night-light or low light for feedings and diaper changes. Be quiet and soothing. Eventually she will learn that daytime is for fun and nighttime is for sleeping.

———————— ☾ ————————

Maria's baby was just such a night owl. After coming home from the hospital, Miguel was fussy for the first four days. On the fifth day, Miguel slept much of the day, waking only three times for feedings. Each time he woke, Maria fed him and changed him. Within ten minutes of changing him, he was back to sleep for three to four hours. Maria was elated, thinking that this was going to be easy. On the sixth day, though, she barely made it through her first sit-down dinner since having the baby before Miguel was awake and screaming. The next nine hours were a blur to Maria, with Miguel awake and fussy much of the time. At best, Miguel was asleep for twenty minutes at a time, and this pattern continued for the next nine days. Maria realized that she had to do something or she was going to lose her mind. The next day, Maria kept Miguel in a bassinet in the family room with her during the day. She turned the radio on and sang along with it. She brought Miguel into the kitchen when she prepared his bottle or got something to eat herself. Rather than putting him down right away after changing him, she held him and sang to him. She invited a friend over and encouraged her to hold and play with Miguel. That night, she put Miguel down in his crib in his room. She closed the shades and turned off the lights. When he awoke during the night, she kept him in his room and turned on only a low light. She kept her interactions with him to a minimum. After three days of keeping to this pattern, Miguel began to sleep longer at night and be more awake and alert during the day. Miguel was still fussy at night but at least he would sleep for several hours at a time.

———————— ✳ ————————

You can often predict whether your baby will be a night owl during pregnancy. If in utero your baby is active at night, she will probably be the same way after birth. If she was active during the day throughout your pregnancy, she will probably be active during the day after she's born. This will not be true for all babies, but it is a good predictor for most babies. Remember, however, that both your schedule and your baby's schedule can get turned around during labor. This is especially true if you go into labor in the middle of the night or had a very long labor.

Sleep and Breast-feeding

One of the things that may fall under the category of "no one ever told me" is that breast-fed babies typically sleep for shorter periods of time and are usually older when they finally begin to sleep through the night.

Why do breast-fed babies sleep for shorter periods? Since breast milk is much easier for babies to digest than formula, it means shorter intervals between feedings. So a baby at eight weeks may still be breast-feeding every two or three hours throughout the night, while a bottle-fed baby may be sleeping for up to seven hours a night. These trends don't hold for all babies, of course. Your baby may do the exact opposite. But as a whole, these are the likely effects of breast-feeding and bottle-feeding on your baby's sleeping pattern.

Breast-fed babies are also more likely to fall asleep while feeding and thus develop a sleep association with nursing. This means that when they wake during the night, they need to be nursed back to sleep. It is also more difficult to break this habit because the mother is so closely associated with breast-feeding. During the night the mother may have a reflexive letdown of her milk when she sees the baby. She also smells like milk. It is hard to tell a baby that nursing is not allowed when he smells the milk. Chapter 7 provides suggestions on how to deal with these issues.

Crying

Face it: Babies cry. For them, crying is a way to communicate. It is their way of telling you when they are hungry, wet, need some cuddling, or just feel grumpy. Babies don't cry just "to exercise their lungs." They always cry for a reason.

On average, babies cry for three hours per day. That is a lot of crying. But you should put your baby's crying in perspective and feel lucky if your baby cries less than this amount. If your baby cries more, think of her as a very communicative baby. It may help you to deal with the crying.

As you get to know your baby, you will begin to be able to determine what her cries mean. A whimper cry may be her way of telling you that she is bored, whereas a scream implies that something hurts. Think of different cries as different words. Each cry can have a different meaning, or a certain cry may have many meanings. It is your job to try to figure out the possibilities, a task that will get easier over time as you get to know your baby.

Babies Cry for Many Reasons

In addition to those just mentioned, there are many other reasons that babies cry, and the following are a few examples.

Pain. Obviously, babies cry when they are in pain. If nothing else works, look for anything that may be causing pain. The strip method is helpful: Strip your baby and look for anything that may be hurting. A common overlooked cause of pain is a hair that is wrapped around a finger, a toe, or some other delicate body part.

Overstimulation. Babies cry when they are overstimulated. You may have just been tickling and bouncing your baby. All of a sudden your baby goes from laughing along with you to crying. This may be the result of overstimulation. It just got to be too much for her. Loud noises, bright lights, or even too much hugging can all overcome a new baby. Having many visitors and being held by too many strangers can also be too much.

Being undressed. Some babies hate to be undressed. They start to cry and then howl as they are getting progressively undressed. It may not be because they are cold or you are inept at changing them. They just hate to be left with nothing close to their skin. The only remedy is to try to be fast when changing your child. Some find it helpful to put a cloth diaper or towel across the baby's stomach and chest when getting her undressed. This may be enough to calm her down.

Being too cold or too hot. Yes, either of these can make your baby cry. Babies often cry when they are first taken outdoors. It may not be the heat or chill per se but simply the change in temperature that makes her cry. A breeze can also upset a baby, no matter how perfect the temperature.

Ways to Respond to Crying

Here are just a few examples of things you can do to respond to your baby's cries.

Feed her. Babies cry when they are hungry. If your baby hasn't eaten in a while, then try nursing her or giving her a bottle. If she just ate, you will need to try another strategy.

Change her. Babies also cry when they are wet or have a soiled diaper. One of the first things you can do when your baby cries is to check her diaper and change her if necessary.

Sucking. Some babies simply want to suck, so try giving her a pacifier or encourage her to suck on her own fingers, and see if that calms her down. Don't always use a pacifier the minute your baby starts crying, but if you have tried everything else, a pacifier can be a real help.

Holding. Most babies love to be held. They are comforted by the physical contact. Don't worry about spoiling your baby by holding him too much. It is natural for your baby to want to be held. In many cultures babies are held all the time. They are strapped onto their mother's back or held by siblings or grandparents when parents aren't available. Studies have also shown that babies who are held more than three hours a day cry much less. So invest in a good sling or pouch and carry your baby around with you. It will be good for your baby and good for you, as your baby will be happy and content.

Rocking. Some babies find gentle motion soothing, so try rocking her, pacing with her, or putting her in a swing. Some parents find a swing a lifesaver, whereas others find it of little help. Babies seem to either love or hate swings. If your baby is a swing-lover, you are in luck.

Moving. Just like adults, babies don't like to be in the same position or look at the same thing for too long. Unfortunately, unlike adults, they can't move themselves during those first few months. So if your baby has been in the same place for a while, try changing her position or move her so that she can look at something new.

Warmth. Babies often find warmth on their tummies to be soothing. Warm a receiving blanket carefully in a microwave or use a hot-water bottle.

Soothing noises. Soothing music, such as a classical piece, or the sound of a vacuum cleaner can calm a crying baby. Tapes that make the sound of a heartbeat can also be helpful.

Vibration. Other babies like the sensation of vibration. Take your baby for a car ride or attach a vibrating machine to her crib.

A new person. After an hour or even fifteen minutes, trying to deal with a screaming baby can get to the best of us. Your baby will sense your fatigue and frustration, which will simply make her more upset. Hand your baby over to someone else. This simple act may just do the trick.

Don't worry. After spending time with your baby, you will begin to learn what your baby wants and what will make her more upset. There will also be times when you will be at your wit's end, when nothing you do seems to help your crying baby. Just remember that she is not crying for the sake of crying but because she is trying to tell you something. It is just as frustrating for her as it is for you.

Colic

Colic is a problem that every parent has heard of and dreads. Colic is defined as excessive crying that occurs during the first three months of life in an otherwise healthy infant. Typically, a colicky infant cries two and a half times more than other infants. And the crying of a colicky infant is usually unrelenting and forceful. They often draw their knees against their stomachs, flail their arms, and struggle when held. Anywhere from 10 percent to 25 percent of all newborns become colicky.

Most pediatricians use the rule of "threes" to diagnose colic. Babies who cry for three hours at a time, three days a week, for three weeks are termed colicky. Surprisingly, this may not be all that different from normal fussy crying. Remember, the average baby will cry for about three hours a day at six weeks of age, which is a lot of crying. What differentiates a baby with colic, though, is that the crying occurs all at once. Other babies may cry for a total of three hours per day, but it occurs in short spurts throughout the day.

Colic, which is usually not diagnosed until at least three or four weeks of age, peaks at six weeks of age. Then, at three months, babies with colic will seem miraculously cured.

Until he was nineteen days old, Calvin was the "perfect baby." He would cry, sleep, and eat, and in fairly predictable ways. His parents thought that he was the best baby ever—that is, until day nineteen, which started like any other day. Calvin woke twice during the early morning to feed. Then throughout the day he woke to feed, spent some time awake in his swing, and cried when he was hungry or needed to be changed. At 4:00 in the afternoon, everything changed. Calvin started screaming. He couldn't be calmed. His mother gave him a bottle, she changed him, she rocked him, she tried distracting him with his favorite toy, and she paced. She even called the pediatrician because Calvin's behavior was so unusual. By the time her husband came home at 6:00, she was frantic. They took Calvin for a drive in the car. They turned on the vacuum cleaner. They did everything humanly possible. Nothing worked. Calvin finally fell asleep from exhaustion at 8:30, after screaming uncontrollably for four and a half straight hours. Life continued this way for weeks. Calvin would be fine all day until, as his parents described it, the "witching hour struck." Without fail, Calvin would start screaming uncontrollably at about 4:00 each day.

No one is totally sure what causes colic. The word *colic* comes from the Greek word *kolikos,* the adjective of *kolon,* which means the large intestine. This term relates to the belief that colic is caused by some type of abdominal or intestinal pain. The cause of colic is unclear and may be different for individual babies. Most people claim that colic is caused by excessive gas. And most babies with colic seem to be gassy, though whether the gas is causing the colic or whether the incessant crying is causing the gas is not clear. Other causes have also been proposed, although there is little support for any of them. Some say colic is related to a milk allergy (very rare), an immature gastrointestinal tract (why then does it occur in some babies and not all?), overfeeding or underfeeding (unlikely), inappropriate handling of the infant by the parent (but colic occurs equally in first, second, and even fifth babies, so experience has nothing to do with it), or heredity (it does not run in families). Or, as is most likely, there is no real cause. The excessive crying is just an extreme variation of normal. If the average baby cries almost three hours a day, that means there are some babies who cry for only one hour and others who predictably cry for six hours.

Colic not only involves lots of crying but can also disrupt sleep. Babies with colic sleep less during the night and wake more frequently—not exactly what you need after dealing with a crying baby all day. Colicky babies are also more restless when they sleep. Their sleep is more disrupted, and they awaken more easily. During the day it is harder to predict when they will nap and for how long. So parents of babies with colic are not only sleep deprived, but it is much more difficult for them to get other things done when the baby is sleeping because it is so hard to predict their baby's behavior.

Along with not knowing the cause of colic, there is no known cure or treatment. But parents will try everything. They change their baby's diet. They change their diet if they are breast-feeding (such as eliminating caffeine, chocolate, or milk products). They change the temperature of the formula if they are bottle-feeding. Some doctors prescribe sedatives or suggest rhythmic movement, such as riding in a moving car or being placed in a moving swing. Try everything! Your attempts may not work or may only work some of the time, but doing nothing can be even more stressful.

The most important person to treat during colic is yourself. Try to get through it while maintaining your sanity. To do so, you need help. You need to get away from the situation. Take a walk. Take a break. Beg every friend you have to watch the baby for a half-hour. Put on headphones.

Unfortunately, even after the colic has resolved, sleep problems may continue. Babies whose sleep is not regular when young often continue to have disrupted sleep. The reasons for this are many. Babies who do not consolidate their sleep during the period of colic may become used to waking frequently. Because of the colic, these babies are less likely to have strategies to soothe themselves back to sleep and can be more likely to require parental attention to return to sleep. Also, it can be hard to distinguish between your baby's continuing to have the colic or simply having a sleep problem. One way to decide is to observe whether your baby has gotten over the incessant daytime crying. If she seems fine during the day, then it is likely that colic has also resolved at night.

Six Weeks to Three Months

Your baby is now six weeks old, no longer a newborn. It is time to start thinking about establishing a sleep schedule. Between the ages of six weeks and three months is also the best time to establish good sleep habits. Physiologically your baby is at the point when she is able to sleep for prolonged stretches of time. This is also one of the easiest times because your baby can't get too far. She can't climb out of her crib yet, and she has not moved to a bed. And you are probably at the point where you are ready to get more than four continuous hours of sleep.

The most important aspect of getting a baby to sleep through the night (see the next chapter for more details) is to have your baby learn to soothe herself to sleep. Babies need to be able to put themselves to sleep without your intervention. The reason is that all babies, as well as all adults, wake during the night. This is normal. What is problematic is not the nighttime wakings but the inability to return to sleep. Your baby needs to learn to soothe herself to sleep so that when she wakes for a moment in the middle of the night, she can immediately put herself back to sleep.

Sometime between six and eight weeks, start putting your baby down to sleep when she is still awake. She doesn't have to be wide awake; she can be groggy, but she can't be sound asleep. Put her down in her crib or wherever you intend for her to sleep all night. Give her something to look at. Some parents have found it helpful to save a favorite toy for sleep times. This will give your baby something to be excited about. The favorite toy can be almost anything.

───────────── ☾ ─────────────

Lisa found that her son Jason loved looking at a funny-looking stuffed animal that a friend gave them. It sort of resembled a bug and a frog at the same time. Whatever it was, Jason loved to stare at it. And this froglike bug helped Jason make the transition into sleep. Lisa would put Jason and the toy in the crib. For a few moments Jason would fuss, until he spotted the animal. Then he would just stare at it and within a few moments, he would start to zone out, eventually sucking on his fingers and falling asleep. Once Jason was able to fall asleep on his own at such a young age, he continued to be a great sleeper. Many other parents were in awe of Jason, who would go to bed at 8:00 at night, not to be heard from again until 7:00 the next morning.

───────────── ✷ ─────────────

The key to getting Jason and all babies to sleep through the night from an early age is to put them down awake!

Another choice to help make the transition into sleep easier is to hang a mirror on the side of your baby's crib so that he can look at himself. A mobile will also work, although it may not be best for you to turn it on so that it spins or plays music, since your baby will want it turned back on in the middle of the night when he awakens. It may seem like nothing to get up, turn the mobile on, and go back to sleep, especially in comparison with being up with your baby for an hour, but this will eventually get old, and you will appreciate longer stretches of unbroken sleep. So if you believe that you are setting your baby up for another bad habit, try to come up with another option.

Begin putting your baby down when he is still awake at bedtime and also at naptimes. The more practice that your baby gets putting himself to sleep, the quicker the process works. He will fall asleep on his own, and you will get the sleep that you need. Remember, however, that breast-fed babies are notorious for taking longer to fall asleep on their own and to sleep through the night. You can begin the process early, but you may not want to start until your baby is eight to ten weeks old. Don't wait too long, though. The earlier the better. Remember, once your baby gets older—that is, at least five or six months— the process of getting your child on a sleep schedule and to sleep through the night gets more difficult.

Soothing Strategies

One thing that you can do during your child's early months is help her learn to soothe herself, as mentioned above. This will make going to sleep much easier in later months. Most babies are very good at soothing themselves. It will just take some minor effort on your part to encourage this activity. And it is important to realize that there is a fine balance between responding to your child's needs and giving him the chance to soothe himself. Both are important. It is just a matter of figuring out when to intervene and when to let him be. You don't want to ignore your child's needs, but you also don't want to smother him and prevent him from developing ways to soothe himself.

Here are some suggestions to help your baby learn to soothe himself:

Sucking. Some babies find sucking on their thumb, fingers, fist, or wrist soothing. When your baby is crying, try gently placing his hand in his mouth to see if it will calm him. If you do not want to encourage your child to suck his thumb, then try another strategy.

Zoning out. Many times we try to distract a crying baby with a toy or by making faces. If you do this and your child turns away or closes his eyes, take this as a message that he needs to zone out. Let him. He may need some peace and quiet. Take the toys away and let him stare at the wall or a spot on the ceiling.

Favorite position. Some babies have a favorite position, such as on their backs, on their sides, or scrunched up against the side of the crib. Once you figure out your baby's favorite position, put him in that position when he is upset and see if it helps him calm down. Additionally, some babies are calmed by being swaddled, whereas others hate being confined.

Leave him alone. If your baby pushes you away or turns from you, he is giving you the message to leave him alone. Don't take this personally. Rather, take this as a positive sign that your baby can calm himself. Turn him away from you so that he can see something else or put him down on a blanket on the floor.

Less noise, please. Some babies simply enjoy quiet. Try turning off the music or the television. Get rid of brothers and sisters who are playing loudly. Imagine yourself in a restaurant or a store where the noise is too loud, making you feel edgy. Your baby can feel that way at times also. This is not to say that you should always be quiet around your baby, but if he is fussy, try toning it down a bit.

Reminders

- The first six weeks with a newborn can be difficult. Get sleep whenever you can.

- Babies cry, and they cry for many reasons. Crying is a baby's way of communicating. Learn what your baby's cries mean and how to respond to your crying baby's needs.

- Coping with a baby with colic is difficult, but it is manageable.

- Between the ages of six weeks and three months is the best time to establish good sleep habits and teach your baby to sleep through the night.

Chapter **5**

BEDROOMS, BEDTIMES, AND
BEDTIME ROUTINES

———————————— ☪ ————————————

*Each night around 8:00, while Zachary is quietly playing, I
begin to dread the ordeal of bedtime. By 9:30, Zachary is
overtired, and it becomes impossible to get him to bed without a fight. By the time he is finally asleep, it is 10:30, and I
am tense and exhausted. This is not the life I envisioned.*

———————————— ✳ ————————————

Set Bedtimes

As mentioned previously, one of the more important things
that you can do for your baby (after proper nutrition and lots
of love, of course) is setting a bedtime. Every night your baby
should be going to bed at about the same time. A typical baby
bedtime is between 7:00 and 8:30 at night.

Keeping your baby up past 8:30 may not be a good idea.
Babies need sleep—and lots of it. However, many parents keep
their baby up longer than they should. In fact, if you have to

struggle to get your baby to sleep, you may be more likely to keep your baby up later. This may be because you can't bear to face the sleep showdown or because you think that if you wait until your baby is tired, he will go to sleep easier and faster. Unfortunately, just the opposite happens. The more tired a baby becomes, the more wired he will be, and the more wired, the harder time he will have falling asleep. Many a parent has commented, "See, he's not tired. It is ten o'clock at night, and he is running around the living room like a banshee." Actually, that is a sign that he is extremely tired. Studies show that young children often become more active the more tired they are. So don't put off your baby's bedtime!

Another reason that some babies go to bed so late is that parents work and feel that evenings are the only time they have to spend with their child. Debbie, the mother of two-year-old Kevin, kept Kevin up until 10:00 every night. Her husband, Tony, rarely got home before 8:00 at night, and she said that if they didn't keep Kevin up late, Tony would never get to see his child. Although this may seem like a good decision for the sake of the parent-child relationship, it is not a good idea to sacrifice your child's sleep. Babies need their sleep, and it is very important to their development.

Having a set bedtime is good for a number of reasons. It helps parents know when to start the bedtime routine and reduces the chance that they will put off getting the baby to sleep. Sometimes when your two-and-a-half-year-old is playing quietly at 7:30 at night—the first time all day—it is hard to get up the nerve to announce that it is bedtime and start the ensuing battle. But putting it off will only make the entire process harder. Then everyone is tired and tempers are short, including yours.

Another important reason to have a set bedtime routine is that it will reset your baby's internal clock. Everyone has a twenty-five-hour circadian rhythm (internal clock). However, we live in a world that only has twenty-four hours a day. This means that in the absence of external cues, your body will tell you to go to bed one hour later each night of the week. Now you are wondering, how will my child ever be tired at his bedtime if his body clock is always shifting. The answer is that you must help him to train his internal clock.

As adults, we have external cues to keep our internal clocks on track. We look at the clock, we eat meals at the same time, we go to work at the same time, and we watch television shows that are shown at the same time every night. Therefore, we are tired at our usual bedtime and most people have no problem falling asleep. Since babies cannot tell time, they need their time clocks adjusted throughout the day. They have no idea what time it is and need us to tell them by our daily activities. They need to eat meals at basically the same time every day, and they need to go to bed at about the same time. This will help to reset their internal clocks to coincide with your own.

Furthermore, it is important for parents to have time to themselves at night. To be a good parent, you need time to yourself, whether that is to spend some time with your spouse, simply to zone out in front of the television, or to catch up with friends or family. This is an additional reason why an early bedtime is good for you and your baby.

Routines

Babies and children love routines and relish schedules. They like to know what is going to happen next. They are also better behaved when things are similar and follow a known pattern. In the early weeks, you will need to follow your child's schedule, but by three months at the latest, provide increasing structure to your baby's day. Have consistent mealtimes, playtimes, and sleeptimes. As you can imagine, if the times of other activities are constantly changing, sleep patterns will also be irregular. Regular routines have many positives. Routines provide your child with a sense of security, and they enable your child to have a sense of control in a world governed by adult demands. Routines also give a framework in which to learn new skills.

Routines help parents, too. They provide some sense of control and expectation of what is going to happen in a particular day. You will know what time your child will have meals and sleep. Knowing that you are going to get some free time at 1:00 during your child's naptime will help you get through a morning when you can't get anything done. It will also provide you with more patience, knowing that a break is coming. Routines also end arguments over what is going to happen next. If your children always watch a video after dinner, then there is no discussion of whether you will play outside with them when you would rather be washing the dishes and cleaning up the kitchen.

You should allow your child to help establish the daily routines. Incorporate something your child does naturally into her daily routine.

———————————— ☾ ————————————

Joanna, sixteen months, likes to put her cup in the sink after every meal. Her mother, Jennifer, encourages Joannna to do this. This daily routine helps Joanna to understand that mealtime is over and it is time to go on and do something else.

☾

Sam, age three, goes around and says goodnight to the family pets before going up to bed. It can take a while to find the family's dog and three cats, but the routine helps Sam make the transition to bedtime.

☾

Your older child can help design the routines. Paul lets his three-year-old son, Teddy, choose whether he wants to get dressed first or eat breakfast first in the morning.

———————————— ✳ ————————————

If your household is chaotic, start by adding routines to the beginning and end of the day. Start with morning time or bedtime. Make a list of what needs to get done, figure out a good order, and start there. Give yourself plenty of time. Trying to cram too much into too little time will only frustrate you and your child. For example, getting dressed and eating breakfast can take a toddler twice as long as you would like. Rather than rushing her, provide more time so that mornings can be relaxing without constant reminders to "hurry up." The same is true in the evenings, before bedtime. Use reminders to let your child know what is going to happen next. "After you brush your teeth, we'll read a bedtime story" or "After this last story, we'll go kiss Mommy good night." As you get mornings and evenings under control, start adding routines throughout the day. Have meals at the same time each day. Make set naptimes and playtimes. Your day doesn't have to be regimented, but with certain specific markers of things happening throughout the day, your entire day will go smoother, and both you and your child will be happier.

Bedtime Routines

Bedtime routines help your baby get ready to sleep through the night. And beginning these practices at a very young age, even by six to eight weeks, will help your baby to sleep and can prevent sleep problems later in life. Your bedtime routine with your baby can be just about anything that you want. There are basically only one or two essential factors that need to be incorporated. One factor is making the end of the routine calm. Another important component is having the last part of the routine occur in your child's bedroom. Many a family uses the child's bedroom only as a place to go when it is time to sleep. For the child, this can feel like a place that he gets banished to. So be sure to spend at least the last ten minutes of your child's bedtime routine in his bedroom. This will help him associate his bedroom with good feelings, a place where cuddling occurs and quality time is spent.

Bedtime routines help children learn to be sleepy at bedtime. They also help make sleep times and wake times significantly different and distinguishable for your child. Putting on special types of clothes, namely pajamas, and having certain rituals, such as taking a bath or brushing teeth, helps your child learn the distinction between daytime and nighttime.

There are many things you can integrate into your bedtime routine. For example, you can give your child a bath and change him into pajamas. If your child hates baths, though, or finds them stimulating, do them earlier in the day. Brushing teeth is always a good habit to start young (be sure to ask your pediatrician about how to do this with new baby teeth). Read a story, sing a song, play a favorite game, imagine nice dreams, or say prayers. Say the ABCs or count to twenty. Talk about what you did today and what you are going to do tomorrow. With older children, discuss any worries or concerns. Talk about what was the "best" thing that happened that day, and what was the "worst." Cuddle. Cross off the day on the calendar. Make up a story. Say silly rhymes.

Whatever your routine is, make it yours, make it special, and make it the same. Starting young with a bedtime routine helps start a tradition that will continue throughout your child's growing years. Everyone will know that this is a special time and that it involves good-quality one-on-one time. It also helps establish a safe space for your child to tell you what is happening in his life.

Be sure that the bedtime routine does not include anything scary. Don't play monsters or the "bogeyman is going to get you" right before bed. No wonder your toddler is scared to be alone in the dark and is having nightmares.

An important aspect of your child's routine is that it is the same every day. Your child will be more relaxed if she knows what is coming next. The more relaxed that she is, the more likely she will go to bed easily and fall asleep quickly. Compare these two routines for these two different children (See chart on page 69).

Clearly, you would expect that Rebecca would go to bed more easily because her bedtime routine is predictable. She

Stacey

Day 1.
Bath, pajamas, teeth, story

Day 2.
Story, bath, teeth, pajamas

Day 3.
Story, pajamas, teeth, kiss good night

Day 4.
Pajamas, teeth, song, drink of water

Rebecca

Day 1.
Bath, pajamas, story, kiss good night

Day 2.
Bath, pajamas, story, kiss good night

Day 3.
Bath, pajamas, story, kiss good night

Day 4.
Bath, pajamas, story, kiss good night

knows what to expect. Not only is Rebecca's routine the same every night, but she is also read a familiar story at bedtime. A favorite story is often better than a new story every night because it is relaxing. Save new stories for daytime hours.

Also be sure to include in your routine everything that is important and necessary. If your child is toilet-trained, then make sure that going to the bathroom is part of the routine.

Get that last drink of water in before you say good night. Make sure that everyone has gotten hugs and kisses, so there aren't any late-night calls for a hug from Daddy or a good night to the dog. If everything is included, then you will know that any requests from your child later are not necessary ones, and you will feel better about ignoring them.

Every family has their own bedtime routines and rituals, and they may change as the child gets older. It will take some time to develop your own particular routine that is enjoyable and relaxing for everyone.

———————————— ☾ ————————————

Steven works all day, often leaving in the morning before his children are even awake. For him, bedtime is his wind-down time with his two children, John, age four, and Karen, fifteen months. Since he works so late in the day, he often misses the children's dinnertime but tries to make sure that he is always home for bedtime. While his wife gives each child a bath, Steven spends some time talking and playing with each child. John loves to build things, so every night Steven helps him build a "bigger and better" tower. While building, they often talk about what happened that day, and simply connect. Karen is a cuddler. Steven usually spends lots of cuddle time with Karen and reads to her from her favorite book, Goodnight Moon. *When both children are in their pajamas, he sings silly songs to both of them. Then it is a kiss, a hug, and "Eskimo kisses" for everyone.*

☾

At one and a half, Joey always knows that the last thing before bedtime is saying ABCs and counting to ten. Joey's mother points to each letter and number on a wall hanging as she says them. Joey always looks forward to this and often asks his mother to do it again. Following the ABCs and counting, last hugs and kisses are given, and Joey goes down in his crib.

Once all teeth are brushed and pajamas are on, Susan reads to the twins, Max and Alex, age two. They are poems from Where the Sidewalk Ends. *She tries to read at least one new one every night, but Max and Alex always insist on hearing their favorites night after night. After all poems are read, Susan sings "Puff the Magic Dragon" to them while cuddling on the overstuffed chair in their bedroom. Susan has been singing this song to them every night at bedtime since they were infants.*

On days that you don't have time for the entire bedtime routine, do an abbreviated one. Sing only one song or read only one poem rather than several. If you don't do any part of the routine, though, you may pay for it because it may take your child twice as long to settle down.

The Bedtime Transition

Many a parent has heard the bedtime plea of "just five more minutes" or "I don't wanna!" Going to bed can be difficult for children. It signifies the end of a day, which is especially hard when it has been an exciting day, such as a holiday or a birthday. Many children also hate to miss anything. They may feel that all of the fun starts after they have gone to bed. Little do they know that much of what is happening is bill-paying and doing the dishes. Another reason that your child may resist going to bed is that he has a hard time with transitions.

To help alleviate bedtime resistance, there are several things that have been found to be helpful. For one, help make the transition easier for your child. Warn her. Five to ten minutes before bedtime should begin, let her know that bedtime is coming. That way she can finish the puzzle she is working on or stop the video at an appropriate place. Obviously, warning a six-month-old doesn't really matter, but by the time your child is eighteen months, it will be helpful. Starting at such a young age will also help her begin to understand the issue of time. Some parents find it helpful to set a timer at the five-minute mark. This helps alleviate the pressure on you. Hey, the timer says it is time to go to bed, not you. This can carry you for a long time before your child realizes that you are the one who set the timer.

Bedtime routines are also a great way to deal with the bedtime resistor, especially if the bedtime routine includes something that your child loves to do, such as having a designated tickle time or reading a favorite story. Bedtime routines give your child the time she needs to make the transition to going to bed.

How do you deal with a dawdler? By twelve months, your child could already be a downright dawdler. One way to deal with this problem is to extend the time you allot to getting ready for bed. This is supposed to be a calm, soothing time, not a mad rush. Hurrying your child may just make her resist more and get her so worked up that she will have a hard time settling down to fall asleep. If you know that your daughter takes twenty minutes rather than ten to get up the stairs and into her pajamas, start earlier and give her twenty minutes to get it done. This way you won't get frustrated by her being a slowpoke. Remember that she can't tell time, so if you start her bedtime routine at 7:00 rather than 7:30, she won't know the difference (unless she has a favorite TV show that comes on at 7:00).

Make getting ready for bed into a game. Play "beat the clock." Set a timer for a reasonable amount of time. If your child is ready before the timer goes off, she gets an extra story or a special treat. Have your child choose how she is going to go to bed. Is she going to walk backwards, skip, tiptoe like a mouse, or stomp like a monster? Playing such a game gives your child some control over bedtime and makes going to bed more fun.

Another idea is to use incentives. Make the last part of the bedtime routine the most enjoyable part. Don't wait to brush teeth until after stories, do it before. Sing your child's favorite song last. Get to have some playtime after putting on pajamas.

Transitional Objects

Many babies make the transition to sleep easier if they have a favorite object with them. These are called transitional objects. The object can be just about anything. For most children it is something soft and cuddly, like a teddy bear or blanket. For example, Amy, age three, had Bunny who went with her everywhere. Bunny went to the store, on car rides, and especially to bed for naptimes and bedtime. But this isn't the case for all children. Calvin's favorite thing in the world was a small hammer that he had found in his father's toolbox. Calvin wouldn't go anywhere without it, especially to bed.

Some studies have shown that incorporating a transitional object into your baby's bedtime can help your baby go to sleep on her own and sleep through the night. One study found that something reminiscent of Mom did the trick. In this study they had women wear a T-shirt all day. At night the women put the T-shirt in the crib with their baby. Amazingly, it worked. The smell of the baby's mother on the T-shirt calmed the babies and helped them fall asleep.

Sarah, a child clinical psychologist, heard about this finding and decided to try it on her twins, Steven and Samuel, who were still not sleeping through the night at four months. Susan had breast-fed her twins for the first three and a half months, wearing a nursing nightgown that had two slits so that she could nurse both twins at the same time. Since she only had this one nightgown, she wore it almost every night and sometimes even during the day in the early months. Sarah decided to take this soft flannel nightgown and cut two large squares out of the material. She placed one in each baby's crib. Miraculously, it worked. The babies instantly bonded to this well-known material that was associated with their mother. At fifteen months, Steven and Samuel still don't go anywhere without their "blankies," especially to bed.

Your baby may already have gravitated toward a favorite object. Don recalls when his daughter Stephanie fell in love with her newfound friend. Pushing Stephanie through a toy store one day, she emphatically pointed to a soft and cuddly dog. Stephanie didn't usually notice much, so Don happily handed it to her. He said it was like watching someone fall in love. She stroked it and hugged it, beaming all the while. Since that day, Stephanie won't go anywhere without "Doggie." Such a profound experience may not happen to your child, but you may find a favorite item that she finds soothing. Don't force this on your child. Some children never develop a strong association with one particular item. In fact, some children relish choosing a different item to take to bed with them every night.

No matter what it may be, a transitional object can help your child settle down so that he can fall asleep easily. The same object can also be used by your child to feel secure in new situations or to help calm him when he is upset, hurt, or angry.

Sharing a Room with Your Baby

In the first few weeks, many parents keep their babies in their bedroom, often in a bassinet or crib within arm's reach. Those first few weeks are often a blur, with little distinction between day and night. It all seems to be a long series of feedings, burpings, and diaper changes with a few stolen moments of sleep thrown in. After the constant need for frequent feedings abates, which can be anywhere from two weeks to three months, you will want to consider whether or not to move your baby to her own room. Of course, this will only be the case if you have a choice. Parents who live in one-bedroom apartments or who reside with other family members may not have this option.

There are both advantages and disadvantages to having your baby as a roommate. The advantages include continued ease in responding to your baby in the middle of the night. When your baby wants to feed or gets fussy, you won't have to get up and go to her. Some parents also find it very nice to be able to look over during the night to check on their baby and just enjoy her presence.

One of the major disadvantages of having your baby as a roommate is that it results in less sleep for everyone. The parent gets less sleep because every time the baby whimpers there is the temptation to respond to her. Basically, how can you not when she is within arm's reach? You are also likely to awaken more frequently just to check on her. Babies also get less sleep when they sleep in their parents' bedroom. Several studies have shown that all babies who share a room with their parents do not sleep through the night. This is probably because you are more likely to pick her up when she fusses, which results in less sleep for her, too. Also, your activities during the night are going to keep her up, just as hers will keep you up.

Another disadvantage is the difficulty in finally moving the baby to her own room. The longer the wait, the harder it will be. The baby will get used to sharing a room with her parents and will find it difficult to make the transition to being on her own as she becomes older. While a two- to three-week-old baby will not know the difference, a six-month-old will.

No matter what you hear and read, though, you need to do what feels right for you. If it feels right to share your room with your baby, then do so. If it doesn't, don't.

Sharing a Bed with Your Baby

Even if you have your baby in your room, you may or may not be sharing your bed with him or her. Some parents prefer co-sleeping, and there are several groups who believe that it is more natural than the typical style in our society of having babies sleep alone in their own rooms. Again, do what is right for you. Don't let others sway you in one direction or another on the decision as to where your baby should sleep.

As with sharing a room, there are a number of positive and negative aspects to it. On the positive side, some believe that co-sleeping is essential to a child's emotional development. Some argue that it is more "natural," as indicated by the high level of co-sleeping in many societies. There also has been some research showing that babies who co-sleep may be at less risk for SIDS than babies who sleep alone. The key may be that babies who co-sleep keep their breathing in tune with their parents'.

There are also several drawbacks to co-sleeping. Babies who share a bed with their parents tend to have sleep problems. They will have difficulties falling asleep at night without their parents' presence and will wake frequently during the night. This is because babies who share a bed with their parents do not learn how to fall asleep on their own, an integral aspect of sleeping through the night. Another drawback is the determination of the point at which co-sleeping should stop. At what age do you decide that your child needs to sleep on his own in his own room? Again, similar to sharing a room, the longer you wait, the more difficult the transition will be for your baby.

Safety is another concern. Although it is very unlikely that you will roll over and harm your baby, babies can be smothered by pillows and comforters or fall between the bed and the wall. Also, if your baby can fall asleep only when sharing a bed with you, you are going to have problems leaving your baby with a sitter.

Another drawback is the potential effect on your marriage or relationship. It is difficult to have an adult or private conversation when a child is sleeping in the same bed. And it is deadly to your sex life. Parents worry enough that their love-making will wake a child who is in the next room. When sharing a room with a child, it is much more of a concern. And when the baby is in the same bed, the possibility of spontaneous lovemaking goes out the window. This may be okay with one of you, but this can also cause tension between you and your partner.

It is also important to decide whether having the baby sleeping in bed with you is for the baby's sake or for your own sake. If you are a single parent or your partner is frequently out of town overnight or works the night shift, you may be continuing the co-sleeping because it is nice to have a warm, cuddly body in bed with you. On the other hand, some people encourage co-sleeping as a way to keep a barrier between themselves and their bed partner. If one of you is not interested in sex, having a baby in bed with you will keep the focus off this issue. If this is the case, it is important to communicate with your partner and not use the baby to avoid dealing with your problems. No matter what the case may be, be sure that the co-sleeping is not a way to avoid facing other issues and that it is not being done to fulfill needs of yours that should be met by other means.

Your Baby's Bedroom and Nightclothes

Many parents have questions about their baby's bedroom. Is it better to be too hot or too cold? What type of blanket should he have? Should I put an undershirt on him with his feet pajamas? Should I get him one of those sheepskin mattress pads that look so comfy?

First of all, there are no absolute right answers to any of these questions. You know your baby best and your living environment best. The rule of thumb is to dress your baby as you would dress yourself. If you would sleep with only a nightshirt and a lightweight blanket, then don't have your baby sleep with an undershirt, heavy pajamas, blanket, and comforter. Young babies do best in an undershirt and pajamas with feet. A lightweight to heavyweight blanket or comforter is appropriate, given the temperature. Babies notoriously kick off their covers but, unlike you, are unable to cover themselves again. So make sure that if your baby becomes uncovered during the night, he is dressed warmly enough to compensate.

Your baby's bedroom should be toward the cool side of comfortable. Studies have shown that people sleep best in cooler bedrooms compared to warmer bedrooms. This does not mean that you should make your baby's bedroom cold. If prior to having a baby you turned your heat way down in the house at night to conserve energy (and money!) and kept warm under numerous blankets, you will need to curtail this severe temperature change. Lower the heat a few degrees if necessary, but don't let the house get too cold. Again, use your judgment.

In terms of your baby's bedding, avoid those comfy-looking sheepskin mattress covers or down covers that go over the mattress. They may look comfortable, but they can be dangerous to your baby. In young babies, these will also increase the risk of SIDS (see Chapter 10). Babies should sleep on a firm surface, which reduces their chance of suffocating.

Reminders

- A set bedtime is important to establishing good sleep habits.

- A bedtime routine is the key to sleeping through the night.

- A transitional object, such as a teddy bear or favorite blanket, can make the transition to sleep easier for your child.

- There are advantages and disadvantages to sharing a bed or sharing a room with your baby.

Chapter **6**

BEDTIME STRUGGLES AND NIGHT WAKINGS

———————— ☪ ————————

*Every night Maryanne puts her daughter, Rachel, eleven
months, down to sleep at 7:45. After changing into pajamas and watching a video, Maryanne puts Rachel into her
crib and gives her a "binky" (pacifier) and her favorite
stuffed dog, Patches. Usually, Rachel is fast asleep within
minutes. On some nights she takes a little bit longer
because as she falls asleep, her pacifier falls out of her
mouth, waking her up. However, even after Rachel has
fallen asleep, she wakes up at least once every night,
sometimes up to three or four times. When she wakes, she
cries, looks disoriented, and sits up. Her parents go into
her room, put her binky back in her mouth, and she
instantly falls back to sleep. The whole process takes less
than five minutes.*

☪

*Bernadette begins the process of putting Robert, nineteen
months, to bed at 8:00. She is lucky if he is asleep by 9:00.*

First, Bernadette rocks Robert to sleep while sitting in a rocking chair. Once he is asleep, she tries to put him in his crib. If she doesn't wait long enough, Robert wakes up and starts to cry. When this happens, she has to start the process all over again. She has gotten to the point where she will sit with him asleep in her arms for twenty to thirty minutes for fear that if she moves she will wake him. During the night, Robert wakes at least twice. He usually wakes up screaming. Each time Bernadette has to rock him back to sleep. This can take up to thirty minutes.

☪

Samantha has tried everything. Her daughter, Roslyn, will not go to sleep at night. For the first year and a half Samantha would rock Roslyn to sleep. It was a good night if Roslyn was asleep within one hour. For the next six months she let Roslyn fall asleep in the living room, watching television. At the age of two, Samantha switched Roslyn from her crib to a bed, thinking that was the problem because Roslyn screamed every time she was put in her crib. Now, at two and a half, Samantha has to stay with Roslyn on her bed until Roslyn falls asleep. For Samantha to finally get out of Roslyn's room, she has to slither off the bed and slowly crawl across the floor, hoping that Roslyn won't wake and catch her. About two hours later, Roslyn wakes up crying and goes into her parents' bedroom. Samantha is so tired at that point that it is easier to simply let Roslyn sleep with her for the rest of the night.

Although these three children seem to have very different sleep problems, actually they all have the same underlying problem. Each child needs his parent or some other type of stimulation to fall asleep. This chapter reviews why babies and toddlers have sleep problems and how to get your baby to sleep easily and quickly and assure that he sleeps through the night.

Bedtime Struggles

There are many reasons that your child may resist going to bed at night, and there are different solutions for each one. The following is a list of the most common reasons and what to do about them.

Staying up later. Children love evening activities. They get to spend time with their parents, which is especially nice if either or both work during the day. They get to play with their brothers and sisters. They may get to watch television. In going to bed, they miss the fun. By arguing, dawdling, crying, or pleading they get to stay up later and do fun things.

Leonard and Tammy, for example, insisted that their two-year-old daughter, Mary, just wasn't tired at night. When they put her in her crib, she would stand there, holding on to the railing, crying for them. After about fifteen minutes, they would go get her, give her Oreo cookies, and let her watch cartoons with them. Why wouldn't she want to stay up if she got to watch television and eat cookies with her favorite people?

The best way to deal with this common bedtime problem is to be firm in setting limits. Have lots of fun in the evening, but bedtime is bedtime. Do not allow your child to get back out of bed once you decide it is time for her to go to sleep. If she is not tired, she can play by herself in her crib or bed. She can have her favorite toy or book. Obviously, you can put a child to bed but you can't make her sleep. Whatever you do, though, don't reinforce her for not going to sleep. Don't let her go downstairs to play or give her treats for not falling asleep. You will only prolong the problem, denying her much needed sleep and you the time that you need at night.

Getting attention. The more you argue, demand, or plead to get your child to bed the more you are reinforcing your child's bedtime resistance behavior. Don't get sucked in to giving bad attention for bad behavior. It is better to give good attention for good behavior. For a reminder of the difference between good attention and bad attention, see Chapter 3.

Many children also find it fun to get out of bed, often getting attention from you, or whoever is putting them to bed. Each time they get up, they get some extra time to spend with you, and they get to see what is going on in the house. Again, be careful not to reinforce your child for getting out of bed. In a neutral and calm manner, return your child to his own bed. Don't spend too much time doing it. Be firm and consistent. Another way to deal with these problems is to tell your child that if he is quiet and stays in bed you will come and check on him in five minutes, or three minutes, or whatever interval is appropriate. Make sure you do check on him. This way you will be providing your child with attention for engaging in good behavior. This often keeps many a wayward child in his own bed. Also, your child will often fall asleep while waiting for you to reappear.

Getting someone to stay. Another trick of the trade if you are a child is that if you appear scared or upset, often someone will stay with you. Children are smart. They know what works. If they asked you to stay with them, you will probably say no. If they appear distressed and pathetic, you will probably say yes. Don't fall into this trap. By staying with your child when he is upset or afraid, you are only reinforcing those bad behaviors. Don't continue to keep going back into your child's room or stay with him when he is crying or acting afraid. Go back in and check on him briefly when he is quiet. More suggestions on how to deal with bedtime fears are presented in Chapter 12.

Sleep associations. Another common reason for children having difficulties falling asleep at night is that they have poor sleep associations. This is usually the most common reason for infant and toddler sleep problems. The rest of this chapter will focus on what these sleep associations are and how to deal with them.

Sleep Associations

Everyone has associations with falling asleep. As adults, these associations are deeply ingrained. Sleep associations are those things or behaviors that are present when we fall asleep. For example, Scott always changes his clothes, brushes his teeth, and reads in bed for at least ten minutes before turning out the light. He always turns a fan on for the constant background noise and closes the bedroom door halfway. He sleeps on his back with two pillows and one lightweight blanket. His wife, Ellen, goes to bed later than Scott. She undresses and takes a shower before going to bed. The sound of the rushing water relaxes her and gets her sleepy. She then turns out all the lights in the house and stumbles her way to bed, being sure not to wake Scott. She removes the second pillow from her side of the bed, gets under the lightweight blanket that also covers Scott and the two extra blankets on her side of the bed, and rolls over onto her stomach.

Scott and Ellen have very different sleep associations. Scott has to read before being able to fall asleep, and Ellen showers. Each sleeps in a different position with a different number of pillows and blankets. Think about your own sleep patterns. What do you do every night before going to bed? Is it relatively the same every night? Think back to before you had children. Were your sleep associations the same then, or have they changed?

Whatever sleep associations are present for you at bedtime also need to be there for you during the night. The reason is that everyone, babies and adults alike, wakes up during the night. If the sleep association is present, you return to sleep instantly. You may notice one of these arousals if you watch someone sleep. He may roll over, change position, or simply scratch his face. He doesn't even appear to wake up. If the sleep association is not present, however, he will wake up and try to rectify the situation. If your blanket fell off the bed, you would pick it up. If the hall light was turned on after you went to sleep, you would get up, turn the light off, and go back to sleep. If you do need to get out of bed, you may be awake for a while, unable to return to sleep quickly. Many people think that they wake up because their pillow fell on the floor or the light woke them up. The opposite is true. They woke up naturally, but the pillow being gone or the light being on makes it impossible to fall back to sleep.

Babies, too, have sleep associations, either positive ones or negative ones. Positive sleep associations help babies fall asleep on their own, whether at naptime, bedtime, or during the night. Negative sleep associations are those that babies can't control on their own. They require the presence of something or someone to help them fall asleep. Think about what your baby always does or needs to fall asleep. How do you get your baby to fall asleep?

Positive Sleep Associations

Positive sleep associations are what you want your baby to have in order to help your baby fall asleep quickly and easily on his own. They should also be present when he wakes during the night. Appropriate positive sleep associations include sleeping in a certain position, sleeping with a teddy bear or favorite object, having the lights off and the door closed, or having a fan running all night. It doesn't actually matter whether a fan is running or the light is off, the important thing is having the bedroom environment constant at bedtime and throughout the night.

Negative Sleep Associations

Negative sleep associations require your presence or are things that will not be present when your baby wakes in the middle of the night. Nursing or drinking from a bottle to fall asleep is probably one of the most common negative sleep associations. You will know this is true if you need to feed her to get her to go to sleep. Do you need to feed her again when she wakes in the night in order to get her to return to sleep? Being rocked to sleep is another common sleep association that interferes with a baby's ability to self-soothe back to sleep. Being sung to, cuddled, or having music playing may be what your baby requires to fall asleep. Whatever the association, a negative one interferes with your baby's being able to fall asleep on her own.

Pacifiers can be a positive or negative sleep association, depending on the baby. They are great for some babies but problematic for others. They are a problem if your baby has a difficult time falling asleep because every time she is on the verge of sleep, her pacifier falls out of her mouth, causing her to wake up. They are also a problem if she can't find her pacifier in the middle of the night and needs you to find it for her.

What Causes Night Wakings?

Your baby waking up at night is normal. Babies (and adults) wake throughout the night. There doesn't have to be any particular reason. Waking is not the problem. The problem is that your baby can't soothe herself and fall back to sleep. Instead she needs to be rocked or nursed back to sleep, or she needs music playing or her blankets adjusted. Your goal, therefore, is to create a situation in which your baby can fall back to sleep.

In the beginning, your baby probably went back to sleep quickly once you rocked her or handed her a pacifier. Hopefully, that is still the case. But some children begin to stay awake for a longer and longer period of time each night. The reason for these prolonged wakings is that your child realizes what is happening. The moment she falls asleep, you put her back in her crib, stop nursing her, or whatever, and leave. It's easy for her to learn that when she falls asleep, you leave. So why should she fall asleep? She will now actually fight to stay awake. If you were told that the minute you fell asleep someone was going to take your pillow or blanket away, you would resist falling asleep, not wanting to lose your pillow or blanket. Your child is doing the exact same thing. She will fight falling asleep so that she will not lose her sleep association. (The same also occurs at bedtime. Why fall asleep in the comforts of the living room when all that is going to happen is that you will wake up in a dark room in a box with slats around it?)

Your baby may also seem angry in the middle of the night when she awakens. She is upset because she is tired and wants to go back to sleep. You would be angry if every night you woke up in the middle of the night and couldn't go back to sleep until someone went and got you a drink of water or straightened your blankets for you.

To put it bluntly:

If you rock your child to sleep, then every time she wakes up, including the middle of the night, she'll need to be rocked in order to go back to sleep.

If you nurse your child to sleep, every time he wakes up, he'll need to nurse in order to go back to sleep.

If you sing your child to sleep, whenever she wakes up, she'll need to have you sing in order to go back to sleep.

Thus, most babies' problems with sleep are the result of negative sleep associations. That is, your baby is unable to fall asleep on her own at bedtime or in the middle of the night when she normally wakes up.

The Basic Bedtime Method

The basic bedtime method is based on the notion of replacing your baby's negative sleep associations with positive sleep associations. Unfortunately, this can be a trying process for a few days until new associations are established. A step-by-step guide is provided here to help you through this process.

• *Step one.* Step one is to have a set time for your baby to go to bed (see more about bedtimes in Chapter 5). Your baby needs to go to bed at the same time every night. This is important to help reset your baby's internal clock every day. Another reason that a set bedtime is important is that babies relish routine, and routine is based on the same things happening at the same times every day. Bedtime is bedtime.

- **Step two.** Step two is to establish a consistent bedtime routine. As discussed in Chapter 5, a set bedtime routine is essential to your child's being able to fall asleep easily and quickly. A bedtime routine helps your child get sleepy and get ready for the transition from daytime to sleeptime. The end of your child's bedtime routine should be done in your child's room so that he perceives it as a place where positive things happen, rather than a place he gets sent to go to sleep. Read the last book in his bedroom, cuddle there, or sing a song there. The reading, cuddling, and singing should end, though, before your child falls asleep.

- **Step three.** This step requires you to spend some time in your child's room during the evening. You need to figure out what it is going to be like for your child when he wakes during the night. What you want to do is establish a consistent bedroom environment, one that is the same at bedtime and throughout the night. Stand in your child's room. Imagine that it is 2:00 in the morning. What does your child see? Is there a light on in the hallway? Is there music playing? Are you there? Are there toys in bed with him? What you want to do is make your child's bedroom be exactly the same at bedtime as it will be in the middle of the night. If there is music playing all night, then play music at bedtime. But if there is no music playing during the night, then there should be none at bedtime because you don't want music to be your child's negative sleep association. One thing that may help you with this step is to think about what may be your child's negative sleep associations. What is it that you need to do at bedtime or in the middle of the night to get your child to sleep? Do you need to refill a cup of water that is placed beside his bed? Do you need to turn a night-light on? Do you have to sing to him? Whatever it may be, either eliminate it altogether or make sure that it is always there. Again, you need to make sure that your child's bedroom is the same all the time when he is sleeping.

- **Step four.** Now it is time to teach your child to fall asleep on his own. Yes, this is the hard part. After your child's bedtime routine is done, put him in his crib or bed, say good night, and leave the room. Don't nurse him. Don't let him fall asleep in the living room. Don't stay with him. Have your child fall asleep alone in his crib or bed. Your child is likely to be upset by the change in his routine. He will probably call for you, cry, or scream. Most likely he will do all three at once. Wait. Then do a simple checking routine. Go back into your child's room. Pat him on the back. Tell him that it is okay. Tell him again that it is time for him to go to sleep. Don't pick him up. Don't cuddle him. Be gentle but firm. Remain fairly neutral and stay for a brief time, no more than one minute. You don't want to reinforce your child's crying by staying long or giving him too much attention. That is, you don't want to make it worth his while to cry for you. Leave. Wait again. Check again. Repeatedly wait and then check on your child. This could take a while.

How long should you wait before checking on your child? It depends on your tolerance level and your child. Most parents can follow the chart on the next page. Start with waiting five minutes and gradually increase that time. Some parents can't bear to listen to their child cry for more than thirty seconds. That is okay. Start there. Wait only thirty seconds. Then wait one minute. Slowly increase the amount of time. You don't ever have to wait ten minutes. Just continue to check every few minutes. The longer you can wait, however, the better. You want to give your child time to soothe himself and fall asleep. Also, some children get more upset seeing their parents than if left alone. If this is the case, wait longer periods rather than shorter ones. Lastly, it may be reinforcing enough for your child to get some attention from you every few minutes. Wait as long as you can to be sure that you are not reinforcing his crying. Remember, the goal is to have your child fall asleep on his own. If you can stand to wait longer than what is listed in the chart, even better. If you can wait twenty minutes or even thirty, then great. It will give your child an even better chance to fall asleep on his own. The goal of this process is not to make your child upset. The goal is to have him fall asleep on his own.

How long should it take until your child finally falls asleep? Most children cry for about forty-five minutes the first night. On the second night, expect it to last longer, about an hour, as your child is basically saying, "Look, last night was a fluke. Tonight I really mean it." In clinical terms this is known as an extinction burst. (For more about this, see Chapter 3.) On the third night expect about twenty minutes. And you can expect your child to be going to bed easily and quickly within the week. Keep in mind, though, that there are some children—those who are strong-willed—who will cry longer, even for an hour or two on those first few nights.

Additionally, it will take your child at least several days to begin to fall asleep quickly with this new routine. Think about it: It would take you a few days to adjust if you were required to establish new sleep associations, such as learning to sleep without a pillow or without a blanket. Some people also find it difficult to make the transition to sleeping someplace new, such as in a hotel room or at a friend's house. Here you are changing all the rules on your child, so expect it to take a few days to a week until the new sleep associations take hold. And once your child is falling asleep quickly at bedtime, don't be surprised if

Minutes to Wait Before Checking on Your Child				
	Night 1	Night 2	Night 3	Night 4	Night 5+
First wait	5	5	5	10	10
Second wait	5	10	10	10	15
Third wait	10	10	15	15	15
And so on	10	15	15	15	15

sleep problems return for a short period. This doesn't mean, however, that the sleep training was ineffective. Remain consistent in your efforts, and your baby will again be falling asleep quickly and sleeping through the night.

What to Do About Night Wakings

Eighty percent of all children who consistently fall asleep alone at bedtime will sleep through the night. However, it may take one, two, or even several weeks until this happens. In the meantime, do what you normally do when your baby wakes up in the middle of the night. If you usually rock her back to sleep, then rock her. If you pace the floor, then pace. Gradually, as your baby learns to self-soothe from her bedtime routine, she will begin to put herself back to sleep more often during the middle of the night.

Why can you intervene during night wakings but not at bedtime? Studies show that teaching your baby to fall asleep on his own at bedtime is all that is required to teach him to sleep through the night. This is because your baby will learn to put himself back to sleep without your help when he wakes during the night. This does not happen immediately, however, and there will be night wakings during the first few weeks. Intervening at these times is easier than letting your baby cry in the middle of the night and will not interfere with his learning to put himself to sleep. The key is to continue to follow the basic bedtime method at bedtime!

What should you do if your baby still doesn't sleep through the night even after several weeks of her going to sleep on her own at bedtime? First, reevaluate what is happening at bedtime. Are there any remnants of negative sleep associations that are causing her to have continued difficulties putting herself back to sleep when she wakes during the night? What is it that your child still needs from you during the night? If it is something that is also happening at bedtime, change your bedtime plan and see if that works. If there seems to be no connection between what happens at bedtime and what you need to do in the middle of the night, you will have to do the checking routine during the night. As at bedtime, wait longer and longer intervals before checking on your child. When you go in to check on her, stay for a brief time, no more than one minute, and keep your contact neutral. Don't pick her up. Pat her on the back and tell her that it is time to sleep. You can use the same chart as given for the basic bedtime method to determine how many minutes you should wait before checking again.

If your child still wakes during the night and doesn't need you anymore to intervene, you may want to consider whether your child is experiencing another sleep problem. For example, if she is waking and screaming inconsolably for a period of time, eventually falling back to sleep, she may be having night terrors. If she wakes coughing and choking, it may be sleep apnea. These and other common sleep disorders are covered in Chapters 10, 11, and 12.

The Story of Max

Sally and Richard arrived at the office, looking exhausted, carrying their fourteen-month-old son, Max. Since the day they brought him home, Max had never slept through the night. Each night either Sally or Richard would rock Max to sleep at bedtime. A few hours later, usually around midnight and again around 3:30 in the morning, Max would wake up, and either Sally or Richard would rock him back to sleep. On a good night this took only about five to ten minutes. On some nights, an hour or two would pass before Max would go back to sleep. Neither Sally nor Richard thought things would ever change.

After much discussion about sleep and both positive and negative sleep associations, Sally and Richard realized that they needed to teach Max how to fall asleep on his own. A bedtime routine that was comfortable for them was established. Max's bedtime was set for 7:30, and his parents began a soothing bedtime routine around 7:00. Pajamas were put on, stories that Max loved to hear were read, and at 7:30 Max was put in his crib with his favorite teddy bear and his parents kissed him good night. Max's parents checked on him every five minutes to make sure that he was fine and to reassure Max that they were nearby.

Sally and Richard were told that on the first night it would take Max about forty minutes to fall asleep, on the second night about an hour (a usual occurrence), and by the third night Max would be asleep within twenty minutes. Once Max began to fall asleep on his own at bedtime, he would know how to fall back asleep naturally when he awakened in the middle of the night.

Sally and Richard went home determined to solve Max's sleep problems and get him to sleep through the night. That night, Sally received an emergency call from work, so they scrapped their sleep plans. Since it was a Wednesday night and they weren't going to start then, they decided to wait for the weekend. On Friday night Sally and Richard geared up. Richard decided to take on bedtime duty the first night because he felt more prepared to deal with Max being upset. At 7:00, Richard announced that it was bedtime. Max and he had fun getting ready for bed. Richard sang while getting Max ready for bed, played his favorite peekaboo game with him, and read Max some of his favorite stories. All was happy until Richard announced again that it was time for bed and put Max in his crib. After being stunned for a few moments, Max began to cry. Richard told him that everything was okay and left the room, feeling that his heart was breaking. Richard waited five minutes and went to check on Max. Again, he told him that everything was okay and it was time to go to sleep. Five minutes later Richard checked again. Seven minutes later Richard couldn't wait any longer and checked again. Seeing that Max was getting more upset when he went in, Richard waited the entire ten minutes the next time. Finally, after exactly fifty-two minutes, Max fell asleep holding his teddy bear and looking exhausted. Max proceeded to wake up twice that night, and each time Richard rocked him back to sleep.

On Saturday night Sally put Max to bed. She did the same routine that Richard did the night before. When it was time to put Max in his crib, he got upset immediately. Sally reassured him and gingerly left the room. At the five-minute mark, Max was sobbing and reaching up to Sally when she went in to check on him. After twenty minutes, with Sally continuing to check on him, Max threw up because he was so upset. Because Sally had anticipated this reaction, she wasn't too concerned. She quickly changed Max and took off the top of two sets of sheets in his crib. Max seemed to settle down a bit after this but continued to cry. He finally fell asleep after an hour and a quarter.

On the third night Sally and Richard flipped a coin to determine who was going to handle bedtime. Neither was looking forward to another night of crying. To their surprise, Max didn't begin crying until after they had been gone for about five minutes. They waited another five minutes before checking on him. Within fifteen minutes Max was sound asleep. The next few nights went similarly, with Max crying less and less. For that first week Max continued to wake during the night and needed to be rocked back to sleep. A few times, though, they heard him whimper and go back to sleep on his own.

Two weeks later Richard commented that "it feels like a miracle." He couldn't believe it. Although the first few nights were difficult, Sally and Richard reassured themselves that they were doing the right thing. By the second *week, life was completely different. Max was going to bed at 7:30, falling asleep quickly, and not waking up again until 7:00 the next morning. Sally and Richard were enjoying life again. They knew that they were likely to encounter problems again with Max's sleep if they went on vacation or if he became sick, but they felt that they knew how to take control and help Max to fall asleep on his own and return to sleeping through the night.*

------------- ✳ -------------

Drinking from a Bottle or Nursing

As mentioned previously, many babies fall asleep while drinking from a bottle or nursing. These children all have a negative sleep association that is preventing them from falling asleep on their own. Children who drink from a bottle or nurse to sleep do not need more nourishment in the middle of the night. All children over the age of three months can get adequate nourishment during the day so that nighttime feedings are not necessary. If you think that your baby needs this final bottle or nursing time, move it to earlier in the evening and break the association of feeding with sleep. Nurse your baby thirty to sixty minutes earlier and then have playtime before bedtime.

Another reason that many children who breast-feed or bottle-feed at bedtime and in the middle of the night do not sleep through the night is that they awaken with a soaked diaper. All of those fluids at night have to go somewhere, and a wet diaper is the result.

If your baby associates nursing or drinking from a bottle with sleeping, you will need to change his negative sleep association to a positive one. The method that will accomplish this is similar to the basic bedtime method; that is, you must stop the drinking or nursing. Rather than stop it abruptly, however, it will be easier on you and your baby if you do it gradually. You can also do the same process at naptime simultaneously. This will help speed up the process and make it less confusing for your child ("Why do I get to nurse before going to sleep at naptime but not at bedtime?").

The Bottle Feeder

The easiest way to get your baby from requiring a bottle to fall asleep at bedtime is to wean him off it. The best way to do this is to reduce the amount of liquid in the bottle given to him at bedtime by one ounce every night. Use the sample charts below and start with the amount you give your baby in his bot-

Weaning from a Bottle at Bedtime	
Night	**Starting with an 8-oz. bottle**
Night 1	7 oz.
Night 2	6 oz.
Night 3	5 oz.
Night 4	4 oz.
Night 5	3 oz.
Night 6	2 oz.
Night 7	No bottle
Night	**Starting with a 4-oz. bottle**
Night 1	3 oz.
Night 2	3 oz.
Night 3	2 oz.
Night 4	2 oz.
Night 5	No bottle

tle. If you give your baby more or less than eight ounces or four ounces, use these charts as a model.

As you can see, if your baby usually drinks an eight-ounce bottle at bedtime, then your baby will be off his bottle by the seventh night. If you are starting with a four-ounce bottle, then the process will take only five nights. You will notice that a one-ounce bottle is skipped in all of these examples. This is because a one-ounce bottle can be a tease to your child and may just make him more upset than no bottle.

When you are rid of the bottle at bedtime, then it is time to move on to the above basic bedtime method. Start putting your child down to sleep when he is awake. Again, having your child put himself to sleep is the key to getting a good night's sleep.

The Breast Feeder

You can use a similar technique for nursing as you would if your baby drank a bottle. Since you cannot tell how much your child gets when nursing, use the number of minutes that he is nursing as your measure. For the next few nights, time how long your baby nurses at bedtime. Once you have that information, you can start to wean him gradually. Decrease the number of minutes your child nurses by one minute per night, as in the example on the next page.

In this example it will take nine nights to eliminate your baby's association of breast-feeding with sleep.

After eliminating your baby's negative sleep association with breast-feeding, it is best if you are not the one who teaches your baby to fall asleep. Your baby will smell your milk, and the sight of your baby will cause letdown. It is almost like teasing a baby with a piece of candy. Here it is, but you can't have it. Try to get someone else to put the baby down and to check on her every few minutes. You can still do your baby's bedtime routine, of course, but leave the last good night to someone else. After your baby has started to get the hang of falling

Weaning from Breast-Feeding at Bedtime

Night	Starting with 10 min. of nursing
Night 1	9 minutes
Night 2	8 minutes
Night 3	7 minutes
Night 4	6 minutes
Night 5	5 minutes
Night 6	4 minutes
Night 7	3 minutes
Night 8	2 minutes
Night 9	No nursing

asleep on her own, you can start putting her to bed again. Expect a minor flair-up at this point since your baby will think that her favorite activity of nursing will resume. But in a few days your baby will start going to sleep quickly and easily for you as well.

Dealing with an Older Child

When your child is a little bit older, toddler age and above, other methods to help him sleep through the night can be employed. Most of these require that your child understands language, has some sense of time, and has a bit of patience.

Stay Shorter and Shorter

Rather than leave your child alone for longer and longer periods of time, you can stay with your child for shorter and shorter periods. Cynthia and Ray did this with their three-year-old daughter, Karley. At night either Cynthia or Ray had to stay with Karley until she was just about to fall asleep. After reading stories to her and getting her a last drink of water, they usually ended up staying with Karley for about twenty minutes. For the first two nights Cynthia stayed with Karley for the entire twenty minutes, but rather than wait quietly and leave when Karley was just about asleep, she told Karley after fifteen minutes that she would be staying for five more minutes. At the five-minute mark, she kissed her good night one last time and left. On the third and fourth nights she stayed a total of fifteen minutes, again telling Karley, after ten minutes, that she was staying another five minutes. On night five Cynthia stayed a total of ten minutes, and on night six she stayed only five minutes. Each time she told Karley she would be staying five more minutes.

When using this technique, it is helpful to emphasize the positive. Cynthia always made sure that she told Karley she would be staying five more minutes; she didn't tell her she would be leaving in five minutes. Setting a timer for five minutes can also be beneficial. This way the timer says that you have to leave, rather than it appearing arbitrary. You won't get into arguments about "just one more minute."

Run Errands

One difficulty many children have at bedtime is that they do not want to be left alone. Your child may need practice before she is ready to be left alone "cold turkey." As your child gets older, she will begin to understand time and the concept that you will return. Use this knowledge to your advantage. Run errands. First, go get a drink or get something from another room. Tell her, "Oops, Daddy forgot his glasses. I'll be right back." In the beginning, if your child has never been left alone in her room at nighttime, leave for very short periods of time, less than twenty seconds. Then start running errands that take longer. Go to another part of the house to get something. Go fold laundry or load the dishwasher. Clean the bathroom. This may even start to work in your favor. Your child will get practice being alone, and you will get some chores done. Make each errand last longer and longer. You can begin with one errand a night or do a few each night. Each time you return, praise your child for staying in her room alone. Tell her how good she is and how much you appreciate her staying in her bed or crib. The key to this strategy is that you must return even if she falls asleep. Don't forget. Set a timer. Don't be distracted by the phone or the television. If you forget just one time, it will encourage your child to yell out to you or, worse, come to get you to make sure that you have not forgotten her.

"I'll Be Back"

What your child wants is your attention, and most of the time he will cry to get it. But you can turn this situation around. Set up a scenario in which your child needs to be quiet and in bed to get your attention. After you say good night, tell him that you will be back in five minutes and give him another kiss good night if he is quiet and in bed. Leave the room and then come back in five minutes. Again, the key is that you have to return! It is harder to remember to return than when "doing errands" because there is no distinct end point of what you are doing. So to make this work, set a timer. When the timer goes off, go check on your child. Give him another kiss good night and tell him how good he is being. Some children require a shorter interval than five minutes, so return after two or three minutes. You can even set the timer for just thirty seconds if that is all you think your child can handle. Should you do this again a second or third time? You can if you think that it will help. For some children just one "I'll be back" is sufficient, but other children will need to see you again. Some children will fall asleep before you get back, but you still must return. You want to tell the truth the next morning if he asks if you came back. He may also be only half asleep waiting for you, so don't put it off or skip out.

What to Do About Naptimes

Many parents ask what they should do at naptime. You have several choices. First, you or your caregiver can do what you normally do: rock him to sleep, nurse him, or drive him in the car. Whatever works. But this can be confusing to your child. If he nurses to sleep at naptime, why can't he nurse at bedtime? Another choice is to do the same checking method at naptime as you do at bedtime. It may not be advisable to do this simultaneously with the basic bedtime method. It may be too much for you and your baby. Instead, do the basic bedtime method only at naptime first and then move on to doing it at bedtime. Or wait until your child has the hang of it at bedtime and then do it at naptime. The ultimate goal is to have your child falling asleep in the same manner and sleeping in the same place at all naptimes, at bedtime, and throughout the night. If you have a child care provider in your home during the day or in the evenings, have him or her put your baby to sleep in the same manner that you do. Make everyone and everything consistent. If your child is in child care outside the home, you may not have as much choice, but do speak to your child care provider about this issue.

Some Important Tips

Tip one: Stick with it. Once you decide to begin to teach your child to fall asleep on his own, don't abandon ship halfway. Once you make a commitment, stick with it. You will only teach your child to scream for a longer time because he will not expect you to follow through. Then the next time that you try again, it will take even longer, and your child will be even more obstinate.

Tip two: Anticipate pitfalls. Anticipate every pitfall that you can so that you know what to do in different situations. Chapter 7 provides a long list of what to do in many different scenarios, such as when your child vomits, tries to jump out of the crib, or gets undressed. It is important that you have a plan as to how you are going to handle different possibilities before you start sleep training.

Tip three: How to cope. The process of teaching your child to be a self-soother and to fall asleep on his own can be stressful. There are many ways to help you deal with this stressful event, including blocking out noise, getting help, and using relaxation strategies. Chapter 8 provides numerous suggestions on how to cope.

Tip four: Don't get upset. When you are in the midst of trying to teach your child to fall asleep on her own, don't get upset with her. Your getting upset will only make things worse. If you are calm, it will help her to be calm. Don't spank your child or yell at her. You need to help her make this transition from negative sleep associations to positive ones. She is not deliberately acting out to get at you. She is tired, and all she wants to do is fall asleep. Keep this in mind when you go in for the seventeenth time or return her to her room for the eighth time. Stay calm and soothing, but neutral.

Tip five: Be creative. As you begin to develop your own strategy to teach your baby to fall asleep on his own and to sleep through the night, be creative. Remember, the goal is to have your baby fall asleep on his own. Whatever you can do to achieve that, go for it. For example, if evenings are crazy in your household, then do it at naptime. Start then, and when your child can fall asleep on his own during the day when he naps, then start with bedtime. It will be faster and easier each time you do it. Some strategies were given above, but you can try different solutions of your own. Figure out what will work best for you and your child. Trust your instincts.

Tip six: Give lots of attention. Give your child lots of attention at other times of the day. Much of the time the reason that your child is crying or acting up is to get your attention. By setting limits on your child's bedtime behavior, it is likely that your child will be receiving less attention overall. This will just make your child want your attention even more. To counteract this, make sure that your child gets more attention at other times. Spend extra time with her in the morning or afternoon. Let her help you make dinner. Make the bedtime routine a longer one and read an extra book or sing an extra song.

Tip seven: When not to try. As important as it is for you to help your baby sleep through the night, there are good times and bad times to start this process. The good times are when you will be home for a period of time and things are calm in your life. The bad times are when typical household routines are altered, such as when you are working overtime or your usual child care provider is on vacation.

If you are about to go on vacation, even if you will not be leaving for two to three weeks, wait until you get back. If a holiday is coming up and your baby's schedule is going to become inconsistent, you should wait. If you are about to have visitors, wait until the house returns to normal. If this is a stressful period at work or at home, then wait. If you are about to move, wait until you are settled in your new residence.

Other Methods

There are other methods that can be used to resolve your child's sleeping problems. Remember, though, that the above basic bedtime method and its variations are tried and true. Much research has supported its effectiveness, and if you do it and follow through, your child will be going to sleep on his own within three or four days and sleeping through the night within two weeks.

Unfortunately, some parents are unable to tolerate their child's being upset at bedtime (but see Chapter 8 on how to cope) and will want to try an alternative method. Below are some other strategies that you may wish to try.

Gradual parent removal. Some parents find the "cold turkey" approach—of completely leaving their child when he is still awake at bedtime—too difficult. An alternative approach is to ease yourself gradually out of your child's presence. Start with sitting in a chair by your child's crib or bed. Stay there until he falls asleep. After two nights of this, move your chair a little farther away. Move your chair two feet away for nights three and four, and then five feet away for nights five and six. On the seventh night you should be sitting in the doorway. On night nine, move into the hallway. Within ten days to two weeks your child should be falling asleep on his own.

There is one major drawback to this method, however. In theory it sounds good, but in reality it may be more difficult than it seems. With the basic bedtime method described above, your child has to get used to only one major change at bedtime: the switch from a negative sleep association to a positive one in which he is falling asleep on his own. With the gradual removal of your presence recommended here, your child has to go through a new transition every other night. Just when he gets used to your being only five feet away, you have now moved to the doorway. And just when he gets used to this, you head into the hallway. So this method can just drag out the inevitable and be more upsetting to your child. It is worth a try, however, if leaving altogether is just too hard on you or your baby. This method may also be helpful if you are worried about your child's hurting himself or jumping out of his crib. You can keep an eye on him while maintaining your distance and teaching your child to fall asleep on his own.

Scheduled awakenings. Research has shown that another technique, scheduled awakenings, can also be effective in helping your baby sleep through the night, but it requires a greater commitment of your time. The first step is to keep track of the time that your baby wakes during the night for one week. You will see a pattern in your baby's awakenings. Once the pattern is clear, figure out what time they typically occur. Betty's five-month-old son, Jason, woke up three times every night, at about 1:00, 3:15, and 4:35.

The next step is to wake your child fifteen minutes before each of these times. Betty was to wake Jason at 12:45, 3:00, and 4:20. She woke him up and then breast-fed him and soothed him back to sleep. Since Betty was usually asleep at these times, she had to set an alarm to be sure that she woke him in time. During the first week, Jason still woke a few times, usually about 2:00. After six days Jason stopped waking up at other times of the night. Once all other spontaneous awakenings subsided, Betty started cutting back on the number of scheduled times that she woke him. By the second week Betty cut back to waking him only two times per night. By week four Jason was sleeping even better, and she woke him only once per night. And by week five she stopped waking him at all. Six weeks later Jason was still sleeping soundly through the night, and Betty did not have to wake him up at any more scheduled times.

As you can imagine, scheduled awakenings require a big effort on the parents' part. If your baby usually wakes after you have gone to sleep for the night, you will need to set an alarm to wake yourself up. Also, some parents have a hard time even thinking about waking a sleeping baby, let alone doing it.

Just let him cry. Many people recommend just letting the baby cry as the best way to deal with a baby who won't go to sleep by himself. Other parents you know may say this, your parents may say this, and your pediatrician may even suggest it. You can try it. It can work. It can also backfire. For instance, you may be ignoring your child when he really needs you. It would be horrible not to go in and check on him and later find that his foot is caught in the crib rails or something has happened to him. Another drawback is that you may not be able to tolerate it. After about fifteen minutes to an hour of crying, you may give in and go get him. And then you will have made the problem worse. You will have taught him that if he cries long enough and hard enough, you will come to get him. The next time he will cry even louder and for a longer time, expecting that eventually you will give in. Another potential problem is that children who are allowed to cry it out seem to cry for a longer time before finally falling asleep. Rather than falling asleep after forty minutes, they may cry for over an hour or even two hours. This makes it harder on everyone. So if you want to, give it a try, just be forewarned of the pitfalls.

Medications. Should you give your child a medication to help her sleep? Some pediatricians recommend or prescribe Benadryl or chloral hydrate to help babies sleep. Does it work? Is this a good idea?

Research has shown that some medications do decrease the number of times a baby wakes during the night, but this is from a statistical point of view, not from a parent's point of view. Thus, rather than your baby waking an average of 3.2 times per night, she will wake only 2.5 times per night. Statistically, this is a significant reduction, and the conclusion made for the study is that the medication worked. For parents, though, this means that rather than waking three times per night, the baby is waking on some nights only two times. This is not the solution that most parents want. Your goal is to get your baby to sleep through the night without ever waking up. Therefore, medications are not the answer. Surprisingly, though, many pediatricians continue to recommend some type of sedative.

It would be wonderful if there was a pill that you could give to your child and have her immediately begin to sleep. Unfortunately, no such pill exists. There is also the concern of side effects with any medication. These types of sedative medications are not usually harmful to a baby, but they can make her groggy the next day. Another problem with medications is that they change sleep, so your baby may not be getting all the different stages of sleep that she needs.

The reason medications don't work is that they do not alleviate the problems of poor sleep associations. Your baby will still need to fall asleep with you rocking her, feeding her, or singing to her. And although she will wake less frequently during the night, she will continue to need you to help her get back to sleep. In addition, once you stop the medication, your baby will go right back to waking as much as she ever did. Some people propose that by giving a baby a sleeping pill for a few days to a few weeks, it will break the cycle. This does not happen. Your baby will simply revert to her old sleeping habits once you stop giving her the medicine.

What Doesn't Work: Don't Even Bother

There are many things that parents do to attempt to get their baby to sleep. Unfortunately, many of these attempts are futile. Here is a list of what not to bother with; some can even backfire and cause more problems.

Solid foods. Some believe that babies wake because they are hungry, and therefore they should be given solid foods at a very young age. No research has supported this belief. Solid foods do not help babies sleep. Remember, all babies wake. It is just a matter of whether your baby can put herself back to sleep. Babies who want to eat during the night have become conditioned to do so. By a relatively young age, babies receive all the nutrients they need during the day. Rather than diet, weight appears to be related to sleeping through the night. Some studies have shown that once a baby reaches twelve pounds, she is more likely to sleep through the night no matter what she eats.

Later bedtime. Parents try to make their baby's bedtime later, hoping he will be so tired that he will fall asleep faster. Again, this doesn't work. When babies get overtired, they get crankier and have a harder time, not an easier time, settling down and falling asleep. Your problems will just get worse if you wait to put your baby down.

Removing daytime naps. In another attempt to get babies to sleep at night, parents try removing daytime naps. Again, don't bother. Nap sleep is independent of nighttime sleep. Babies need their naps, and if denied their naps, they will be more tired and have more problems falling asleep at night and sleeping throughout the night. What may also happen if you or your caregiver tries to keep your baby awake all afternoon is that she will fall asleep at 5:00. Now you are really in trouble because there is no way she will go to sleep for the night at 7:30. Also, have you ever tried to keep a baby awake when she is determined to fall asleep? It's an almost impossible task.

Growing out of it. Babies don't grow out of sleep problems. Studies show that most babies with sleep problems at one year of age will still have sleep problems at four years of age if nothing is done. Regrettably, though, this advice is often given by grandparents, neighbors, friends, and even pediatricians. Don't waste weeks and months of sleepless nights waiting for something that probably won't happen. Do something about it now and relish those nights of sleep ahead.

Just Short-Term Solutions, Unfortunately

Parents try many other solutions, but unfortunately most of them turn out to be short-term solutions. Remember that what will get your baby to go to sleep quickly may lead to a poor sleep association. With this negative sleep association, your baby will not be able to fall asleep on her own without the association being present.

Driving in the car. Parents often find that their baby is likely to fall asleep if they put her in the car and go for a drive. The rhythmic motion of a moving car and the constant noise of the engine lulls the baby to sleep. Some parents resort to this on a daily basis, taking their baby for a drive to get her to take a nap or to fall back to sleep in the middle of the night. In the short term, this works. In the long term, however, it does not teach your baby how to fall asleep on her own, and you will be doing a lot of driving in the months ahead.

Vibrating crib mechanisms. Several mechanisms on the market are made to soothe your baby to sleep. Some simply vibrate the crib. Others vibrate the crib and come with a tape of a mother's heartbeat. It may or may not work for your baby. At this time there is no scientific evidence that these really work. Even if they do, they will help only in the short run. They may get your baby to sleep today and tomorrow, but they won't help for next week or next month. Remember, your baby needs to learn how to be a self-soother so that he can put himself to sleep at bedtime and throughout the night when he wakes up. A vibrating crib simply instills a negative sleep association.

Constant noises. Parents are ingenious at figuring out ways to put a baby to sleep. Placing your baby in a car seat on the dryer while it is running works. If you ever try this, do not leave your baby alone! There is a very high likelihood that the car seat will fall off the dryer because of the vibration.

Teddy bears that make a noise that mimics the mother's heartbeat fall into the same category. One family referred to their vacuum cleaner as "Betty the Baby-sitter." They had just moved into a new home and were trying to get it painted. While they were painting, they put their five-week-old baby in a car seat on the floor and turned on the vacuum cleaner. Within moments their baby was asleep, and off they would go to paint.

Again, these things work, but they should be considered only short-term solutions. You do not want to teach your baby that she needs the constant vibration or noise to fall asleep, or you will have to turn the vacuum cleaner on every night at bedtime and do so throughout the night.

Warning

The hope and belief that most parents have is that they will have to deal with sleep issues only once and that when their baby is sleeping through the night, their worries are over. Unfortunately, this isn't the case. You will almost certainly have to deal with sleep issues again (see Chapter 9 on obstacles to continued good sleep and solutions to these common problems). A child's sleep will be disturbed by illness, vacations, and the development of separation anxiety (an aspect of normal development when your child will not want to be apart from you). There will even be times when your baby won't sleep for no apparent reason. That is the bad news. The good news is that each time your baby's sleep begins to be problematic, if you have a set bedtime routine and put her to bed awake, she will return to sleeping through the night quicker and with less fuss each time.

Reminders

- There are many reasons that young children resist going to bed, including wanting to stay up later and getting attention.

- Poor sleep associations are the primary reasons that children have sleep problems.

- Waking at night is normal; the problem is falling back to sleep.

- Replace your child's negative sleep associations with positive sleep associations.

- The basic bedtime method will get your baby going to bed and falling asleep quickly and easily.

- The basic bedtime method needs be employed only at bed-time. If your baby wakes during the night, you can respond as usual. Once your child can self-soothe to sleep at bed-time, sleeping through the night is sure to follow.

- Although your child will take longer to fall asleep at bed-time for the first three to five days of using the basic bed-time method, sleep problems will resolve within one to two weeks.

- Be creative when teaching older children how to fall asleep on their own.

- There are other methods to change your child's sleep prob-lems, including gradually removing yourself and scheduled awakenings.

- Avoid using medications, changing your baby's naptimes or bedtime, or moving your baby to solid foods to solve your child's sleep problems. They won't work.

Chapter 7

"WHAT DO I DO IF . . . ?"
Coping with Difficult Situations

————————————— ☾⋆ —————————————

I tried to get Peter to sleep through the night, but breast-feeding makes everything more difficult.

☾⋆

I tried not to interfere, but when Cindy threw up, I had to take her out of the crib.

————————————— ✳ —————————————

Some parents fail to change their child's sleep habits because of a particular situation, such as breast-feeding, or because something unexpected occurs, such as their child vomiting. Such situations or events make it more difficult to follow a program designed to teach a child to put himself to sleep over a period of weeks. I find that many of the parents I see in my clinical practice do not know what to do when something unexpected occurs, and it is helpful to have parents practice solving every situation that they think could possibly occur.

Vomiting

Anne is the mother of fifteen-month-old Eric, who has rarely, if ever, slept through the night. On the first night, following implementation of the changes suggested in Chapter 6, everything went smoothly and according to plan. On night two, however, Eric cried so hard that he vomited all over himself and his crib. At that point Anne gave up, not knowing what to do about this unexpected event. She immediately ran into Eric's room, took him out of his crib, cleaned him up, and rocked him to sleep. Eric then continued to wake several times a night for the next three weeks. Anne was afraid to leave him for too long or to allow him to cry for more than five minutes because she was concerned that he would vomit again.

Vomiting is no big deal for infants and toddlers, although it can be quite upsetting for parents. For young children, vomiting can even be fun. And it is common for infants and toddlers to vomit after crying for a long period of time. Unfortunately, children can also learn to vomit at will if vomiting is reinforced. It gets parents to respond. And it gets the child out of the crib.

Vomiting can be dealt with just like any other behavior. If your baby vomits after crying, don't worry about it and don't reinforce it. Be neutral. Change the sheets, clean up the baby as well as you can (preferably without picking him up), and leave the room. One helpful hint is to make your baby's crib with two sets of sheets (with a liner in between) so that when he vomits, you can quickly and easily take off the top set and leave the bottom set on. Sheets that fasten to the bars of the crib with Velcro and all-in-one sheets also make this process easier. (See Appendix B, Resources for Parents, for places that sell these sheets.)

If, however, your child is vomiting at other times of the day, you should call your pediatrician. But if this is the only time he vomits and he has appeared fine all day, it is likely to be a behavioral problem rather than a medical problem.

Rolling Over

———————— (————————

Sally, my two-month-old, has learned how to roll from her back to her stomach but can't roll the other way yet. Unfortunately, she sleeps on her back, so once she rolls onto her stomach, she can't turn over and can't fall asleep.

———————— ✳ ————————

By the age of two months, some babies can roll from their back onto their stomach. This is a problem if they can fall asleep only when on their back. If it is sleep time, the minute they roll over onto their stomach they will cry for you to turn them back over. There is not much you can do about this other than to go in and turn the baby over. You may try to teach your baby to roll back the other way, but you can't really speed up motor development in a baby this young.

By nine or ten weeks babies are able to roll themselves onto their backs from their sides, so if you were putting your baby to sleep on his side, you have now lost control of keeping him there. Again, there is nothing that you can do about it other than go in and put him back on his side. It is also important that you don't restrict his movement by swaddling him or putting him in clothes in which he is unable to move around. This is not a solution to the problem of his rolling over.

Standing Up in the Crib

———————— (————————

My seven-and-a-half-month-old son has a new trick. After I put him to bed and leave the room, he pulls himself up, stands there holding on to the railing, and cries. The problem is that he can't sit back down. What can I do? This has been going on for days!

———————— ✳ ————————

Standing up and holding on to things is a developmental milestone. Some babies begin to pull themselves up to standing as early as five months, whereas others may not do so until they are a year old. In either case, these babies often have a difficult time sitting back down. They become frustrated and begin to cry several minutes after pulling themselves up to standing because they are stranded. They then have to wait for someone to help them down, or they simply collapse. Once helped down, they invariably pull themselves back up immediately and get stuck again. This can become tedious and frustrating for parents.

When your baby begins to pull herself up to standing, start to help her down slowly and gently so that she learns how to do it herself. This learning process should take only a few days, although some babies may take a few weeks to learn this new skill. In the beginning you will have no choice but to rescue her. If your baby is doing this at naptime and bedtime, go in and, in a neutral manner, sit or lie her back down. If you get too involved, she will keep standing up and crying to get your attention. During the day, at times other than bedtime, have her practice pulling up and sitting back down. Once you are sure that she has the ability to sit back down, stop rescuing her when she is in her crib or it will become a game to her.

Also, be sure to safety-proof your baby's crib. Don't leave any hard objects, such as busy-boxes, on which she can bang her head if she falls.

Jumping Out of the Crib

———————— ⟨⋆ ————————

Billy is two years old. He has just figured out how to get out of his crib. He puts his right foot up on the rail and pulls himself over. The first two times that he did this he fell down and banged his head on the floor. He has since become an expert and can climb out swiftly and easily. It has gotten to the point where he climbs out the moment he is put down for a nap or at bedtime.

Maggie is three years old. She had never even tried to climb out of her crib. The other day, though, Maggie all of a sudden appeared at the top of the stairs at the end of her nap, yelling, "I'm done!"

There are two groups of babies: those that jump out of their crib and those that don't. Hopefully, your baby will never try this stunt. Jumping out of the crib is something that understandably causes many parents concern. They worry that their child may get hurt, and they worry because they don't know what to do when it happens. Some babies try to climb out of their crib as early as eighteen months of age. Other children won't even attempt it until they are at least two and a half. And then there are those who never do.

A parent's immediate reaction often is to give up on using a crib and move their baby to a bed. This doesn't have to be the answer. There are other solutions to this problem. But first, make sure that your child will not get harmed if he does decide to take the leap. Put pillows on the floor around the crib. Remove any nearby objects, such as toys or pieces of furniture (especially toy chests), on which your child can bang his head.

Here are some suggestions that many parents have found helpful.

Lower the mattress. Move the crib mattress to its lowest setting to make climbing impossible. If your child can't physically manage to climb out, he won't. This works especially well for younger toddlers or when your baby is small in size.

Remove all crib toys. Take all large toys out of the crib, as well as the crib bumpers if they are still in the crib. Your baby will use these as a step stool to give him a boost up and over.

Don't make it worth it. The major reason that babies climb out of their cribs is that they get something out of it. Don't let your child climb in bed with you after climbing out. Don't give him lots of attention. Very calmly and neutrally return your child to his crib and say in a firm voice, "No climbing." After several more attempts, your child will realize that it is not worth it. He is just going to be put right back in his crib.

Be firm. This is not a behavior about which you can be wishy-washy. There is too high a chance that your baby will hurt himself. Don't let him rule the roost just because he climbed out once. Take a stance, set limits, and be firm.

Catch 'em early. If your child makes a habit of climbing out of the crib, catch her at it early. Stand where you can see your child, but she can't see you. The moment your child starts to put her foot on the rail or over the rail, say immediately and firmly, "No climbing." If you startle your child enough and do it several times, she will stop trying to climb out.

Install a crib tent. Many manufacturers make mesh crib tents (See Appendix B, Resources for Parents, for places to purchase these tents.) These tents attach to the crib rails with Velcro. They work great against little climbers, making it impossible for them to climb out. They are simple to install, and it is still easy to get at your baby quickly. (The tents can also be used to keep pets out of your baby's crib.)

When all else fails. If you have exhausted all other remedies, you may want to lower the side bar and push a stool up next to the crib to prevent a bad fall. This way your child has a safe way to get out of the crib and doesn't have such a great distance to cover to get to the floor. If your child is likely to start wandering around the house, install a gate at the bedroom door. You can also attach a bell to the bedroom door to alert you that your child is trying to leave her bedroom. This may be even more important if your bedroom is on a different floor from your child's room.

Losing a Pacifier

If your child has finally gotten to the point of having no problems either falling asleep or with night wakings but does use a pacifier to self-soothe, he may get into trouble when the pacifier gets lost. If this is a problem for your child, strategically place a bunch of pacifiers around his crib. If one gets lost or thrown out of the crib, he should be able to find another one without your assistance. Do not tie the pacifiers to the slats of the crib because this can be dangerous. Babies can strangle themselves on the string, especially if they roll over with the pacifier in their mouth.

If your child uses a pacifier to fall asleep and is having no sleep problems, there is no need to intervene. However, some babies remain awake for long periods because every time they are on the edge of falling asleep the pacifier falls out of their mouth, which wakes them up. If this is the case, your child has made an association of being able to fall asleep only while sucking on his pacifier. (Other children need to be rocked or to drink from a bottle to fall asleep.) You will therefore need to teach your child new, positive sleep associations to replace the negative sleep association of sucking on a pacifier (see Chapter 6 for more details). This will also help your child to sleep through the night.

Getting Undressed

———————————— ☾ ————————————

Rudy is two and a half. She has always been a good sleeper, going to bed without a problem at 7:30 and sleeping until 7:00 in the morning. Once she wakes up in the morning, she even plays in her crib quietly and happily for another half-hour. She naps every afternoon for a solid two hours. Rudy's mother, Alicia, considers herself lucky. In the past few weeks, however, Rudy has begun stripping, taking off all her clothes and her diaper. She has done this several times in the morning and during many of her naps. Unfortunately, she is also not toilet trained, which means the crib is often soaked. Amazingly, whenever Alicia goes in to get Rudy, Rudy immediately begins telling her mother, "C-c-cold," and doing a shivering routine. But this hasn't stopped Rudy from getting undressed.

———————— ✳ ————————

Young children usually undress for one of two reasons. They do it because they are bored, or they do it to get attention. If your child is wide awake when put to bed or wakes earlier than everyone else in the morning, she may undress to keep herself amused. This may mean that you are leaving her in the crib too long in the morning or at naptime, or you are putting her to bed too early, before she is tired at night.

If your baby is getting undressed because she is bored, put lots of toys in her crib to keep her amused. If she throws her toys out of the crib, attach a busy-box to the crib rails or hang interesting objects from a mobile. You can even change these objects on a frequent basis to hold her interest.

If she gets undressed to get your attention, ignore the behavior. In a few days, when getting undressed doesn't get your attention, she will stop. At that point it won't be worth it to her anymore.

Another way to deal with your child's getting undressed is similar to the advice given above for climbing out of the crib. Stand where your child can't see you. The moment that she begins to undress herself say "no" in a firm, loud voice. As long as you are consistent, the undressing should stop.

Some parents have resorted to putting their child in clothes that they can't undo. Also, some pajamas can be turned around so that all fasteners are in the back, where little hands can't reach. Obviously, you won't be able to turn feet pajamas around.

Getting Out of Bed

It is much more difficult to teach your child to be a good sleeper when he is in a bed rather than in a crib. A crib is a bit like a baby containment area. It is better at keeping a baby safe and sound, and, most important, in one place. Once your child has moved to a bed, it becomes more difficult. He is now more mobile. He can get out of bed whenever he wants. This may occur once, twice, or seventeen times in one evening.

Thinking back to Chapter 6, remember that the trick to having your child sleep through the night and fall asleep easily at bedtime is to teach him to fall asleep on his own in his own bed. This obviously requires that your child be *in* his bed. Amazingly, most children do stay in their bed when they make the move from a crib (see Chapter 8 for more information on switching from a crib to a bed). Your child, however, may be one of those who simply will not stay.

As discussed in Chapter 3, the two basic principles of changing your child's behavior is to use reinforcement and be consistent. Oh, yes, and remain calm—which is probably the hardest part. Decide on a night when you are going to start insisting that your child remain in his bed. Do it on a night that you don't have to get other things done, such as pay bills or make phone calls, because this may take a while. You may even want to start when you know you have a few nights to devote to this endeavor.

First, perform your bedtime routine. Put your child to bed and leave the room. When he gets out of bed, calmly return him to bed and tell him that he must stay in bed. When he is in bed, tell him what a good boy he is for being in bed. Say good night and leave the room. Do this again and again and again. Remain calm. Keep your interaction with your child to a minimum. You want to reinforce him for being in bed, not for getting out of bed. If he is getting something, such as more attention or upsetting you, he is more likely to do it again. After numerous times, he'll get the message. He will realize that it is simply not worth it. On those occasions when he has remained in bed after you left, go back in and praise him for staying in bed.

On night two, repeat the process. Don't be surprised if it

takes longer on the second night. To your child, the first night may have been a fluke, and he will want to let you know that he is not kidding. He does not want to stay in bed. He will test the limits. Be strong and stick to your guns. If you eventually give in and allow him to stay out of bed, you are going to have quite a battle on your hands in the future. You will have taught your child that if he is persistent, you will eventually give in, and he will then keep getting out of bed.

Some parents have found that staying close to their child's room will help their child stay in bed. He will know that you are close by and that he is safe. If you choose this method, stay shorter and shorter periods of time. Start by staying for fifteen minutes. Decrease the amount of time that you stay by two or three minutes per night. Within a week you can probably leave easily. For more anxious children, this process may take several weeks. This method can be extremely useful if you have recently moved to a new house or if your child is sleeping in a strange place.

Coming Out of the Bedroom

Your child may not only get out of bed, but he may also come out of the room. When this happens, follow the same routine as when he gets out of bed. There are also other ways to keep your child in the bedroom. One method that has been successful for many families is to install a bell or an alarm that rings when their child tries to come out of their room. Bells that hang over doorways or burglar alarms that go off when the doorknob is touched are inexpensive and easy to install. In this way you will know that your child is out of his room, without the necessity of locking the door. This can be very helpful for a family where the child wakes in the middle of the night and leaves the bedroom without the parents being aware of it. Many parents comment that they wake up in the morning only to find their child in bed with them. If this doesn't bother you, then fine. If it does, you will need to devise some system to awaken you when your child is up and wandering.

Another alternative is placing a baby gate in your child's doorway. This will help keep your child in his room and is especially useful with toddlers. However, a young child's crying and holding on to the gate can be a pathetic sight, and it may be difficult for you to resist rescuing him.

Parents often wonder whether they should lock the door to their child's room. This can work for some families. It gives the message to the child that the parents mean business. It is easier than holding the door shut and getting into a power play with your child. Some families find that they remain calmer doing this than returning their child to the bedroom umpteen times.

An alternative to locking the door is to tell your child that if he is in bed, the door stays unlocked or even partially open. Once he gets out of bed, however, the door gets locked. If you are going to do this, be consistent. The moment your child is back in bed open the door.

Locking the door has many drawbacks, however. First, it can be dangerous. If there is a fire or an emergency, your child cannot get out. If you lock the door only to keep your child in his room at bedtime, unlock it once you know that he is asleep. Another problem is that your child can get hurt when left in a room without supervision. Make sure that there is nothing in the bedroom that can cause your child injury. Remove all dangerous objects. Your child may also destroy the room. You may return to the room to find your child asleep on the floor and everything pulled out of the closet and every drawer. Before you resort to locking the door, try alternative methods, and be firm and consistent.

Breast-feeding

Tara is the mother of seven-month-old Jason, who has been exclusively breast-feeding since he was born. Jason falls asleep each night between 7:00 and 8:00 while nursing. Tara usually goes to bed shortly after Jason because she knows that he generally wakes at about 11:30 and again between 2:00 and 3:00 in the morning. Each time she breast-feeds him back to sleep.

As mentioned in Chapter 2, there are several reasons that breast-fed babies take longer to sleep through the night than bottle-fed babies. Since breast milk is easier to digest than formula, a breast-fed baby will digest the milk faster and get hungry again quicker. Thus, there will be a shorter time span between feedings. You may therefore find yourself needing to wake more times during the night to breast-feed your baby. Keep in mind, though, that once your baby is several months old, you can be sure that he is getting enough nutrition during the day that he doesn't need to breast-feed during the night. Check with your pediatrician if you are concerned about your child's growth or are worried that your child still needs middle-of-the-night feedings.

Another reason for the increased sleep problems is that there is often a strong association between nursing and falling asleep. Your baby is likely to fall asleep while nursing. Don't lose hope, though. There are ways to deal with babies who can fall asleep only while breast-feeding; usually, that is the easy part. It is dealing with the middle-of-the-night feedings that are more problematic. Remember, the key is to reduce the association of feeding with falling asleep. There are several ways to deal with this special issue.

Decrease breast-feeding gradually. As discussed in Chapter 6, one solution that has worked for many nursing mothers is to decrease the length of time that they breast-feed at naptimes and bedtime. To do this, you will need to time how long you usually breast-feed at bedtime. If you usually nurse for ten minutes, decrease breast-feeding by one minute each subsequent night. So on night one, nurse for nine minutes. Night two, eight minutes, and so forth. End at either two or three minutes. It becomes cruel to nurse for just one minute. If you usually nurse for a very long time at bedtime, you may want to decrease by two minutes each night.

Change the time you nurse. Rather than wean your child gradually, simply change the time that you breast-feed so it is not near the time that your child usually falls asleep. Nurse when your baby awakens from a nap rather than when he falls asleep. Nurse first thing in the morning. If you usually breast-feed your baby at 7:30, expecting him to be asleep and in his crib between 7:45 and 8:00, then breast-feed at 6:30 and have an hour of playtime before going to sleep for the night.

Involve others. If your baby usually falls asleep while breast-feeding, it will be hard for him not to associate sleep with breast-feeding. To counteract this, get someone else involved in putting your baby to sleep and responding to him in the middle of the night. Once your baby begins sleeping through the night you can go back to responding to him. Your baby will have developed other soothing techniques and have other ways to cope with going back to sleep, other than just wanting to nurse. You can ask the baby's father, a sitter, a friend, or a grandparent to put your baby to sleep and go to him during the night when he wakes for several nights.

Wake the baby. I know, I can hear you saying: "Are you crazy? Wake a sleeping baby?" Yes, wake the baby. If your baby falls asleep while you are nursing him, wake him before putting him in his crib. To succeed at getting your baby to sleep through the night put him in his crib awake so that he puts himself to sleep. Your baby may not like having you wake him and may even cry, but this will last only for a short time. In a few days you will not need to breast-feed at sleep times and can simply put him in his crib awake.

Teething

Parents often comment that their baby was sleeping fine until he began to teethe. Surprisingly, however, teething is probably not the main cause of sleep problems. First teeth usually begin to come in sometime between six months and ten months. Although teething may cause some problems with sleep, it is more likely that it is coincidence. Studies have shown that sleep problems increase at this age and are related to normal development. Thus, it is often coincidence that your baby begins to have problems sleeping right at the time that he begins teething. In addition, babies continue to get teeth until the age of two or two and a half. But most babies do not continue to have problems sleeping, supporting the contention that there is little relationship between teething and sleep problems. But if your baby is having some problems sleeping when teething, there are some things to try.

Babies will be fussy when they are teething. It does not feel good. They will drool more and want to bite on things. Provide your baby with lots of soft things to chew on. There are teething toys specifically made to ease teething pain. Most are placed in the refrigerator or freezer. The coldness helps soothe the baby's gums. Children's Tylenol can also be helpful, but be sure to check with your pediatrician before giving your baby any medication.

If your baby is having sleeping problems at the same time he is teething, be sure that he doesn't have a fever or other symptoms of illness. If all seems fine except for the teething, be consistent about sleep issues. Even a few nights of changing the rules can lead to many a sleepless night for you and your baby.

Toilet Training

"I have to go potty!" is a statement that few parents can ignore. And young children quickly learn that when toilet training begins, "going potty" takes precedence over almost anything else. The moment that you get a child all bundled up into a snowsuit, the child will declare that she has to go potty. The moment that you are a mile from your home and are late for an appointment, your toddler will claim a desperate need to go potty. And the same thing happens at sleep times. The moment that your baby is settled into her crib or bed, she will insist that she needs to go to the bathroom, even if she just went.

There are two ways to deal with this situation. The first is to make sure that your child always goes to the bathroom before going down for a nap or to bed for the night. The second way is to allow your child one extra time going to the bathroom. Plan for this and expect it to happen. This way you won't get frustrated when she claims the need to go. When she does call out, get her and take her to the bathroom or give her permission to go on her own. This method is also good practice because she will learn what to do when she is in bed and really does need to go to the bathroom. The novelty of trying this out at bedtime will soon wear off. (Remember, at the beginning of toilet training, going to the bathroom is a novel and exciting thing to do.) After the first time (or second time if you decide this is reasonable), don't allow any more trips to the bathroom. If you make this rule, be firm and follow through. You should therefore make a decision as to how you are going to handle the call for the potty, and stick to it.

"Just One More"

"I need a drink of water."
"Just one more hug."
"I just wanted to tell you that I love you."
Children are ingenious. They will always try for one more, and they will figure out what works. When asking for a drink of water or just one more story doesn't work, they will resort to "I just wanted to tell you that I love you." And they will do it with the most precious little face imaginable.

Children pull these stunts for several reasons. They may actually want a drink of water, or they may have forgotten to bring to bed their favorite stuffed animal. They may do it to make sure that you really are nearby and will come if they need help. They may do it to avoid going to sleep, especially if they think that you are having fun without them. And, of course, they may do it for the attention that they get. Even if you just end up yelling at them, that is still attention—not as much fun as positive attention, but attention nonetheless.

How do you deal with this? First, try to figure out exactly why your child is doing this. If she really just needs her covers straightened, she will do it rarely and will stop calling you once the problem is solved. If your child seems nervous that you are not around or because she can't see you, she may really need to know that you are nearby and she is safe. For these children, simply responding to them verbally by saying something like "It's okay. Go to sleep" may do the trick. For those children who simply don't want to go to bed or are getting rewarded for their bedtime behavior, you will have to set some limits.

First of all, children should always get one chance. Even if your child always pulls this stunt at bedtime, she may actually really need to go to the bathroom or has lost her favorite doll. By responding to her once, she will also know that you really are there when she needs you. After that, be firm. Reply that now it is time to go to sleep. Be neutral. Don't yell. Don't lose your temper. Remember, yelling is still attention even if doesn't seem that much fun to you. (Make sure you read Chapter 3 on how to manage children's behavior.)

If you say, "This is the last time," then mean it. Those words are meaningless if you are willing to return or will come in and pick up the dropped pacifier numerous times.

You also have to remember that children love rules, and they love to have limits set. After testing the rules and understanding how far they can go, they will understand what they are supposed to do and be better behaved.

The Early Riser

One common parental complaint is that their child wakes too early in the morning. And while getting up early in the morning is part of being a parent, getting up with your child at 5:00 in the morning is stretching it for most people.

There are two groups of children who wake early in the morning. The first group are those who wake up before they get enough sleep. The second group are those that get enough sleep, and their normal waking time is early in the morning.

Waking Too Early Without Getting Enough Sleep

Some children wake up early in the morning before completing their last sleep cycle. Since there are many transitions in sleep in the early morning hours, many things can awaken your child. For instance, something in your child's environment may be causing the problem, such as early sunlight or the sound of someone getting up to go to work. Being hungry or having a wet diaper can also awaken your child. The problem is that children who require their parents to be present to fall asleep at bedtime may demand this attention to return to sleep early in the morning.

One way to tell if your child is waking before getting enough sleep is to look at her behavior during the day. Does she seem more sleepy than usual? Does she return to sleep an hour or two after her early morning rising? Remember, it is rare for an infant or toddler to need less than nine or ten hours of sleep per night. So if your child is waking after less than ten hours of sleep, look for reasons.

If there is something in your child's environment that is waking her or keeping her awake after a partial arousal, then remedy the situation. Install room-darkening shades in her bedroom if the sunlight is streaming in at 5:00 in the morning. If there is too much noise from the garbage trucks going by in the morning, try to dampen the noise with a fan or vaporizer. If your child is waking early in the morning, only to return to sleep quickly, changing a poor sleep association as outlined in earlier chapters will get her sleeping to a more reasonable hour. A wet diaper can be resolved by double-diapering or putting your child in super-absorbent diapers made for nighttime. The extra expense of these types of diapers is well worth the better night's sleep.

――――――― ☾ ―――――――

Laura and Steve's child, Jessica, began waking at 5:00 in the morning. Steve was a medical resident and was on a rotation that meant he had to be at the hospital by 5:30 in the morning. His getting up and showering at 4:45 was waking Jessica, and then Laura had to get up with her. There wasn't anything that they could do about Steve's schedule, but Steve started changing his morning routine. Rather than shower and get dressed upstairs, he started showering downstairs. He also took his change of clothes downstairs the night before so that in the morning all he had to do was get up and go directly downstairs. He also started picking up coffee on the way to work rather than making it at home because the smell of the brewing coffee would wake Jessica. With the change in Steve's morning routine, Jessica soon returned to sleeping until her usual waking time of 6:45.

――――――― ✳ ―――――――

The Early Riser Who Has Had Enough Sleep

――――――― ☾ ―――――――

Stephanie, age two, is in bed and asleep by 7:30 every night. Unfortunately for her parents, she is up and ready to face the day by 6:00 in the morning.

――――――― ✳ ―――――――

This second group of children, who are up and raring to go early in the morning, are those who have gotten a full night's sleep by 5:30 or 6:00 in the morning. Typically, these children go to bed by 7:00 or 7:30 in the evening. This is good for the parents because it frees them for activities at night, but it takes away their ability to sleep later in the morning. Your child can sleep only so much. So choose what works best for you: an early bedtime or a later waketime in the morning.

Children can learn that just because they are up, it doesn't mean that others must get up, too. Children need to learn to respect the fact that others are asleep. Parents can establish a clear signal as to when it is okay to start the day. A clock radio can help solve this problem. When the alarm goes off and your child hears the music, that is when everyone can get up. Before that she must play quietly without waking the rest of the family.

Parents should also decide what their child is allowed to do in the morning before everyone else is awake. If you do allow your child to be up early, make sure that he does not have access to anyplace where he can get hurt and that he is unable to let himself out of the house to play outdoors. Determine whether he is allowed to watch television or turn on a video. A special place for morning toys, such as books and puzzles, can be set up. Add a bowl of cereal if your child is usually hungry first thing in the morning. For younger children, busy-boxes and toys in the crib can help entertain them. You can even put several toys in your child's crib once he is asleep that he can play with once he wakes in the morning. You cannot expect him to stay quiet without something to amuse him.

Allison and Roger solved this problem with their early riser, Nathan. By age three they had taught Nathan how to turn on the heat in winter months, get out a bowl of Cheerios that they had left for him downstairs, and look through books. In the morning when they got up, they would find him happily ensconced on his favorite stool next to the heat vent in the kitchen, munching on Cheerios and "reading" to himself.

If your child cannot be left without supervision, then someone is going to have to get up when he gets up. If you have a partner, negotiate taking turns with this early morning duty so that each of you gets to sleep in sometimes.

The Night Owl

In contrast to parents of early risers, there are some parents whose major concern is that their child goes to bed too late at night. These night owls are perfectly content to stay awake until 10:00 or 11:00 at night, and sleep until 9:00 in the morning. On being put to bed earlier in the evening, these children will toss and turn, unable to fall asleep until their usual later bedtime. On mornings that they need to get up early, they will be difficult to waken. Night owls are not resistant to bedtime, they are just literally not sleepy or ready to go to bed until a much later hour.

You cannot simply move a night owl's bedtime to an earlier hour. If you put your child in bed at 7:30 when he is unable to fall asleep until 10:30, he will lie awake for three hours. Thus, he will not associate his bed with sleep but rather with being awake and bored. To move a night owl's bedtime earlier, you will need to do it gradually. Start with the time that your child normally falls asleep. Use this as your first bedtime. For the next three nights, put your child to bed at this starting bedtime. Your child should fall asleep easily and quickly. Next, move the bedtime earlier by fifteen minutes. After three nights, move it earlier again by fifteen minutes. Continue this pattern of moving your child's bedtime earlier by fifteen minutes every three nights until you reach the desired bedtime. With children who can't tell time, moving bedtime earlier in a gradual fashion will not lead to any resistance. They won't even know they are going to bed earlier.

———————— G· ————————

Stanley was successful at moving his two-year-old son's bedtime to an earlier time by using this gradual approach. Previously, Charles was not going to bed until 11:00 at night. After three nights, Stanley moved Charles's bedtime to 10:45. Three nights later, bedtime was 10:30. After several weeks, Charles was going to bed at 8:30 at night, and Stanley and his wife were finally able to have some time to themselves. They also found that Charles was happier in the morning, and he did not resist getting dressed or eating breakfast.

Twins . . . or More

Twins can be twice as much fun and twice as much work. Sleep problems with twins can also be twice as difficult, especially since each baby will have his or her own idiosyncratic sleep issues. And one twin invariably seems to wake the other. Take twin issues one step further if you have triplets or more.

One of the most frequent questions asked by parents of twins is whether or not to have the twins share a room. Most parents opt to keep them together. If multiple babies start sleeping in the same room from the very beginning, they won't wake each other up. They will learn to tune the other one out. So if one starts fussing, don't take her to another room. The other twin will likely sleep until he is ready to get up.

Another commonly asked question is whether to put them on the same sleep schedule. The answer is a resounding YES. It is best to enforce simultaneous naptimes and bedtimes. The babies will do better being on a schedule, and more important, you need the quiet time to energize yourself for when they are both up.

From early on, put twins or triplets down to sleep when they are awake. As with single babies, twins need to learn from an early age to fall asleep on their own and to be self-soothers. When there is more than one of them, there will always be times when they will need to soothe themselves and be patient. You have only one lap and two hands. Even with two adults, twins are a handful. As difficult as it may seem, try to schedule all sleep times and all naps together. Give yourself plenty of time to get both changed and ready before being put down to sleep. The risk with twins or triplets is that while you are busy with one, the other one will fall asleep in a swing or a high chair. You don't want this to happen. And even though she fell asleep on her own, she needs to do it in the right place: the crib.

Dealing with twins becomes even more interesting when they reach the age of six to nine months. That is when each one discovers the built-in playmate. Before, you had worried that one's crying would wake the other. Now it is the fun and laughing that you need to worry about. Discourage twins from waking up and playing together during the night or in the early hours of the morning. One trick that Sylvia used with Gregory and Matthew was to place a quiet toy in each of their cribs once they were both asleep. This way when one woke up in the morning, he would have a quiet toy with which to play without waking the other. Stuffed animals and busy-box–type toys are good choices.

As your twins or triplets get older, another problem that is multiplied is their getting out of the crib. One getting out of a crib is bad enough; two can be dangerous. With two there is a higher likelihood of someone's getting hurt because they are more likely to try to get into things that they shouldn't. Also, an unsupervised aggressive toddler can be a serious danger to another toddler. Be firm in your rules that no one is allowed out of his crib without permission. You may also want to keep twins in their cribs as long as possible to contain their antics.

Sharing a Room

Many children share a room with a brother or sister or with someone else in the household. There is often concern that the two people sharing a room will wake each other. Surprisingly, this rarely happens. After a few weeks of sharing, most individuals, children included, rarely hear the other person.

In some situations, though, the child with a sleep problem will disrupt the person sharing their room. In these cases, creative solutions are necessary. One solution is to move the sibling out of the room until the child with the sleep problem is sleeping through the night. In a full-force effort, this should take only one to two weeks. Another possibility is to begin sleep training at other times of the day, such as at naptime. In this way the process will not disrupt the other person's sleep.

Felicia did just that in dealing with her son Jim's sleep problems. Jim was seventeen months old and shared a room with his older brother, Michael, who was three. At bedtime Felicia would get Michael ready for bed and tuck him in. When he was all taken care of, she would turn the lights off and rock Jim to sleep. Throughout the night when Jim would wake, Felicia would take him out of his crib and rock him back to sleep. The few times that she didn't, Jim's cries woke Michael. On a few nights she put Jim down in his crib awake. He cried so much that it upset Michael, so she had given up. After months of getting little sleep, Felicia was at her wit's end. Her solution was to spend a week putting Jim down for his naps awake in his crib. He was very upset for the first three days, but by the end of the week he was falling asleep quickly. She was then ready for dealing with bedtime. The first two nights she put Michael to sleep in her bed. Since this was a special treat, Michael thought it was great. She then put Jim in his crib awake. The first night was difficult, but Jim had gotten the message. Once Jim was asleep, she moved Michael back into his own bed. On the third night both boys were put to bed in their room. Jim was fussy, but Felicia was surprised to hear Michael telling Jim that it was okay and to go to sleep—the exact words that she had used!

Single Parents

As a single parent, there are times that you are going to need help. Face it: It is hard enough in two-parent families, but when it is only you—and especially if you have more than one child—it can easily become overwhelming. Single parents need even more support from others than do dual parents. A single parent needs a sounding board to help make parenting decisions. Single parents also need downtime. Day after day and night after night of constant childrearing is difficult to do. No matter how much you love your child, you need a break. So figure out ways to get help. Pay a baby-sitter to watch your child, whether you go out or stay home. A less expensive alternative is to swap child care time with other parents. All parents appreciate the time off. If you know of a group of parents with children of similar ages, establish a baby-sitting cooperative. A record can be kept of who has given baby-sitting time and who owes baby-sitting time. Everyone gets free child care, and everyone gets time off.

One issue that some single parents grapple with is guilt. They feel guilty that their child does not have a mother and a father. To compensate for this guilt, some single parents are reluctant to set limits, and they allow their child more free rein. This is a recipe for sleep problems. It is often easier for a single parent to just give in: What difference does it make if the child stays up a half-hour later or sleeps in the parent's bed just this night?

Well, it does matter. Children need routines and they need to have limits set whether they have two parents, one parent, or another type of caregiver. So be sure to have a daily routine and set bedtime rules.

Apartment Living

Families who live in apartments may have more problems teaching their babies to sleep than those living in single homes because of worries about disturbing the neighbors. It may be virtually impossible to let your baby cry at 2:00 in the morning with neighbors nearby. This is especially true in the summertime when windows are open. Some parents even state their concern that their neighbors might even think that their baby is being abused or neglected because they are letting him cry for such an extended period of time.

If you have these or similar concerns because you live with others or close to others, there are solutions. Remember, the important part of getting your baby to sleep through the night is teaching him to fall asleep on his own. This does not have to happen at one specific time. Rather than teaching your baby to self-soothe at bedtime, do it at naptimes. And do it during the week when most people are gone for the day. You can also choose your days. Begin sleep training on a Friday night so it will only disturb weekend sleep. And by all means warn your neighbors. Explain your predicament and what you are trying to do. (Beware, though, that you may be the recipient of lots of unwanted and contradictory advice about how to manage your baby's sleep problems.)

Reminders

- Anticipate pitfalls to teaching your child good sleeping habits.

- Developmental milestones such as rolling over can interfere with your baby's ability to fall asleep.

- Be firm about your child's climbing out of the crib and getting out of bed.

- Breast-feeding can make sleep issues more complicated.

- Be prepared to deal with "I have to go potty" and "Just one more hug."

- Parents in special circumstances—whether it is having twins, being a single parent, or living in an apartment—need to anticipate common obstacles to sleeping through the night.

- No matter what the situation, find solutions that promote positive sleep associations and do not reinforce negative sleep associations.

Chapter **8**

"AM I DOING THE RIGHT THING?"
How to Cope

―――――――――――――――― ☾ ――――――――――――――――

Michelle and Tom's sixteen-month-old son, Sean, had never slept through the night. Every night either Michelle or Tom would rock Sean to sleep while he drank from a bottle. On the first night of sleep training, Michelle put Sean in his crib awake after reading him a story and singing him a song. After listening to Sean cry for ten minutes, Michelle herself started crying. Both Michelle and Tom felt guilty, listening to Sean cry when he seemed to really need them and doing nothing. They kept reading the instructions over and over again on what they were supposed to do, reassuring each other that they were doing the right thing. Eventually Sean did fall asleep, and within three days he was falling asleep quickly at bedtime and was sleeping through the night.

―――――――――――――――― ✳ ――――――――――――――――

A difficult issue that many parents face is how to cope with a screaming baby. Here you have a two-year-old who has been sobbing for Mommy or Daddy for forty-five minutes, and you know that if you just rocked him for five minutes, he would calm down and immediately fall asleep. This is where the going gets tough and why parents often do not succeed in making the necessary changes to help their child sleep through the night.

Guilt

One thing that seems to come with being a parent is guilt. Am I doing enough for my baby? Am I a good parent? These are difficult questions, without also having to cope with setting limits and possibly upsetting your child at times.

Unfortunately, setting limits for your child is part of being a good parent. Children are born as clean slates. They don't know anything, which is an overwhelming concept to realize. This means that you have to teach them everything. You have to teach them to dress themselves, to feed themselves, how to do laundry, and even how to calculate the tip at a restaurant. You have to teach them to distinguish between right and wrong. You also have to teach them how to behave. For example, you don't hit people. You don't jump up and down screaming in church or synagogue. You don't scratch yourself in certain places in public. And on and on. It's a tough job, so don't feel too guilty when your child doesn't like what you just told him to do. It comes with the territory of being a parent.

Another guilt issue felt by many working parents is that they do not spend enough time with their children if they send them to bed shortly after getting home from work. Ken was worried that he wasn't spending any quality time with his fifteen-month-old, Justin. Ken would get home each night at 7:00, just when Justin was getting ready to go to bed. Stacey had the same concern, but with an added issue: She wondered whether it was fair to her three-year-old, Bobby, to put him to bed early without spending any time with her after having been in day care all day. She felt that it was just another instance when Bobby got pushed aside and didn't get to spend time with her.

The concerns of these parents are very real and very common. But keep in mind that it is just as important for your child to get adequate sleep at night. Numerous studies have shown the negative consequences of sleep deprivation and the positive effects of sleep on development. Proper sleep will not only put your child in better spirits but will allow him to learn more and enjoy the time that he does spend with you. It is important that your child gets adequate time with you, but these times can be early in the morning or on your days off. He will be at a disadvantage, though, if he doesn't get adequate sleep—even if it is just for one night.

Questions Parents Often Ask

Going along with the issue of guilt, parents often ask themselves lots of questions and can doubt their parenting at times.

"Am I a bad parent?" A bad parent is someone who doesn't provide for his/her child or abuses his/her child. A good parent is someone who takes care of his/her children's needs and does the right thing. Teaching your child how to fall asleep on his own is doing the right thing. He will need this skill as a baby and in the years to come. You may feel that your child needs you at bedtime when he is crying and upset, but the opposite is actually true. He needs you to help him learn how to fall asleep on his own.

"Will this cause my child harm?" As long as you provide your baby with lots of attention during the day, you will not harm your child by letting her cry when she wakes during the night. Some say that suggestions on how to deal with sleep problems simply give parents permission to allow their baby to cry. This is not exactly true. One aspect of dealing with sleep problems may involve your baby crying, but that is not the largest component. The major components are teaching your child how to be a self-soother and how to put himself to sleep. Prevention

of sleep problems is even more important. By preventing future problems, you are helping your child, not harming him.

"Will my child be scarred for life?" Some parents instantly imagine their child on the psychiatrist's couch talking about the damage his parents did to him by leaving him abandoned at bedtime to cry on his own. This will not happen. Research has shown that children who sleep well, with limited bedtime problems and night waking problems, are better adjusted, better behaved, and do better overall. One study done in our laboratory found that those children between the ages of two and three who had bedtime problems were more likely to have a whole spectrum of behavior or psychological problems. That is, they were more likely to be aggressive and noncompliant. They were also more likely to appear depressed and withdrawn. So rather than scarring your child, you will be helping him. Children who sleep are well-adjusted and have fewer overall problems.

"Will my child still love me in the morning?" Don't worry, your child will still love you in the morning. He is not upset with you personally when he is crying at night, he simply wants to fall asleep. The next morning he will be just as happy to see you as always.

The Emotional Aspects of Sleep

For some reason, sleep is different from most other behaviors. We seem to attach much more emotional weight to sleep than practically any other aspect of our children's lives, and there are probably many reasons for this. A few of these reasons will be explored here. It is important to understand these reasons so that they can be dealt with in a forthright manner and not interfere with what you decide is best for your child. One reason is that we all have long-standing images of an adorable sleeping baby. Some of our favorite pictures are of our child asleep. In sleep, babies seem vulnerable and sweet. When dreaming of having one's own child, many individuals have the image of cuddling a baby to sleep while rocking in a chair in a peaceful, quiet place. So when their child is sobbing at bedtime, it runs counter to these pleasant images.

Second, we tend to give dramatic meanings to the cries of a baby alone in a crib. With older children we learn why they are upset because they can tell us. With young babies, however, we really don't know why they are crying and often attribute their cries to something else such as hunger, sadness, separation anxiety, or any number of concerns. Rather than simply thinking the baby is saying, "I don't want to be here. Take me out of my crib," we believe our child is saying something completely different, such as "You have abandoned me." Thus, we often interpret our baby's cries as separation anxiety or abandonment, which may not be the case at all.

We also don't like to think about our children being sad and alone. The picture of our child standing all alone in his crib and crying invokes in us a need to comfort our child. It is difficult to stand by and let this happen even when we know that it is best for the child.

Be careful not to project too many of your own feelings onto your baby when he is crying. Your baby does not hate you, and you are not abandoning him. You are trying to do what is best for him, and that includes finding a way for both of you to get a good night's sleep. Your baby needs you. He needs you to help him learn how to fall asleep on his own.

In thinking about these reasons, it may be helpful to remind yourself that learning to fall asleep alone is a skill that has to be learned. This may help you deal with sleep problems. You can equate learning to fall asleep alone with learning to walk. When your baby is learning to walk, he will probably fall down a few times. This may scare him and make him cry. Being scared and crying doesn't mean, however, that you will never let him try to walk alone. That would be harmful. Try to see sleep the same way. Your baby may be upset at first, but eventually, with some practice, your baby will acquire this new skill and have it for a lifetime.

———————————— C· ————————————

Vanessa was stunned when this transition happened for her two-year-old daughter, Denise. Bedtime had been a struggle since Denise was very young. Vanessa decided that she needed to replace a stressful bedtime routine with a calm one that would help her daughter go to sleep happy and relaxed. After developing a set bedtime routine and helping Denise fall asleep on her own, the world became a different place. There were no more crying spells when Vanessa announced it was bedtime, and Denise seemed much happier in the evenings and during the day. Three weeks later Vanessa had the shock of her life. Dinner was over, and she was reading Denise a story in the living room. Halfway through the story, Denise turned toward her mother, lifted her arms, and said, "Bed." Thinking that she had misheard, Vanessa asked her to repeat what she had said. In a more definite tone, Denise announced that it was time for bed.

———————————— ✳ ————————————

Your child may not go to this extreme, but she will stop dreading bedtime and enjoy the peacefulness of crawling into a snug bed after a busy day.

Babies Know What Works

Babies know how to get what they want. One way is by being incredibly cute and incredibly pathetic. Babies need to be able to look pathetic. That is one of their surefire ways of getting what they want. They are completely helpless and dependent on others. On top of all that, for the first few years of their life they have a very difficult time telling people what they want. So being pathetic works.

There is nothing more pathetic than a crying baby all alone

in his crib. Your immediate reaction is to pick him up and save him. Remember, looking pathetic works. As your child gets older, he will learn even more tricks. My favorite one is "I just wanted to tell you I love you." How can you stay mad at that? So what if it is your seventh time stamping up the stairs to see what your child wants. And then by about three years old they learn those magic words: "I have to go potty." Again, you can't ignore that.

Parents with Two Different Styles

Some couples work well together dealing with their child's sleep problems. As one mother said, "We had a common enemy." For others, this may be an issue over which they strongly disagree. One may be willing to let the baby cry, while the other may not be able to tolerate it. One may not like having the baby share their bed, while the other may not mind. Leslie and Mark were such a couple.

------------------------------ ☾ ------------------------------

Leslie and Mark's son, Danny, woke several times a night. By the time Danny was seven months old, Leslie decided that it was time to do something. She couldn't take the sleepless nights much longer. One Thursday night, after putting Danny down in his crib, she left him. After five minutes of listening to Danny cry, Mark stormed upstairs to get Danny, saying that he couldn't take it. This led to several weeks of arguing over what they should do. Both thought that something should be done, but while Leslie could tolerate Danny's being upset, it was too difficult for Mark.

------------------------------ ✳ ------------------------------

How can this issue be resolved? Communicate. Compromise. Negotiate. Marriage can be difficult even in the best of times. And when sleep deprived, even the best of us gets cranky. In developing a strategy, both individuals need to have input. If not, it will not work. Both people have to come to an agreement.

This will require communication on both parts. Don't simply agree for the sake of avoiding an argument—the process will backfire. One of you will end up insisting on a different course of action in the middle of dealing with your baby at bedtime. That course of action is usually to give up and get the baby when he is upset. This will make the situation worse, especially if the baby has been crying for a long time. It will teach your baby that if he persists and really screams, someone will come to get him. You have just taught him to cry longer and louder. The next time that you try to implement a strategy, your baby will be upset twice as long. Therefore, for you and your partner's sake, it is vital that you discuss what you are going to do, develop a strategy, and stick to it. This process will be good practice for years to come. Developing a strategy to deal with your child's sleep problems will just be the first of many times that you will need to do this, whether it is because your child bites, is acting up in school, or keeps breaking his curfew.

There is another practical way to deal with two parents who have different styles. As mentioned above, often one parent can deal with a sleep problem while the other parent can't. If this is the case in your family, then allow the parent who can cope to do the sleep training the first night or two. And plan to do it when the one who can't cope is out of town or at least out of the house. He or she can go to the movies, visit a friend for a night or two, go for a long walk, or listen to music with headphones on. After the first night or two, that parent can rejoin the bedtime routine.

One other hint: It is important that each parent put the child to sleep at different times. If not, your child may not be able to fall asleep for the other parent.

How to Cope

There are many ways to cope with teaching your baby to sleep through the night. You will probably need a repertoire of coping strategies because one method will not work in every situation. Here are some suggestions that many parents have found helpful in coping with a crying baby at bedtime.

Block out the noise. The simple sound of your baby's crying is likely to make you feel stressed. That is nature's way of making sure that babies are taken care of. Unfortunately, the sound of your baby's crying will raise your level of stress whether it is an emergency situation or simply your baby being fussy or unhappy. One way to decrease your response is to block out the noise. Don't block out all the noise, since you do want to make sure that you don't ignore a baby who is in danger. But if you know that your baby is simply unhappy and likely to be crying for a while, then dampen the noise.

Here are a number of ways to block out the noise: Go to another part of the house. Just being farther away will dampen the noise and help you cope. Turn on anything that will block out the sound. Turn on a fan or the air vent in your kitchen. Turn on the vacuum cleaner. Take a shower or simply sit in the bathroom with the shower or sink running. Put some music on or turn up the television. Blow-dry your hair.

Many parents worry that the noise that blocks out the baby's cries will keep the baby awake. Don't worry; as long as you're not making too much noise, any constant sound is likely to help your baby sleep. It is also much less likely to keep your baby up than hearing you wandering around the house.

Don't be a clock watcher. Remember the old saying, "A watched pot never boils"? This is true about babies also. A watched baby will never seem to stop crying. When your child is crying, don't watch the clock. This will make the crying seem to go on forever. Don't sit on the stairs listening. Leave. Do something else. Put the dishes in the dishwasher. Flip through a magazine. Put on your favorite music. Call a friend for support while your child is crying (and be sure to explain what is going on!). Go get the mail from the mailbox. Do anything but watch the clock.

Humor yourself. One of the best ways to deal with a stressful situation is to use humor. Humor is a great stress reducer, and it will help you keep your perspective. When it is 10:00 at night and your baby has been cranky all day and you are now on your eleventh trip to check on your crying baby, it is easy to lose all perspective. You will feel as though you will never have a moment's peace again. But try to remember that this is just a temporary situation. As your grandmother probably once told you, this, too, shall pass.

So use humor to keep your sanity. Cut out cartoons about babies who don't sleep and put them on the refrigerator. Look at them to remind yourself that you are not alone. Put notes up around the house. Put a sign on the door to your baby's room saying CRYING BABY—ENTER AT YOUR OWN RISK. Put a sign for visitors in a prominent place: WE ARE TEACHING SAM TO SLEEP THROUGH THE NIGHT. EXPECT DIRTY DISHES, CRYING BABIES, AND UNHAPPY PARENTS. PLEASE PROVIDE SUPPORT.

Smile. Smiling is the best thing to do when you are feeling low. You cannot feel stressed or be unhappy when you are smiling. Even if you don't feel like smiling, do it anyway. Smiling will make you feel better and give you more reason to smile again. It may feel stupid at first, but try it. It really works.

Play music. Music is great for our moods. Research has shown that music can have strong effects on our moods, in both positive and negative ways. Loud, obnoxious music will put us in a bad mood. Our favorite music will put us in a good mood. When you are feeling down or overwhelmed, or when the baby just won't seem to stop crying, put on some favorite music. Put on soft, soothing music if you are feeling stressed. Put on fun, energetic music if you don't feel that you have the energy to go on. It is a great way to motivate yourself to clean the house or to just dance. It will help put older children in a good mood, too. Get everyone into the dancing mode.

A Calm Parent Equals a Calm Baby

While a calm parent equals a calm baby, the opposite is also true: An upset parent equals an upset baby. Your baby will sense your mood. If you are upset, she will be upset. If you are tense, she will be tense. But if you are happy, she will be happy.

Your baby looks to you for cues on how to react to the world. If you start to feel tense as bedtime is approaching, your baby is going to sense that and think there is something she should be worried about and afraid of. However, if you approach bedtime with a feeling of serenity, she will sense this and feel serene as well.

Challenge Those Thoughts

Our thoughts are very powerful. What we are thinking can make us happy or can make us stressed. Dealing with a crying baby, especially one who won't sleep, makes us think negative thoughts. Imagine that it has been forty minutes of constant crying for the second night in a row. You might start thinking, "This is never going to work." Everyone thinks that at some point. Your thoughts may be irrational: "He is never going to stop crying" or "It's not fair that my baby won't sleep when everyone else's does." You may be angry at your baby for not sleeping and not letting you sleep. Such thoughts make it even harder to cope with the situation. Are you one of those people? Are you caught up in negative thoughts that are just making you feel worse? Your negative thoughts are not going to make the baby stop crying or start sleeping. Instead, they are going to make the situation worse. Your baby will sense your stress and become even more upset. To get out of the vicious cycle of your thoughts affecting how you feel, you need to combat your negative beliefs.

The first step to combating negative thoughts is to notice what you are thinking. Write your thoughts down. You may be surprised at the ideas that are going through your head. Once you have identified your thoughts, you can begin to challenge them. Argue with yourself. Present the logical side: "My baby will stop crying. Eventually he will have to fall asleep" or "I am not a failure as a parent simply because my baby has problems sleeping. Otherwise, my baby is happy and healthy" or "His not sleeping is not my fault, and it is not his fault. He has simply gotten into some bad habits" or "Why would this program not work for my baby? It has worked for so many other babies. I can do it."

Teaching your baby to sleep through the night is not an easy process. It takes work and will probably involve some tears (likely on everyone's part). When you notice that you are telling yourself negative thoughts, combat them. Stress the positive: "This is going to work" or "It is only the second night. Next week at this time everyone will be sleeping." By saying positive things you will feel better and will be better able to cope.

Get Sleep Yourself

One important issue for both you and your partner is to make sure that you get some sleep. It is very difficult to cope with anything when you are sleep deprived. Try to work out a system with your partner to share the duties and let each of you get as much sleep as possible. One person should take late-night duty, and the other be on in the morning. That way one person can get to sleep early at night, and the other can sleep in the next morning. And swap off nights; take turns in getting up with the baby. On weekends, one can do Friday night and the other Saturday night.

Two problems frequently occur when attempting this system. The first is that the parent who is on duty does not wake up when the baby cries. In this situation, the other parent ends up saying that by the time the partner who is on duty wakes up (or is awakened), the other partner is already wide awake and may as well take care of the baby. You will need to work out a solution to this dilemma. Wake your partner and make him or her get up. Put the baby monitor on that person's side of the bed. After a while, if you keep getting up with the baby, your partner will learn to sleep through the noise and will never wake to the cries, so it is important that the person be awakened. With a little training the adult on duty should begin to wake when the baby does.

The other issue is what to do when one parent works and the other parent stays home. Usually in this type of situation the person who remains at home always gets up with the baby because the other person is expected to function at work the next day. But people do not always realize how much work it is to stay home with a baby. Yes, you can remain in your night-clothes all day long, but taking care of a baby or a toddler takes enormous effort, physically and emotionally. A fairer solution is to compromise, but the compromise does not have to be exactly fifty-fifty. The working partner (in the more traditional sense) can take over on Thursday nights, when only one day is left in the workweek, and on weekends. Another solution is for the working person to take every third night rather than every other night. At the very least, the working parent can take the duty on the weekends to give the stay-at-home partner a break. Working out a solution for this problem is important. We all need suffi-cient sleep to be at our best. The working parent also benefits from solving this problem because he or she will not be coming home to an overtired and cranky partner.

Coping with Loss of Sleep

If you are sleepy, be careful. Don't take long drives in the car. Be careful in the kitchen. Accidents can happen when you are tired. Often we are expected to get things done, no matter how much sleep we got the night before, the week before, or even the month before. Before you just jump in and do whatever is expected, think about whether or not you realistically can. Will you be safe? Will you be endangering others? For example, more car accidents are caused by sleepy driving than by drunk driving. These accidents are more likely to occur in the middle of the night, as you might expect. But, surprisingly, the next most dangerous time is between three and five in the afternoon. Turning up the radio or rolling down the car window is not going to help much in the event that you are falling asleep at the wheel. The only thing to do is stop and take a quick nap, ten to fifteen minutes. Of course, if you can take a longer nap, then do so. If you are not getting enough sleep, figure out the limits on what you can reasonably and safely achieve.

Relaxation Strategies

Psychologists have had a great deal of success in developing techniques that help people relax in stressful situations. These strategies are often used by people with anxiety disorders, people about to undergo a stressful medical procedure, or those who need to learn stress management techniques. Try out a few and decide what works best for you. Using a relaxation strategy will help you cope when dealing with an upset baby.

Progressive muscle relaxation

Some say that progressive muscle relaxation (PMR) is the gold standard of relaxation strategies. It takes practice, but once learned it is an excellent way to reduce stress. Progressive muscle relaxation teaches you to identify and relieve tension in your muscles. When you are stressed or upset, you may not even notice how much you are tensing your muscles. This technique will help you identify times when you are tense and teach you to relax.

In PMR, each muscle is sequentially tensed and relaxed to help you identify tension and then release it. In the beginning, progressive muscle relaxation takes between twenty and thirty minutes. The more you practice, the less time it will take. By the end you will be able to relax in a matter of moments.

Follow the script that is outlined. You can tape it on a tape recorder if you want. If you are like many people who don't like to hear the sound of their own voices, get someone else to do this for you. The person should speak in a slow, soothing manner. The exact words used are not important; it is the process that is important. You don't even need to follow an exact script as long as you sequentially tense and relax your muscles. Each time that you tense a muscle, keep it tensed for about ten seconds.

Progressive Muscle Relaxation Script

Muscle Group	Tensing Exercise
Lower arms	Make a fist
Upper arms	Make a muscle
Lower legs	Point toes
Thighs	Squeeze legs together
Stomach	Tighten stomach muscles
Chest	Take a deep breath
Shoulders	Raise shoulders to ears
Neck	Lower chin to chest
Jaw	Bite down firmly
Lips	Press lips together
Eyes	Close eyes tightly
Forehead	Frown, draw eyebrows together

To begin this exercise, find a comfortable place. It can be lying on a bed or sitting in a reclining chair. Remove your glasses (if you wear them), get comfortable, and close your eyes. You are to keep your eyes closed throughout the relaxation process.

Here is a sample script that you can use to practice progressive muscle relaxation:

Begin by taking a few deep breaths. Breathe relaxation in and breathe tension out.
(Wait 20 seconds.)

Now tense the muscles of your right hand by making a fist. Feel the tension . . . study the tension . . . and relax. Notice the difference between the tension and the relaxation.
(Wait 20 seconds.)

Now tense the muscles of your right arm by making a muscle. Feel the tension . . . study the tension . . . and relax. Notice the difference.
(Wait 5 seconds.)

Just let yourself become more and more relaxed. Feel your muscles becoming loose . . . heavy . . . and relaxed. Just let your muscles go.
(Wait 5 seconds.)

Now tense the muscles of your left hand by making a fist. Feel the tension . . . study the tension . . . and relax. Notice the difference between the tension and the relaxation.
(Wait 20 seconds.)

Now tense the muscles of your left arm by making a muscle. Feel the tension . . . study the tension . . . and relax. Notice the difference.
(Wait 5 seconds.)

You are becoming more and more relaxed, sleepy and relaxed.
(Wait 5 seconds.)

Now tense the muscles of your right leg by pointing your toes. Feel the tension . . . study the tension . . . and relax. Notice the difference between the tension and the relaxation.
(Wait 20 seconds.)

(continues)

Now tense the muscles of your left leg by pointing your toes. Feel the tension . . . study the tension . . . and relax. Notice the difference.
(Wait 5 seconds.)

Just continue to relax.
(Wait 5 seconds.)

Now tense the muscles of your upper legs by pressing your thighs together. Feel the tension . . . study the tension . . . and relax. Notice the difference between the tension and the relaxation.
(Wait 20 seconds.)

Now tense the muscles of your stomach. Feel the tension . . . study the tension . . . and relax. Notice the difference.
(Wait 5 seconds.)

The relaxation is becoming deeper and deeper. You are feeling relaxed, drowsy and relaxed. With each breath in, your relaxation increases. With each exhalation, you spread the relaxation throughout your body.
(Wait 5 seconds.)

Now tense the muscles of your chest by taking a deep breath. Feel the tension . . . study the tension . . . and exhale. Notice the difference between the tension and the relaxation.
(Wait 20 seconds.)

Now tense the muscles of your shoulders by hunching your shoulders toward your ears. Feel the tension . . . study the tension . . . and relax. Notice the difference.
(Wait 5 seconds.)

Let yourself become more and more relaxed.
(Wait 5 seconds.)

Now tense the muscles of your jaw by biting down firmly. Feel the tension . . . study the tension . . . and relax. Notice the difference between the tension and the relaxation.
(Wait 20 seconds.)

Now tense the muscles of your lower face by pressing your lips together firmly. Feel the tension . . . study the tension . . . and relax. Notice the difference.
(Wait 5 seconds.)

Now the very deep state of relaxation is moving through all the areas of your body as your muscles completely relax.
(Wait 5 seconds.)

Now tense the muscles of your eyes by closing them tightly. Feel the tension . . . study the tension . . . and exhale. Notice the difference between the tension and the relaxation.
(Wait 20 seconds.)

Now tense the muscles of your forehead by frowning and drawing your eyebrows together. Feel the tension . . . study the tension . . . and relax. Notice the difference.
(Wait 5 seconds.)

Let yourself become more and more relaxed.
(Wait 20 seconds.)

Now relax all the muscles of your body; just let them become more and more relaxed.
(Wait 20 seconds.)

Remain In your very relaxed state. Begin to notice your breathing. Breathe through your nose. Notice the cool air as you breathe in and the warm moist air as you exhale. Just continue to notice your breathing. Now each time you exhale, mentally repeat the word *relax*. Inhale, exhale, relax . . . inhale, exhale, relax.
(Wait 20 seconds.)

(continues)

Now you are going to return to your normal, alert state. As I count backward, you will gradually become more alert. When I reach "two," open your eyes. When I get to "one," you will be entirely alert. "Five . . . four" . . . you are becoming more alert . . . "three" . . . you feel very refreshed . . . "two" . . . now open your eyes . . . "one."

How do you feel? You should be extremely relaxed. Continue to practice. That is the only way to get good at this technique. Even if you feel completely relaxed after the first time, you will feel more and more relaxed each time you practice. After a number of sessions (over at least two weeks), cut back the number of muscle groups by half (both fists together, both arms together, both legs together, thighs, chest, neck, lips, eyes). Practice again for two weeks. Cut back the muscle groups again by half (both arms, both legs, chest, lips). By now you should be an expert at becoming relaxed. Once you are good at PMR, the word *relax* will be well associated with a completely relaxed state. Use the word *relax* in your everyday life to help you relax in tense situations. It is a good time to try it when the baby is crying.

Diaphragmatic Breathing

Slow, even breathing is also an excellent way to relax. There are, however, two ways that people breathe. The first way involves breathing from your chest. This type of breathing can cause you to hyperventilate. A better way to breathe is from your diaphragm. This technique will take only a few moments to learn.

First, lie down on your back on the floor or on a firm bed. Place your hand on your chest and breathe using your chest muscles so that you feel your chest rise and fall with each breath. Now place your other hand on your stomach, leaving your first hand on your chest. Continue to breathe from your chest and feel that your stomach muscles hardly move. Now breathe from your diaphragm. This will require you to take deeper breaths. When you breathe from your diaphragm, your chest will hardly move and your stomach will rise and fall. Continue doing this for a few minutes and get the feel for it. Once you think you have it, sit up, leaving your hands in place on your chest and stomach. Continue to practice diaphragmatic breathing, that is, breathing from your diaphragm. When you are ready, stand up. Again, keep your hands where they are while you get the hang of it. If you think that you lost the feel for it, return to a lying position.

In the beginning, when you go to use this technique, you will need to place your hand on your stomach to make sure that you are breathing from your diaphragm. As you get better and better you will no longer need to do this. When doing diaphragmatic breathing, take slow, deep breaths. Don't breathe too fast, or you may hyperventilate, which will make you feel even more stressed. Take several deep breaths. Breathe normally. Take several deep breaths again. Within a few minutes you should feel calmer and more ready to face the world, or at least a crying baby.

Diaphragmatic breathing is not just specific to calming down when facing a crying baby. Diaphragmatic breathing is an excellent stress reducer in any situation. If you are about to give a presentation at work and are feeling stressed, do your diaphragmatic breathing. Upset with your spouse and feeling stressed? Do a few minutes of deep breathing. This type of deep breathing can be done anywhere. No one will even know that you are performing a stress relaxation technique. You can do it at home, while in a store, or out at a restaurant. Deep breathing will send messages to your body to calm down. It will change your body's reaction to stress.

Guided Imagery

Guided imagery is another excellent way to relax. At times, we all imagine ourselves to be somewhere else. If you imagine yourself in a stressful situation, such as having to do a stressful presentation or being in danger, you will become tense. Your body will react as if you are actually in that situation. Your heart will pound, your pulse will race, and you may feel jittery all over. This will also happen if you imagine yourself listening to your baby crying. The opposite is true if you imagine yourself in a pleasant, relaxing scene. Your breathing will become more even, and your pulse will slow. Imagining yourself in such a pleasant situation will therefore help you to relax.

The first thing you will need to do is develop a pleasant scenario. Lie back, close your eyes, and think of your favorite place. For example, this is the scene that Michael developed for himself: "I am lying on the beach in Hawaii. The sun is warm. The beach is quiet. I can hear a few people talking and laughing in the distance. I can hear the waves crashing. I can smell the salt water in the air and hear the birds. The sand is warm under my hands, and my whole body is relaxed, relishing the moment." Michael is able to think of this scene any time that he is feeling stressed. He thinks of it when he begins worrying about finances or is in a stressful meeting at work. He can even go there in his mind when the baby has been screaming for twenty minutes.

Maybe your relaxing place is on top of a mountain or sitting in front of a fireplace. Whatever your scene, think of it in terms of all your senses. What do you hear? What do you smell? What do you feel? The more senses that you incorporate into your scene, the easier it will be to imagine. Once you have developed your scene, imagine yourself there two to three times a day. Embellish it until you can actually feel yourself there. With practice you will be able to imagine yourself in your peaceful setting almost instantaneously and will quickly feel relaxed. And when the baby is crying or you are stuck in traffic, put yourself at your scene and enjoy the sensation.

Other Relaxation Strategies

There are many other ways that people relax. Some people do yoga. Others meditate. Whatever works for you, do it.

Being relaxed is important for your mental well-being. It will help you cope with teaching your baby to sleep on his own and, amazingly, it will make the process go faster and smoother. The calmer you are, the calmer your baby will be, and a calm baby will quickly become a sleeping baby.

Reminders

- Teaching a baby to sleep through the night can be stressful for parents.

- There are many ways to cope, including using humor, adjusting your thinking, and remaining calm.

- Relaxation strategies, including progressive muscle relaxation, diaphragmatic breathing, and guided imagery, are all excellent ways to deal with stressful events.

Chapter **9**

IT'S OFF TO GRANDMA'S HOUSE WE GO
Obstacles to Continued Good Sleep

Ellen's two-year-old son, Nathaniel, finally started sleeping through the night at fourteen months. But for the past few weeks he has refused to go to bed and won't sleep in his room. All of these problems began after the family returned from a summer vacation.

Kathleen and Brian recently separated. They have joint custody of their three-year-old daughter, Courtney. Courtney spends weekdays with Kathleen and weekends with Brian. Both Kathleen and Brian find that Courtney has difficulty falling asleep on the first night that she sleeps at either's house.

Once a baby is sleeping through the night, parents often feel that the worst is over. And while this is true, there may still be obstacles to face. Such obstacles include vacations, overnights at grandparents', baby-sitters, special occasions, and times when the baby gets sick. Other common obstacles include managing an older child's sleep after the birth of a new baby or the divorce of parents. Each of these situations, and more, can create sleeping problems for your child.

Switching to a Bed

One obstacle that all parents face is how to manage the change from a crib to a bed. The two major questions that arise are "when?" and "how?"

When Do You Make the Switch?

There is no set time that you should get rid of your child's crib and switch to a bed, although most children make the move sometime between one and a half and three and a half years. The exact time can be triggered by many things. The most common time is prior to the birth of another baby. If this is the reason, you may want to make the switch at least six to eight weeks before your next child is due. You want your older child well settled in his new bed before he sees the new baby taking over his crib. An alternative is not to make the switch until the new baby is three or four months old. Before that time, the newborn may be sleeping in a bassinet anyway. Then, by waiting, your older child will have adjusted to the new baby, making the transition easier.

The second most common reason to make the switch is when your child tries to climb or jump out of the crib. Many parents become concerned about their child's harming himself. This may or may not be a good time to switch to a bed. On the positive side, you will not have to worry about your child's hurting himself in the middle of the night by falling from the crib. On the negative side, switching to a bed does not remove the concerns about your child's being able to get up and move about during the night without your knowing it. You will also have lost all control of detaining your child during the night. If your child is very young and you would rather not move him to a bed, the ways to handle the issue of getting out of the crib are given in Chapter 7. You can also simply keep the side of the crib down so that your child can easily get out without having to switch to a bed.

Another reason that many parents decide to make the move to a bed is that their child is in the midst of being potty trained or is already potty trained. While your child is being potty trained, you will want him to be able to get to the bathroom when necessary. Being in a crib may make this impossible. One solution, though, as mentioned previously, is to raise the crib mattress to its highest position and put a stool by the side of the crib. This allows your child to climb out whenever necessary, but still allows him to continue sleeping in a crib. If this sounds dangerous, or you are not sure if your child can handle it, do some test trials and have your child practice. Remember that he may already be climbing up on counters or onto high objects where you don't want him to be, so the climb from the crib may be relatively easy.

Parents sometimes decide to switch their child to a bed because it seems like the right time or their child appears to be outgrowing the crib. These are good reasons to make the move.

How Do You Make the Switch?

For some children the transition from crib to bed goes smoothly. For others it is more difficult. It usually goes smoother than the parents expect, however. One of the most creative ideas that I have heard was from a parent who threw a "big boy bed" party for her three-year-old. She had him go with her to choose the bed at the store and then talked it up for a week in advance. On the day of the big event, she had a party and invited friends and grandparents. There was a cake and balloons. He was so excited about getting a big boy's bed that everything went smoothly.

But while many children relish the move, others are resistant. Each child is different. Your first child is the most likely to resist the transition. He may be very attached to his crib, and it is likely that the switch will be made around the time that a new baby is coming. Switching to sleeping in a bed is one of the many changes that will occur in his life, such as no longer being the baby of the family and the center of attention. It may also coincide with toilet training, another pressure for him to "grow up." Later-born children often make the transition easier because they want to be just like their older brother or sister. Since their older sibling sleeps in a bed, they will also want to sleep in a bed. To a younger child, a crib may be for "babies."

Should you leave the crib still standing? This is a difficult question to answer. It really depends on your child. The usual suggestion is to take the crib down when you put up the bed. Some people have no choice because they have no room to do otherwise. But even if you have the room, leaving the crib standing may cause difficulty for your child. She may become ambivalent about where she wants to sleep, and the choice may put even more pressure on her during this potentially stressful time. Even if you are expecting another child within a few weeks, you may want to take the crib down for this short time, until your child no longer recognizes it as his and as the place where he sleeps. If you do take the crib down, put the new bed in the same place as the crib to avoid additional changes for your child. And your child may find it soothing to continue to sleep with her old crib blanket even if it is too small for the bed. For some children, though, it won't matter what you do. They are ready to move to a bed and will relish this change in their status.

No matter how prepared your child may be to move to a bed, you should always put up a guard rail to prevent him from falling out of the new bed. Some children may become resistant to having the guard rail up at bedtime. Jessica was this way. She moved into a "big girl's bed" at three. Two months later she insisted that her mother not put the guard rail up at bedtime even though she had fallen out of bed several times when it had been left down. Rather than fight, her mother simply left it down at bedtime. After Jessica had fallen asleep, her mother went back in and put it up. This ensured that Jessica was safe but also stopped the arguments at bedtime. Jessica did catch on eventually, but by that time her mother had decided to take the guard rail off the bed completely. Jessica was more used to sleeping in a bed by then and didn't need the guard rail.

In the beginning, after your child has moved to a bed, be alert when your child sleeps in beds other than her own, such as at others' houses or while on vacation. Put up a bed rail or construct a wall of some type so that she doesn't fall out of the bed. At a minimum, place blankets or pillows on the floor to cushion the fall so she won't be hurt if she does fall. Falling out of bed is even scarier for children who are sleeping in a strange bed.

Falling out of bed can also occur at other times. Sarah's mother couldn't understand why Sarah suddenly began falling out a year after being moved to her bed. Then she came to realize that after she had rearranged Sarah's bedroom furniture, a different side of the bed was against the wall. Before, Sarah could safely roll to the right because the wall was on her right side. With the new furniture arrangement, the wall was now on her left side. In her sleep she would still roll to the right, thinking it was safe, but instead she now landed on the floor. Sarah's mother put a guard rail back on the bed for a few weeks until Sarah got used to this new arrangement.

The Birth of a New Baby

The birth of a new baby can lead to sleep problems in older children. Children will often have a period of adjustment to the presence of a new baby in the house. As one mother said about her twenty-month-old, "I swear, he keeps giving me dagger looks and wants to know when 'she' is going to be returned." Having a new baby disrupts everyone's routine. A new baby and a toddler can be even more difficult. A newborn is demanding, especially for the first few months. At the same time, your older child or children need just as much attention as before. And if you and your newborn stay awake much of the night, you won't have the opportunity to sleep during the day because your older child will be running about.

There are some things that you can do, however, to make the transition easier. First of all, prepare your other children for the arrival of their new baby brother or sister as much as you can. Obviously, this will depend upon the age of your older one(s). Read lots of books about being a big brother or sister. Talk about Mommy being gone for a few days and coming home with a new baby. Talk about the new baby in Mommy's tummy. As you set up the nursery for your new baby, have your older child help. Involve him in the process as much as possible.

When it comes to sleep, there are several things that you can do to make the transition to older sibling easier. Remember, your other child may feel displaced by the new baby in terms of your time and affection. Keep that in mind when your older child starts to act up. Children need lots of attention during this time. Yes, I know that you are saying, "How in the world am I going to do that?" The easiest way is to get help if you can. Your partner will be even more essential in helping out after the birth of a second or third child than with the first. A helper can be a huge benefit in caring for the newborn. To be honest, a one-week-old baby does not care much who changes her diaper, while a two-year-old will care a great deal about who puts him to bed. To keep your older child sleeping through the night, make sure that you make bedtime and bedtime rituals sacred. Try to get someone else to watch the baby while you spend some quality time with your older one. Read books in peace. Put on pajamas and have some fun with your older child. In the beginning you may not be able to do it all alone, especially if you are not allowed to lift anything, but that is okay. Do as much as you can and have someone else lift him into his crib.

Another good idea is to keep bedtime rules consistent. Obviously, someone else will be taking care of your older child(ren) while you are off having the next one. Make sure that you have left instructions on your child's sleep rituals. As much as possible, keep everything the same while you are gone. Your child will be better off.

Once you are back home, your child will test the limits. He'll want to check that you are the same parent as before. If only two requests for extra hugs were allowed at bedtime before, then give only two extra hugs now. Four hugs to try to reassure him will only confuse him and make him more concerned. In his mind something must be really wrong if he is getting away with misbehaving. He wants to be sure that all is the same, and setting limits will be reassuring. It will not upset him more.

Another issue that may come up is whether one child will wake the other in the middle of the night. Usually, the older child wakes the newborn rather than the other way around. If your new baby is waking your older child, though, reassure the older one and put him back to bed as quickly as you can. You don't want to reinforce night wakings. It may take older children a few weeks to get used to the sound of a newborn baby crying in the middle of the night, especially if it results in parental attention, but be assured that this, too, will pass and things will return to normal. Keep the faith and don't get too overwhelmed and discouraged. All will settle in, and everyone will get some sleep eventually.

Vacations

When Becky was eight months old, Francine and George decided to go on vacation, their first since Becky was born.

They went to Florida and stayed with George's parents in their condominium on the beach. Before the vacation, Becky slept very well. They would put her to bed at 8:00 and wouldn't hear from her again until she woke at 6:30 in the morning. On vacation her sleep began to become problematic. Because his parents' condominium only had two bedrooms, Becky slept in the same room as Francine and George. In addition to sleeping in the same room with her parents and being upset by being in a new place, Becky's sleep schedule was disturbed because they would often stay out late visiting friends or going out to dinner. By the end of the vacation, Francine and George were ready to return home and to their routine. What they didn't expect was that Becky continued to have sleep problems. The first night was difficult because they had an evening flight and therefore did not get home until 11:00 at night. The next morning Becky slept until 9:00, which threw off her nap schedule. Then bedtime became difficult. Before, Becky would go right to sleep on her own. Now she demanded that someone hold her until she fell asleep. She was also waking two to three times per night. Francine and George vowed never to go vacation again until Becky was eighteen!

Vacations are known to disturb babies' sleep schedules. There are a number of reasons for this common problem. Francine and John's story is fairly typical. Often on vacation, parents have the baby sleeping in the room with them. They may also have to respond to their baby during the night because they are concerned about the baby's crying since they are in a hotel or staying at someone's house. The baby's sleep schedule is often changed because of plans that disrupt normal naptimes and bedtime. There are things to do during the day and places to go in the evening. Baby-sitters may not be available, so the parents are often forced to bring the baby along with them. Because the baby is sleeping in a strange environment, she may be more inclined to have problems falling asleep at night and difficulties with waking during the night. As a parent you are also much less likely to set limits because you know that it is difficult for the baby to be sleeping in a new place. You yourself may even have problems sleeping in a new place and can sympathize with your baby's problems. Another issue that may interfere is a change of time zone if you travel far; this will wreak havoc with everyone's schedule, especially your baby's.

Upon returning home, most parents expect that sleep will return to normal. It often doesn't. Your baby has quickly become used to being rocked to sleep or at least having you stay with her or responding to her during the night. She may also be used to sleeping in the same room with you, something she may thoroughly enjoy whether you did or not.

Never going on vacation again is not the best solution. There are things that you can do to minimize sleep problems associated with vacations. The key to sleeping through the night on vacations is to make things as similar to home as possible. Here are some suggestions.

Room arrangements. If possible, try not to share a room with your baby (that is, only if you don't share a room with your baby at home). Obviously, you may not have a choice. But if you do, opt to have your baby stay in her own room rather than share with you. This will be more like what she is used to and will help ease the transition. If you are concerned about hearing her during the night, bring along a baby monitor. If you can afford it, get a suite at a hotel so that the baby can sleep in a separate space. Some hotel rooms have separate sitting areas, a less expensive option than a suite or two rooms. Staying at a small inn or bed-and-breakfast may also help. This way, in the evenings, you can be in the sitting room enjoying the fire and maybe reading, or having a late dinner in the inn's restaurant, while your baby is in your room asleep. Be sure to bring along your baby monitor so you can hear what is going on with your baby. (And prior to making the reservations, confirm that babies are allowed at the inn.)

Bedding and favorite items. Bring your baby's blanket or other bedding with you. This may be inconvenient to carry, especially if you are traveling by plane, but you'll find it truly worthwhile. Your baby will sleep better in her own familiar bedding. The smell, feel, and texture will help soothe her. Also, if your baby sleeps with a favorite stuffed animal or other item, be absolutely sure that you do not forget it. Many a family has had to turn the car around halfway to their destination because they forget "bunny" or "teddy."

Sleep schedules. Although this can be difficult while on vacation, try to keep sleep schedules as similar as possible to your baby's schedule at home. Try to keep all naptimes and bedtimes the same. Although this may interfere with your vacation plans, you will be happier with a baby who is not cranky and overtired. This may require hiring a baby-sitter or splitting baby duty with your spouse. One of you may need to stay with the baby while the other goes off to play. Switch off baby duty so that everyone has time for fun. Yes, vacations will be different from what you were used to, but then adjusting to a baby requires certain changes.

Bedtime routine. Hopefully, you have established a bedtime routine at home. Keep to the same routine on vacation. If your baby's routine is to take a bath, put on pajamas, read a book, and sing a song, then by all means while on vacation bathe, change, read, and sing away. While everything is so new on vacation, your baby will appreciate some familiar routines.

Travel schedules. When making travel arrangements, keep your baby's sleep schedule in mind. If you have only a two-hour car ride or train trip, do it when your baby usually naps. This way your baby will sleep on the ride and will be right on schedule when you get there. If you are flying, travel during the day—again, if possible, during usual naptimes. Try to avoid red-eye or late evening flights, which will force your baby's bedtime to be several hours later than usual. You may not have much choice, of course, if you are traveling a long distance.

Returning home. The key to getting sleep back to normal is to return immediately to your usual routines the moment you get home. Put your baby down awake at her usual time and go through her usual bedtime routine. Don't stay with her "just this once" if you usually don't. If you do, she is going to assume that new rules apply, and you will have a battle on your hands. If you go back to the typical home mode right from the start, she will understand that even though things may have been changed when you were away, home sleep rules still apply. Of course, your baby may take a night or two to adjust to being back home, but be assured that she will go back to sleeping through the night (that is, if she slept through the night before).

Overnights

Staying over at someone else's house or at a hotel can be a challenge. Many adults have difficulty sleeping in new places, so don't be surprised if your child has problems, too. On the other hand, to many parents' frustration, their child may sleep better at someone else's house. This is usually true only if neither parent is present.

———————————————————— ☾ ————————————————————

Lorraine's baby, Timmy, would never go to sleep in his crib but always insisted on being rocked. He would usually wake two to three times every night, usually between 2:00 and 4:00 in the morning. Whenever Timmy stayed at his grandparents', though, he would go to sleep easily and sleep through the night. As you can imagine, Lorraine wondered if she was doing something wrong, and she found Timmy's sleep problems even more frustrating at home since she knew he really could sleep through the night.

✳

The reason your child may sleep better for others is that your child does not have the ingrained sleep associations elsewhere that he has with you. If your child needs you to nurse or rock him to sleep, he will need to figure out some other way to soothe himself to sleep when you are not available. Take this as a good sign. It means that your child has the ability to comfort himself and put himself to sleep. You just need to train him to do this in his own home.

For babies who have problems sleeping at other places, there are a few things that you can do. First, make sure that your child has familiar items with him. Send along his favorite blanket or stuffed animal. Tell the person that he is staying with about his usual routine. If you are with him at someone else's house, take the time and don't scrimp on his bedtime routine. Your baby will sense if you are rushing him, and you will pay the price when he resists going to bed. No matter how well or poorly it goes when your child is sleeping someplace else other than home, return immediately to your usual routine when you get back home. Don't build in a transition night. This will only confuse your child. You need to help your child learn that certain limits apply when at home. Just one night of giving in and staying with him until he falls asleep will limit your ability to follow through on subsequent nights.

Remember, it is important for your child to be able to sleep at other places. Just because he has a difficult time sleeping elsewhere and then has problems making the transition to being home doesn't mean that you should just give up and never let him stay anywhere other than home. He just needs some practice, and after several times of dealing with the transition, things will start to go more smoothly.

Baby-sitters

For the past two weeks you have been working diligently at getting your baby to go to sleep without fussing, and he is finally sleeping through the night for the first time in eight months. This coming Saturday night, however, you have to be at a family event, and so you have a baby-sitter coming over. You are worried that all of your hard work will have been wasted and you will end up right back where you started. What should you do?

The best thing to do is be prepared. Although your child may have gotten to the point where he is sleeping great for you, the first night with someone different putting him to bed can be difficult. But remember that even if your child has problems sleeping the night a baby-sitter is caring for him, he will return to sleeping well for you. It may take a little practice, though, for your child to understand the difference between your rules and a baby-sitter's rules. But instead of worrying about that, try to prevent that type of situation from occurring. If it is your standard baby-sitter, have the person arrive early. Explain what you have been doing and about your child's new sleeping habits. Give the baby-sitter step-by-step instructions on your child's new bedtime routine. Inform the baby-sitter that your child is to be put to bed awake; tell him or her what to say, when to leave the room, and what to do if your child fusses or cries. Give support on how this may be difficult and how to cope with crying. Explain thoroughly why you are doing this and why it is important.

If it is a paid baby-sitter, you shouldn't have too many problems getting him or her to implement your instructions. If the baby-sitter is a family member, especially a grandparent, it may be more difficult. Family members are much more likely to express their opinion on this process and may not like what you are doing: "How can I let my grandchild cry? It is so cruel." You have two choices in this situation. Choice one is to explain the process and emphasize the positive strides that have been made. The other choice is to leave it alone. Your child will still go to sleep for you as long as you are consistent, although it may take a night or two to adjust to your new rules after a pushover night with Grandma and Grandpa. Also, once your child is going to sleep easily, the grandparent will see the change and want things to go as smoothly. Your baby will also get to the point of insisting on his usual bedtime routine so that he can fall asleep. Good sleep associations are just as hard to break as bad ones.

Special Occasions

One of the things that seems to go along with special occasions is staying up later at night. Whether it is a birthday celebration, the Fourth of July, or another holiday, children often stay up later and miss out on their bedtime routines. They also may stay up later, fall asleep on the car ride home, and then get put to bed already asleep.

When your child stays up late, he may become overtired and cranky. This can make settling him down for bed more difficult. Don't forsake a bedtime routine because it is so late. You may want to shorten it a bit, from two stories to one, but don't eliminate it entirely. Your child needs his routine to fall asleep and sleep through the night. Without a routine, you may pay the price with a middle-of-the-night waking. Also, don't try to rush your child. It will just unsettle him and can make the entire process take longer if he balks at being rushed.

What should you do if your child has been out late somewhere other than home and falls asleep before getting home? Some parents find that their child will sleep better if they wake him after getting home and do at least a part of the bedtime routine. Your child may not want to wake up and may be a bit crabby, but it can help the transition. It will also make it easier for your child when he wakes up in the middle of the night and finds himself in his bed at home when the last thing he remembers is being in the car. There is no need to wake an infant, but it can be beneficial for a child over the age of one. For some children, however, waking them causes more problems because they will be overtired and cranky, and then stay awake for a long time before settling back down again. It will take some experimentation to see what works best for your child.

Illness

---✦---

Janine, eight months, has frequent ear infections. Whenever she gets an infection, she starts having trouble falling asleep at night and wakes frequently throughout the night. Since Janine is so young, her parents sometimes have a hard time determining when the ear infection has cleared up and whether Janine is just waking from habit.

---✳---

Illness always wreaks havoc on sleep. During an illness your baby will most likely have a difficult time falling asleep, will be waking frequently throughout the night, and will likely be cranky on top of everything else. Then, once sleep patterns get thrown off, it will take a while to return to normal. And it is often hard to tell when the illness is over and your baby is again feeling fine.

When your baby is sick, you have no choice but to go to her during the night when she wakes up. She doesn't feel well and may be in pain. She is going to need soothing. However, once you are sure that she is well again, go right back to your normal bedtime routine and return to setting limits on her behavior during the night. After several bouts with ear infections or colds, she will begin to understand the rules. When sick, you get attention. When not sick, bedtime rules apply. If you are in the midst of sleep training or have just finally gotten your child sleeping through the night, don't despair. Once well again, your child will quickly resume the progress that she has made.

Don't be surprised if your baby has sleep problems if she is often sick. Research has shown that babies who are often sick or who are colicky are the least likely to sleep through the night. But don't despair; you are not alone.

Time Changes and Longer Days

Your child's usual sleeping patterns may get thrown off when the clocks change. In the spring, the clocks get moved forward. This means that if your child goes to sleep at 7:30, after the time change it will really be 6:30 when you put him down. Your child will probably not be tired and may take a long time to fall asleep. Don't change his bedtime to compensate, or else the adjustment will take even longer. Just keep putting him to bed at his usual time, when the clock says 7:30. To help him make the transition more quickly, keep waking him at his normal wake time rather than letting him sleep in to compensate for the lost sleep. He may be cranky from being tired, but this should last only a day or two.

In the fall, the clocks get moved back. What used to be 7:30 is now 8:30. Bedtime should not be a problem. Your child will be tired and definitely ready to go to bed by his bedtime. The problem parents face in the fall is that their child is now waking too early in the morning. Rather than getting up at 6:30, he will be ready to get up for the day at 5:30. Again, this will work itself out with time. It may take several days to a week, but if you stick to his usual bedtime and wake time, all will return to normal.

Along with the clocks changing, another thing that can affect sleep is longer days and shorter nights during summer months. This is especially true the farther north you live. With longer summer days, it may seem strange to put your child to bed at 7:00 at night while it is still bright and sunny outside. Do it anyway. Your child needs his sleep. If the light seems to be bothering him, get room-darkening shades. Remember, babies are used to sleeping when it is light out. They do it all the time when they nap. If they can sleep at naptime when it is light out, they can sleep at bedtime when it is light out. The theme throughout this book is to be consistent. Be consistent and it will all work out.

Going Back to Work

One thing that mothers often agonize over is returning to work. Mothers go back to work either because they need to or because they want to. No matter what the reason, your return to work may be a difficult and emotionally trying time. One result of this change is a possible disruption of your baby's sleep schedule. If your baby wasn't having sleep problems before, he may begin to have them now. On the other hand, if your baby wasn't sleeping before, the problem will remain the same and may even get worse.

Your baby's sleep schedule is affected by your return to work for several reasons. First of all, your baby's routine changes. Whether he is in day care or being cared for at home by someone else (even the baby's father), everyone does things slightly differently, and your baby will notice the difference. His usual naptimes may be at different times of the day, especially if his early morning schedule is affected by your return to work. He is likely to be put down to sleep in a different way. Rather than being nursed or sung to, he may be given a bottle or just cuddled. No matter what, this will be a time of transition for your baby. This is not a bad thing. Babies need to be able to adapt to different environments and different people.

Another thing that often happens is that the mother's behavior changes. Your behavior will likely change simply because of the changes in your life. You are now juggling several roles and multiple demands. You are likely to be more tired. In addition, many mothers feel guilty about returning to work and leaving their baby. This guilt may cause you to project your feelings onto your baby. You may think that your child is suffering because he needs you or that he is sad when you depart. And while these things may be true, your child will adjust—and he'll probably adjust quicker than you will. You may even worry that your child is adjusting too well while in someone else's care. This does not mean that you are not needed. You may try to overcompensate for your absence by not setting limits. Many parents feel that they do not get to see their child enough during the day, so they keep him up later at night. Also, your behavior is likely to change. You will be more likely to respond to your child in the middle of the night, worried that your child needs you and will feel totally abandoned if you are not available at all hours of the night and are gone during the day.

------------------------------- ☾ -------------------------------

Donna had a difficult time with the transition back to work. Donna worked for a large corporation where she had to return to work when her baby, Megan, was six weeks old. Soon after her return to work, Megan began to suffer from colic. For the next two months Megan screamed every day from 3:30 in the afternoon to midnight. The only time that Donna had good quality time with Megan was from 4:00 to 6:00 in the morning when Megan would awaken and Donna would nurse her. These were difficult times. It was stressful for Donna to be at work and away from Megan during the day. Then when she got home at 5:30, she would find a screaming baby, an exhausted baby-sitter, and a six-hour-long siege with a crying baby. During this time Megan became a nighttime baby. She slept much of the day and was awake much of the night. She reluctantly took a bottle during the day when she was with her baby-sitter, but she refused to take a bottle during the night when Donna was around. Even after the colic resolved, Megan continued to be a nighttime baby. She would sleep from 8:00 in the morning until 3:00 in the afternoon, waking only for a four-ounce bottle around 11:30. When Donna came home, she would nurse

Megan, who would then go back to sleep from 7:00 until 10:00 in the evening. Megan would then wake up every two hours throughout the night to nurse and play. Donna felt guilty not being around during the day and believed that Megan was suffering because basically the only time that she would eat was when Donna was there to breast-feed her. At six months Megan seemed to be thriving, but Donna was exhausted.

——————✳——————

The experience that Donna had with Megan is common. Returning to work often occurs before everyone is ready. The mother may not feel that she is fully recovered and may not feel emotionally ready to be away from her newborn. The baby may not yet have a set routine. And guilt often takes over. To help with the guilt, make sure that you feel comfortable and confident with the person(s) caring for your baby. This will make the time that you are away easier. Then, once you have gotten adjusted to your return to work, step back and evaluate your life and your baby's life. Is everyone getting what they need? Is there a better way to achieve these needs? Is your baby waking during the night because she truly needs the nutrition or because this has become a learned habit? Your baby needs a happy and functioning mother more than she needs to see you at 3:00 in the morning. This may be a difficult transition period for you, but everyone has to be happy and functioning for a family to work.

Employees who work evening or night shifts may have even more difficulties with their baby's sleep. These individuals often have problems with their own sleep because they adjust to a day schedule on their days off. They also may not be able to get enough sleep because other demands are made on their time off during the day, such as child care. For those with changing shifts, their work schedule may create absolute havoc on their sleep. Their own sleep schedule may be so disorganized that it will inevitably affect their baby's schedule. Although there may not be much that you can do about your own daily schedule, try to keep your baby's schedule as consistent as possible. No matter whose care she is in, get her to bed at the same time every night and keep a tight schedule for her naps. This may take some work to accomplish, but it will be well worth it for your baby. She needs to keep a regular and consistent schedule for her to develop and grow up happy and content.

Separation and Divorce

Unfortunately, separation and divorce occur. The period surrounding these separations can be a time of great upheaval for both parents and children. Children often do not understand what is going on. Many children blame themselves for Mommy or Daddy's moving out. They will believe that they did something wrong that caused the separation or divorce. Young children often become much more clingy. If there is a great deal of arguing, children may become withdrawn or may tend to act out more. Although this is a difficult time for parents, much attention must be given to the children in this situation.

Sleep problems are likely to occur during and after the separation for a number of reasons. Your child's daily routine may be upset, and therefore she is less likely to have set naptimes and bedtimes. You may become more lenient with your child and less likely to set limits. Parents who are going through such upheaval may be more likely to allow and even want their child to share their bed. Also, when there are two separate homes, there may be two separate sets of rules regarding sleep and other matters concerning the child.

Don't worry: If you do all the wrong things in the beginning, it is understandable. But once things have calmed down, you must begin to deal with issues such as sleep problems. Remember, though, that prevention is the best solution to most problems. If you can prevent either the onset or the continuation of problems, that is best for you and your child.

First of all, if your child was already a good sleeper, then stick to what you always did. Your child will feel much more secure if things stay the same. Try to retain your child's normal daily schedule. Have naptimes the same. Put her to bed the same time every night. Have the same nightly routine. If the parent who was involved in the nighttime routine is no longer in the home, the other parent should try to do the same routine. If parts of the routine are not comfortable for that parent, then he or she should simply do what is comfortable and substitute something else for what would be uncomfortable. For example, if your wife always sang your baby a song at night and you can't sing, then come up with something that you can do, such as reading a book or telling a story.

Things can become difficult if your child sleeps at different times at each parent's home. For both your own and your child's sake, learn to communicate about parenting issues with the other parent. Parenting issues are not the ground on which to wage the battle concerning your marital problems. Your marriage may be over, but you will be joint parents for life. The best thing that you can do for your children is to maintain some semblance of peace about how to manage them. Try to set the same limits about sleep. Your child may have a difficult time sleeping at first, so try to have each parent maintain the same time for going to bed and a similar bedtime routine.

Be careful about giving in over sleep and letting your child stay up later or not having to sleep in his own bed. Good quality time with your child should occur at non–sleep times, not after bedtime. To help your baby sleep at both homes, make sure that your baby's favorite blanket and toy travel with her. If she sleeps in a crib in one household, have her sleep in a crib in the other. If she sleeps in a bed, have the same at the other residence.

Should you let your child begin to sleep with you after a separation or divorce? If your child has always slept with you, then go ahead and continue. If not, though, you need to ask yourself why is it happening now. Is it for your sake or the child's? As a parent, it is nice to have a warm body next to you in the middle of the night, especially when there used to be one. However, don't have your child be a substitute for your spouse. The other issue is that sleeping with you all of a sudden can be confusing for your child. This is especially true if your child is blaming herself at all for the divorce. She may feel that she is replacing the parent who moved out. Psychologically, this is not good for your child. It will lead to ambivalent feelings about her relationship with both parents and her role. Remember, she is the child and should remain the child in the relationship. For a more complete discussion of co-sleeping, be sure to read Chapter 4.

If your child has always had sleep problems, this is not the time to decide to do something about them. Yes, sleep problems should be corrected, and your child needs to be taught to put himself to sleep and to sleep through the night. However, this is not the time. Wait until things have calmed down, some time after the separation. On the other hand, if the separation or divorce occurred a while ago, don't put off doing something about your child's sleep problems. Don't use the separation or divorce as an excuse to delay.

Death in the Family

A death in the family, whether sudden or unexpected, is a tragic event. Your child will likely be experiencing grief, no matter what his age. Whether he is four months or three years, your child will understand that something is wrong and will miss the person who died. If it is a grandparent or other relative whom your child did not know well, he will still sense your grief and the sense of crisis. When it is a parent, it is even more difficult. (Because this book is focused on sleep, only those pertinent issues will be discussed. However, be sure to get information on how to deal with death and grief in connection with your child.)

One of the most important things regarding sleep is that people often explain death to young children as sleep. "Grandpa went to sleep and isn't going to ever wake up." Children are concrete. This means that they take things at absolute face value. Your child is going to believe that anyone who goes to sleep may not ever wake up again—and that includes you and your child. Your child may suddenly become terrified to go to sleep at night, afraid that he will die in his sleep. He may be afraid that you will die in your sleep. So whatever you do, don't explain death in terms of sleep.

After a death, the sleep issues that are likely to arise are similar to those discussed above for children experiencing their parents' separation or divorce. Many of these problems revolve around changes in routine. During the period after the death and throughout the time of the funeral and mourning period, your child's schedule is apt to be different from the usual. Naptimes may get missed and late nights are likely. In many cases your child may not be sleeping at home in his own crib or bed. If the funeral is out of town, your child may have to adjust to sleeping in a hotel or at a relative's or friend's home. Even if the funeral takes place where you live, some families find it easier to have their children stay at others' homes. If any of these are the case, try to bring along something comforting and familiar for your child. Take your child's favorite stuffed animal and his blanket and pillow. This sense of familiarity will help make the transition easier. If possible, try to maintain your child's usual naptimes and bedtime. If you will be unavailable to put her to sleep, have someone do it that your child knows and feels comfortable with. If the death is of a parent—and especially if it is the parent who usually does the bedtime routine—try to mimic your child's usual routine as much as possible. Do things in the same order. If the child insists, "That's not the way Daddy did it," go along with your child's wishes. This is not the time to establish all new ways of doing things. Expect your child to act up during this time, especially at bedtime. He is most likely not getting as much attention as usual, he may be overtired and cranky from missed sleep, and he may be reacting to the surrounding stress and tension. If possible, spend an extra few minutes cuddling; don't rush through the bedtime routine, and remain calm if he gets overly silly or cranky. If your child dawdles or gets obstinate, take this as his way of reacting to the death rather than perceiving it as belligerence.

Another issue that may arise following a death is whether to allow your child to sleep with you. If this is your usual practice, don't insist on your child's sleeping alone all of a sudden. If your child normally sleeps in his own crib or bed, however, then you will need to consider the ramifications of this change in sleeping arrangements.

Another sleep problem that is common when a death occurs is for children older than age two to begin having nightmares about death and about the person who died. Your child may even dream about others dying, not just the person who has actually died. He may dream about dying himself or being lost. Nightmares of other bad things are also apt to occur. This is the time for lots of reassurance. For other suggestions on how to deal with nightmares, see Chapter 12.

Death is an issue that everyone has to deal with at some time. It can be especially difficult for young children because their understanding of death is limited. Expect this time to be difficult on everyone, and anticipate how you are going to deal with any sleep problems that arise.

Reminders

- Even after your baby is sleeping through the night, anticipate obstacles to continued good sleep, such as vacations and illness.

- Switching from a crib to a bed can be an easy transition for you and your baby.

- Returning to work can disrupt everyone's schedule, as can the birth of a new baby.

- Changes in the family, including death, separation, or divorce, can disrupt sleep.

————————————————————✳————————————————————

Chapter 10

SNORING AND SNORTING
Sleep Apnea

———————————————— ☾ ————————————————

"Doctor, you have to help me. Every night my son, Stevie, stops breathing. It lasts so long that I think he won't start breathing again. I have him sleep with me so that I can shake him to make him breathe whenever he stops. I have called our pediatrician because some nights he stops breathing for so long it scares me. But the doctor says he is perfectly fine."

————————————————————✦————————————————————

What Is Sleep Apnea?

Sleep apnea, also known as obstructive sleep apnea, is a serious disorder in which there are pauses in breathing during sleep. Sleep apnea is generally thought of as an adult disorder, but it is often experienced by children. For some children, like Stevie, apnea is serious, and the parents, while aware of the problem, don't know where to turn for help. In many instances, however, the parents aren't even aware that their child has sleep apnea and do not seek medical help.

Symptoms of Sleep Apnea in Children

There are a number of symptoms to look for that are common in children with sleep apnea. Some children will have most of these symptoms, whereas others may have only one or two.

1. *Snoring.* Almost all children and adults who have sleep apnea snore, so this is a good place to start if you want to know if your child has apnea. However, not all children with apnea snore. And not all children who snore have sleep apnea.

2. *Breathing pauses.* Breathing pauses are the hallmark of sleep apnea. Rather than breathing in an even and consistent manner, your child may appear to stop breathing for a few moments and then start breathing again. If you observe this behavior, it is almost certain that your child has sleep apnea.

3. *Difficulty breathing while sleeping.* Rather than observing breathing pauses, you may notice that your child seems to have difficulty breathing while asleep. His breathing may not appear regular and even, or he may be a noisy breather.

4. *Mouth breathing.* Most children with obstructive sleep apnea breathe through their mouths at night—and often during the day as well.

5. *Coughing or choking.* If your child frequently starts coughing or choking in his sleep, this may be a sign of a breathing problem.

6. *Restless sleep.* Many children with sleep apnea are restless sleepers. Each time they have a breathing pause, they will arouse and move.

7. *Sleeping in unusual positions.* Some children with sleep apnea sleep in an unusual position, for example, with their head hanging over the side of the bed or with their head raised on several pillows or on stuffed animals. They do this subconsciously to try to keep their airway open to help them breathe while asleep.

8. *Sweating.* Many children with sleep apnea sweat profusely while they sleep. It is unclear as to the exact reason, but it may be because the body has to work so hard to breathe during sleep.

9. *Nightmares or night terrors.* Children with sleep apnea may be more prone to these two sleep problems because they are nore likely to be making the transition from one sleep stage to another or to be waking more frequently. This is because they are waking to breathe. The next chapter discusses both nightmares and night terrors.

10. *Night wakings.* Frequent night wakings in infants and toddlers are usually related to sleep associations as discussed in earlier chapters. However, some children's night wakings are caused by sleep apnea. If your child has other symptoms discussed in this section and awakens at night, it is worth considering whether or not your child has sleep apnea. Remember, though, that for these children the waking may be caused by the sleep apnea, but they should be able to fall back to sleep on their own. If they are not, be sure to also consider a sleep association problem.

Daytime Symptoms Often Associated with Sleep Apnea in Children

1. *Appearing sleepy during the day.* Children with sleep apnea are not getting enough sleep because their nighttime sleep is interrupted so frequently. Thus, your child may be

sleepy during the day beyond what is normal for his or her age.

2. *Appearing hyperactive during the day.* Many children who do not get enough sleep do not look and act sleepy. Instead, they become wired and hyperactive. This is common. And, don't fool yourself by saying that your child is never tired because he is in constant motion. This may actually be a sign that he is overtired.

3. *Daytime behavioral problems.* Some children may have daytime behavior problems. For example, some children with sleep apnea are irritable, cranky, or easily frustrated. Others may have difficulty focusing their attention.

4. *Behavior has changed significantly.* If your child's behavior has changed significantly during the day, such as appearing more cranky, irritable, or sleepy, and he also has other symptoms that are discussed above, the problem may be associated with sleep apnea.

5. *Falling asleep at inappropriate times or at times other than naptime.* Another sign that your child is not getting enough sleep is if he is falling asleep at inappropriate times. For example, does he always fall asleep while riding in the car, no matter whether it is for a two-minute or twenty-minute drive? Does he fall asleep at meal times?

6. *Health problems.* Many children with sleep apnea have a history of chronic problems with tonsils, adenoids, and/or ear infections. These medical problems may be causing the sleep apnea.

7. *Eating.* Some children with sleep apnea are noisy eaters, probably because they have difficulty breathing solely

through their nose while chewing. Other children with sleep apnea are slow eaters, and some even have problems swallowing, especially if they have very large tonsils.

8. **Slow growth.** Another potential problem that your child may have if he has sleep apnea is growth impairment. Children with growth impairment are usually under-weight and short for their age. Sleep apnea may cause some cases of growth impairment, as growth hormone gets released during sleep. If your child is not sleeping because of the apnea, there will be a reduction of growth hormone released. In these cases, these children will have a sudden growth spurt when the sleep apnea is treated, and they will catch up to other children their age.

Symptoms Associated with Sleep Apnea in Older Children (Ages Six and Up)

1. **Bed wetting.** Older children with sleep apnea often continue to wet their beds beyond when you would expect them to stay dry all night. If your older child is continuing to wet his bed, check to make sure that he doesn't have any of the symptoms listed above.

2. **Morning headache.** Some children will complain of having a headache in the morning. The headache is caused by the decrease in oxygen to the brain during the night. This diminished oxygen is not harmful, although it sounds scary. This symptom may also occur in infants and toddlers, although it is difficult to know whether they have a headache.

3. **Difficulty in school.** In older children the effects of sleep apnea may result in poor performance in school. These children may be labeled slow or lazy and may have difficulty focusing their attention on their schoolwork.

Will She Stop Breathing Altogether?

"Several times during the night my two-year-old seems to stop breathing. I am scared that she won't breathe again!"

Other than in cases of SIDS (see below), your baby will always start breathing again. The body has its own internal mechanism to make sure that breathing continues. The pause in breathing triggers the body to awaken, which results in a return of muscle tone to the airway and breathing resumes. These wakings are so brief that you and your child may not even be aware of them.

Causes of Sleep Apnea in Children

The most common cause of obstructive sleep apnea in children is enlargement of the adenoids and tonsils. During sleep there is a considerable drop in muscle tone, which affects the airway and breathing. Many of these children have little difficulty breathing when awake; however, with decreased muscle tone during sleep, the airway becomes smaller, making the flow of air more difficult and the work of breathing harder. (An analogy can be made of breathing through a small, flimsy straw with the straw occasionally collapsing and obstructing airflow.) These obstructions result in frequent brief arousals from sleep. Many of the short pauses (lasting only a few to twenty seconds or so) cause a brief arousal that increases muscle tone, opens the airway, and allows the child to resume breathing. Although the actual number of minutes of arousal during the night may be small, the repeated, chronic, but brief disruptions in sleep can lead to significant daytime symptoms in children. (A comparable image would be answering a wrong number on the telephone fifteen to twenty times a night.) The child is usually unaware of waking up, and the parent often describes the child as having very restless sleep but not necessarily waking up completely.

Who Is at Risk for Sleep Apnea?

There are a number of things that put children at risk for sleep apnea. A selection of these will be reviewed here.

Tonsils and adenoids. As mentioned above, most children with sleep apnea have enlarged tonsils and/or adenoids. Once the muscles in the neck relax during sleep, the big tonsils or adenoids block the airway and get in the way of breathing.

Illness. Children with frequent ear infections, sore throats, and tonsillitis are also more likely to have sleep apnea. Allergies can also contribute to sleep apnea, as breathing becomes more difficult.

Weight. Sleep apnea is also more common in children who are overweight. This is because the extra weight around their necks can make their airways smaller. Not all children with sleep apnea are overweight, however. Many children of normal weight have sleep apnea, and children with sleep apnea can even be underweight.

Physical structure. Other children who are at high risk for sleep apnea include those with abnormal bone structure in the jaw area. For instance, children who have a receding chin may have a smaller airway. Another potential cause may be a cleft palate, particularly if it has been repaired.

Down syndrome. Children with Down syndrome are at risk for sleep apnea because they are often slightly overweight and because they often have an enlarged tongue that can block the airway during sleep. Studies have shown that almost half of all children with Down syndrome have sleep apnea.

Prevalence of Sleep Apnea in Children

Although it used to be considered rare, recent studies have shown that sleep apnea is more common in children than previously thought. It is suspected that sleep apnea occurs in about 2 percent of all children. That is, 1 out of every 50 children have sleep apnea, a total of about 640,000 children between the ages of one and nine in the United States. Sleep apnea can begin as early as the newborn period, but the average age of onset is fourteen months. There is no sex difference in the prevalence of sleep apnea; that is, boys and girls are equally likely to have sleep apnea.

Family History

──────────── C⋆ ────────────

"My husband snores and so does our eleven-month-old baby. Is snoring inherited?"

──────────── ✳ ────────────

Sleep apnea often runs in families. Many of the children I see and diagnose with sleep apnea have one or both parents with the same problem. Therefore, if you have been diagnosed with sleep apnea, it is a good idea to determine whether your child has any of the symptoms that were discussed above. (For further information on sleep apnea in adults see Chapter 14.)

Who Should You See for Help?

Children with suspected sleep apnea should be seen by a sleep specialist who can evaluate and treat it. An extensive interview, physical examination, and an overnight sleep study will likely be conducted. To find out about a sleep disorders center near you, call the American Sleep Disorders Association at (507) 287–6006.

Assessment of Sleep Apnea in Children

──────────── C⋆ ────────────

Tara is two years old. Her parents noticed that she always seemed to be sleepy during the day. At first they thought that Tara just needed more sleep than other children her age, but then they realized that even if she slept for long periods at night and took long naps, she still seemed sleepy. She always fell asleep in the car and often nodded off in her high chair at mealtime. She would even fall asleep watching her favorite video, Beauty and the Beast. *Tara's parents began to watch her sleep and noticed a number of unusual things. First, Tara was a mouth breather, and she was noisy when she slept. She was also a very restless sleeper and would be all over the crib throughout the night. Finally, concerned about Tara's sleep, they mentioned the problem to their pediatrician. Their pediatrician referred them to a sleep disorders center.*

Tara's mother called the sleep disorders center and made an appointment for the next week. They received a packet in the mail that included information about the center and a ten-page questionnaire about Tara and her sleep. The questionnaire asked about Tara's evening activities, such as television watching, bedtime, and bedtime routines; how long it took for Tara to fall asleep; details of any unusual behaviors during the night; and the number and duration of any night wakings. The questionnaire also asked about the time that Tara woke up in the morning, how sleepy she appeared during the day, and whether she took naps. Tara's parents completed the questionnaire before their appointment. They also had to keep track of Tara's sleep by keeping a sleep diary from the time they got the packet to the time of their appointment. During the first appointment, the doctor asked every conceivable question about Tara's sleep and even about their own sleep. Tara was also given a brief physical examination that included checking her height and weight and looking in her ears and throat. The doctor at the sleep disorders center found that Tara had enlarged tonsils and thought that her symptoms indicated she had sleep apnea. To be sure, though, they wanted to perform a polysomnography (PSG) during an overnight sleep study at their sleep center.

Tara's overnight study was scheduled for three weeks later. Her parents were instructed to bring her to the sleep center at 6:30 P.M. Since Tara liked to wear one of her father's T-shirts to sleep in at home, Tara's mother had to go out and get her pajamas that had a separate top and bottom to be worn during the study, as recommended by the doctor. They were all set. They had toys for Tara to play with, her stuffed bunny that she slept with, and lots of juice and snacks. It was decided that Tara's mother would stay with Tara overnight because she could take the next day off from work.

Getting Tara hooked up for the sleep study, which involved gluing a number of electrodes to her, was a challenge. She was scared at first and didn't like sitting still for that long. But the technicians at the sleep center were very good. They explained to her that the electrodes were not needles; they would not pierce her skin but, rather, would be glued or taped on. They helped Tara get over being scared by first putting some electrodes on her mother and then having Tara put them on her bunny. They also gave her lots of breaks to play. She was finally hooked up and sleeptime was to begin. Tara was fussy for about ten minutes after being put into a strange crib with a bunch of wires attached, but she quickly calmed down and went to sleep. During the night, the monitors kept track of Tara's oxygen levels, how much air was going in and out of her nose and mouth (oral and nasal airflow), respiration, arm and leg muscle activity, and her brain waves by way of an electroencephalograph. The next morning when Tara woke up, all the electrodes were removed, and she and her mother were free to leave. Tara was off to day care.

Tara and her parents returned a week later for a follow-up appointment and were told that Tara definitely had sleep apnea. They were referred to an ear, nose, and throat specialist. Eventually, Tara had her tonsils and adenoids removed. Her sleep problems were cleared up, as *were her problems with sleepiness during the day. Shortly after this, her father entered the sleep center to be evaluated because he also snored and was sleepy during the day.*

As with Tara, a thorough evaluation at a sleep disorders center typically involves: (1) obtaining a complete history of your child's sleep, (2) the keeping of a sleep diary for one to two weeks, and (3) an overnight sleep study if an underlying physical problem is suspected. Following the collection of all this information, a diagnosis and a treatment plan are made. The sleep disorders center staff will also send all this information to your pediatrician.

Treatment for Childhood Sleep Apnea

For most children with sleep apnea, removal of enlarged tonsils and adenoids is the first treatment. An ear, nose, and throat specialist will evaluate whether your child should have a tonsillectomy and/or adenoidectomy. The tonsils can be seen by any doctor, but special equipment is needed to see the adenoids. Once the tonsils and/or adenoids are removed, the airway will not be blocked, and breathing during sleep can occur normally. The surgery is usually done on an outpatient basis, meaning that your child will go to the hospital in the morning for surgery and be released that afternoon. Some children with moderate to severe sleep apnea, though, may be kept overnight to be sure that any postsurgery swelling does not make the child's apnea worse. Once the swelling has dissipated, the apnea usually disappears. There are few risks involved in this type of surgery, but it is always important to ask your doctor about any possible complications.

If other physical reasons are present that may be causing obstruction, other operations may be recommended. For example, if your child has nasal polyps or any other growths in his nose or throat, these will need to be removed. When the doctor is evaluating for a tonsillectomy and/or adenoidectomy, a complete inspection for these types of growths is done at the same time. Sometimes a child will need correction of a deviated nasal septum, usually the result of a broken nose. In severe cases, correction of malformations of the jaw or upper palate may be necessary.

If the cause of your child's sleep apnea is related to allergies, these need to be brought under control. An allergy specialist should be seen for these types of problems. For some children, weight loss may be beneficial in eliminating sleep apnea, but consult your pediatrician before starting any weight loss program for your child.

Another effective treatment that is commonly prescribed for adults with sleep apnea is continuous positive airway pressure (CPAP), and this treatment is now becoming more common for children. In this highly effective therapy, a mask is worn over the nose during sleep, and pressure from an air compressor forces air through nasal passages and into the airway. This air pressure keeps the airway open and allows the child to breathe normally during sleep without the disturbing arousals.

Sudden Infant Death Syndrome (SIDS)

Any coverage of infant sleep is not complete without a discussion of Sudden Infant Death Syndrome (SIDS), a tragedy that occurs most often while a baby is sleeping. It is not likely to happen to your baby, but it is a possibility that you should take into account and do what you can to prevent.

------------------------------ ❋ ------------------------------

After two years of trying, Lisa finally got pregnant, and she and John were happy to welcome a 7-pound 2-ounce baby girl whom they named Courtney. Although the first few weeks were difficult for John and Lisa, mostly because of sleep deprivation, Courtney was "perfect." She was healthy and gaining weight. Everyone said that she was adorable, and her pediatrician proclaimed her healthy and normal. She started smiling and holding her head up on time. She began sleeping through the night at nine weeks. John and Lisa were ecstatic about finally becoming parents. On a Tuesday night when Courtney was thirteen weeks old, Lisa put Courtney to bed at 8:30 at night. All was quiet throughout the night, as it usually was. By 8:00 in the morning Courtney was still not awake, which was unusual. When Lisa went to check on her, she found that Courtney was not breathing and was lifeless. The paramedics came but said there was nothing they could do. The police came, and an autopsy was done. Nothing was found to have caused Courtney's death. The final conclusion was sudden infant death syndrome, otherwise known as SIDS.

Unfortunately, babies do die in their sleep. Sudden Infant Death Syndrome, also referred to as crib death or cot death, is the leading cause of death in infants between the ages of one month and one year. In the United States, about five thousand to ten thousand babies die each year from SIDS. This represents about one to two babies per one thousand born. The definition of SIDS, according to the National Institutes of Health, is "the sudden death of an infant under one year of age which remains unexplained after a complete postmortem examination, including an investigation of the death scene and a review of the case history." Thus, there is no clear cause of death.

Most babies with SIDS are between the ages of two and four months. Almost 90 percent of babies who die of SIDS are under six months of age. Although it can happen at any time of the year, SIDS occurs most often in the winter. It usually occurs when the baby is thought to be asleep.

SIDS is not caused by child abuse. It is also not caused by vomiting or choking, or by minor illnesses, such as colds or infections. It is not contagious or hereditary, and is not caused by immunizations for diseases, such as diphtheria or tetanus.

What Babies Are at Risk for SIDS?

It is impossible to identify exactly which babies are at risk for SIDS. We do know, however, about a number of trends regarding SIDS. For instance, babies born to younger mothers are more at risk for SIDS. Mothers who smoke are more likely to have babies who die of SIDS, as are those who use illegal drugs during pregnancy, have a history of sexually transmitted disease or urinary tract infections, or who receive poor prenatal care. Bottle-fed babies are more likely to be victims of SIDS, compared to breast-fed babies. Babies who have a sibling close in age are more at risk. Twins and triplets are more at risk, as are babies who had a low birth weight. Brothers and sisters of SIDS victims are also more likely to suffer from SIDS, especially if there was more than one SIDS victim in the family. And, lastly, baby boys die from SIDS more often than baby girls.

Surprisingly, most babies who are victims of SIDS were considered healthy prior to their death and were well developed and nourished. Most babies were also full-term, meaning that they were not born substantially early. Many do not even have any of the risk factors mentioned here.

What Causes SIDS?

No one really knows what causes SIDS, and in fact it is likely that rather than being one cause, there are many reasons why babies die from SIDS. It is known that SIDS appears to be related to some type of breathing and heart problem, at least at the time of death. Some of these babies are found to have very high body temperatures or are covered with sweat, so problems regulating temperature may be the cause of some of these unfortunate deaths.

Because SIDS involves sleeping and possible problems in breathing, sleep apnea has been suggested as having a role. Studies do not support this hypothesis, however. Fewer than 10 percent of SIDS victims were known to have apnea before death. Remember, though, that not all parents are aware that their children have sleep apnea.

What Can Be Done to Prevent SIDS?

Unfortunately, we don't know of a way to prevent SIDS completely. The following recommendations, however, will help reduce your baby's risk of being a victim of SIDS.

Sleep position. First, have your young infant sleep on his or her back or side. Babies who sleep on their stomachs are more susceptible to SIDS. In the past, pediatricians recommended that babies sleep on their stomachs or sides because there were concerns that babies may choke if they vomit while asleep on their backs. This now appears unlikely, as over forty studies have failed to support this belief. However, studies have found a significant decrease in SIDS in babies who sleep on their back or side; in fact, getting infants to sleep on their backs is the basis of the national campaign called "Back to Sleep," which is an attempt to inform parents that this is the preferred sleep position for babies.

Some inexpensive devices are available to help keep your infant on her side while sleeping (see Appendix B, Resources for Parents), although the American Academy of Pediatrics does not recommend them because they can conceivably entrap your baby. An easier method is to place your baby so that her back is against the crib and the arm she is lying on is extended out from her body so that she can't roll over. Her lower shoulder, the one on the mattress, should be farther forward than her upper shoulder so that if she does roll over, it will be onto her back. Never strap your baby into position or completely pad her crib with blankets. She could easily get caught in the strap or smother in all those blankets if she rolls over.

If your baby prefers to fall asleep on his stomach, you can let him fall asleep this way, then gently turn him over onto his back. At some point your baby may decide that he wants to sleep on his stomach and will keep rolling into this position throughout the night. Most babies who are able to roll over onto their stomachs are past the high-risk SIDS period. Speak with your pediatrician if this happens, though, to be sure that your baby is not at risk for SIDS. With the pediatrician's approval your baby can sleep this way.

Stop smoking around the baby. Studies have shown that mothers who smoke throughout pregnancy and following the birth of their baby triple the risk of their baby's dying from SIDS. Surprisingly, women who quit smoking during pregnancy but return to smoking once the baby is born have babies who are twice at risk for SIDS. So smoking should not take place near your baby.

Use firm bedding. Babies should sleep on a firm, flat mattress. Babies should not sleep on beanbag cushions, sheepskins, foam pads, quilts, pillows, or any other soft item. These soft items can be dangerous because your baby can easily smother.

Avoid overheating your baby. SIDS has been associated with babies who are overheated by too much clothing, too many blankets, or too warm a room. This is especially true for a baby with a cold or infection. You can tell if your baby is overheated by whether she is sweating, has damp hair, a heat rash, or rapid breathing. Dress your baby in as much or as little clothing as you are wearing. Keep bedrooms at a consistent 68 to 70 degrees Fahrenheit.

Breast-feed your baby. Babies who are breast-fed are less likely to die of SIDS. This may be because breast-feeding helps prevent gastrointestinal and respiratory illness.

Home apnea monitoring. Some parents utilize home monitors, which alert them if their baby stops breathing or if there is a problem with the baby's heart rate. These monitors are helpful, although they are not guaranteed to avert all SIDS occurrences. Typically, the babies who are most likely to be placed on home monitors include those who have had a past life-threatening event, premature babies with apnea, the twin of a SIDS victim, babies born to families in which there have been two or more prior SIDS victims, and infants with existing heart or breathing problems. Home monitoring is not recommended for normal infants and healthy preterm infants.

The Impact of SIDS

SIDS occurs unexpectedly and suddenly. Babies are not supposed to die. The first few months after a baby is born is a time of joy and bonding with the new baby, and the unexpected death of a baby is especially traumatic. The first reactions are usually numbness and bewilderment. As one parent simply stated, "This wasn't supposed to happen." Since there is no one to blame for the death, parents often blame themselves, thinking, "If only I had checked on him." The parents often perceive themselves as failures and question why they hadn't noticed any problems or done anything to protect their baby. And as if to compound the pain, some SIDS deaths involve legal investigations into the baby's death, sometimes with fingers being pointed at the parents.

After the initial shock, many parents become severely depressed. They may have difficulties concentrating and sleeping. They may become tired and irritable. They may have difficulty functioning, at home and at work. If there are other children in the family, parents may become overprotective, never letting them out of their sight.

Another common occurrence after the death of a child to SIDS is moving to a new home. Many couples can't live with any remembrances of their child and try to change as many aspects of their life as they can. This is often an attempt to escape. Fears about future pregnancies and having another baby are also extremely common.

The death of a baby to SIDS will impact the other children in the family as well. The death will be just as traumatic for them. Some children will feel that it is their fault, especially if they felt any resentment toward the new baby who was the center of attention. They may worry that they will die in their sleep. Most will be confused about the death and unable to understand what happened. Some children will become withdrawn. Some will feel that they need to live for themselves and the other child. The other children in the family are going to need support. They will need to have the death explained to them at a level that is appropriate for their age. They will need to understand that it is important to grieve and feel sad. Parents will need to help their children deal with their own feelings.

If your baby is a victim of SIDS, get support. Most parents whose babies die of SIDS feel guilty, but you must remember that it is not your fault and there was nothing that you could have done to prevent it. Be sure to contact a local chapter of the SIDS Alliance. Another place to get more information on SIDS is the SIDS Clearinghouse. Phone numbers and addresses for these organizations can be found in Appendix B, Resources for Parents.

If you know someone who has lost a child to SIDS, you should realize that the parents need support. This does not mean that you need to make the person feel better. Pain and grieving, which may continue for months and years after the death of the child, are important aspects of their recovery. Parents of SIDS victims often want to talk about the baby, and they don't mind when others talk about their child. Don't be reluctant to talk about the baby. This will not upset the parents. The baby did exist, and parents often enjoy talking about him and appreciate someone listening to their stories. The parents may also appreciate tangible reminders of their baby, so feel free to give or make something, such as a framed picture of the baby. Give a donation in memory of the baby or plant a tree in his honor. All of these gestures will be appreciated. Being a friend and listening, though, are probably the best things you can do.

Reminders

- Sleep apnea is a serious disorder in which there are pauses in breathing during sleep.

- Common nighttime symptoms of sleep apnea in children are snoring, breathing pauses, mouth breathing, and difficulty breathing while asleep.

- Common daytime symptoms of sleep apnea are changes in behavior, such as appearing sleepy, hyperactive, or falling asleep at inappropriate times.

- Sleep apnea in children is usually caused by enlarged tonsils or adenoids.

- A diagnosis of sleep apnea should be made at a sleep disorders center.

- Sudden Infant Death Syndrome (SIDS) is the leading cause of death in infants between the ages of one month and one year. There are some things that you can do to help prevent SIDS.

Chapter **11**

BABIES WHO GO BUMP IN THE NIGHT
Parasomnias

———————————— ☾ ————————————

*Every night around 10:30 Billy bolts out of bed and starts
screaming uncontrollably. I often find him running around
his room looking frantic. I try to hold him, but he just
pushes me away. I don't understand what is happening. He
looks terrified, and it frightens me.*

———————————— ✳ ————————————

Unusual behaviors that occur during sleep are called parasomnias. Billy's nighttime behavior is known as a sleep terror
or night terror. They are common in babies and toddlers. In
time, most children grow out of these unusual sleep disturbances. For parents, however, watching their toddler have a
night terror can be a very frightening experience.

Parasomnias

The term "parasomnia" refers to a wide variety of behaviors
that occur during sleep. The most common type of parasomnia

is the "disorder of partial arousal," which includes confusional arousals, sleepwalking (somnambulism), and sleep terrors. Experts believe these types of arousal disorders are related and share some symptoms. Essentially, they arise when the child is in a mixed state, being both asleep and awake, generally coming from the deepest stage of nondreaming sleep. The child is awake enough to act out complex behaviors, but asleep enough not to be aware of or remember them. These events are usually infrequent and mild. However, they may occur often enough or be sufficiently severe or bothersome enough to require medical attention.

Confusional Arousals

Confusional arousals usually begin with crying and thrashing around in the crib or bed. Your child will appear awake and may look confused or upset. She may moan or cry out for you, but if you try to comfort her, she may resist you and not allow you to console her. You will realize that she is half-asleep, and she will be difficult to awaken. These episodes may last up to half an hour. They usually end with your child calming down and returning to a deep sleep. Sometimes a child will awaken briefly from a confusional arousal, only to return to sleep quickly.

Most infants and toddlers have at least one confusional arousal. It may have happened to your child without your even realizing it. It may just seem to you that your child seemed to wake up, fuss for a while, and then fell back to sleep. As stated before, most children have confusional arousals. They are extremely common and primarily occur in children under the age of three.

Sleepwalking

Sleepwalking is often seen in older children, peaking in children between the ages of four and eight. Almost half of all children have at least one episode of sleepwalking. Some children will simply get up out of bed and walk around the room, whereas other children may sleepwalk for a long period and may go to another part of the house or even outside to the yard or garage. The sleepwalker may return to bed or awaken in the morning in a different part of the house, such as in a closet or someone else's room. Sleepwalkers can even carry on conversations, which are difficult to understand and make little or no sense. Children who are sleepwalking are capable of acting out complicated behaviors, such as rearranging furniture, but usually the activities make little sense. It is quite common for children to urinate in closets or other strange places while sleepwalking. When your child sleepwalks, his eyes will be open, but they may appear "glassy." Injuries during sleepwalking are uncommon because your child is able to see when sleepwalking. (This will be discussed in more detail later in this chapter.)

Sleep Terrors

Sleep terrors, or night terrors as they are often called, are the most extreme and dramatic form of partial arousal disorders. They are also the most distressing to witness. Sleep terrors almost always begin with a "bloodcurdling" scream or shout. During one of these events your child will look as though she is experiencing extreme terror. Her pupils may be dilated, she will breathe rapidly, her heart will be racing, and she may be sweating. Overall, she will look extremely agitated. During a sleep terror a child may bolt out of bed and run around the room or even out of the house. During the frenzied event, children may hurt themselves or someone trying to calm them. As disturbing and frightening as these events appear to the observer, children having them usually are totally unaware of what they are doing and do not remember the incident in the morning. In fact, sleep terrors are much worse to watch than to experience. For the child, a sleep terror is less traumatic than a typical nightmare or bad dream. An easy way to distinguish between sleep terrors and nightmares is to determine who is more upset the next morning. If your child is more upset, then it was a nightmare. If you are more upset, then it was a sleep terror.

About 5 percent of children have sleep terrors, with most sleep terrors occurring when the child is between five and seven years, although younger children can also have them. And sleep terrors run in families. Studies find that 96 percent of children who have sleep terrors have another family member who has experienced a disorder of partial arousal.

While the term "parasomnia" refers to a wide range of sleep disorders, for the rest of this chapter parasomnia will refer to the disorders of partial arousal: confusional arousals, sleepwalking, and sleep terrors.

Crucial Features

Confusional arousals, sleepwalking, and sleep terrors all have a number of things in common that distinguish them from other sleep disorders. Once you know about these features, these disorders are relatively easy to identify.

Time of night. Parasomnias usually occur within one to two hours of falling asleep. They also occur like clockwork. That is, you may be able to predict almost to the minute what time your child is going to have one. Don's son, Matthew, goes to bed every night at 8:30 and falls asleep by 9:00. At 10:15, Matthew starts screaming. This happens at least twice a week. If Don hasn't heard Matthew by 10:30, he knows that there will be no night terror that night.

Amnesia. Another feature of parasomnias is that your child will have no memory of these events. In the morning, to them, it will be as if it had never happened. Some children, if they have them often enough, may have some fuzzy recollection of being up but no more than that.

Avoid comfort. Children who are upset usually cling to their parents. Children having a parasomnia do not. They may not appear to even notice you. They are likely to scream more if you pick them up or try to hold them. They may get more upset if you talk to them and try to calm them down. Just leave them alone. Watch them, but don't interfere.

What Parasomnias Are and Are Not

We don't exactly know what parasomnias are, but we do know some things about them. All parasomnias occur out of non-REM sleep (which was discussed in Chapter 2). They occur during transitions from one sleep stage to another. They usually occur coming out of stage three or four sleep, what is referred to as deep sleep. The person is basically stuck halfway between being asleep and awake. He is not fully asleep nor fully awake.

Some children sleepwalk or have a sleep terror every night. For other children, it will wax and wane, with "good" weeks and "bad" ones. Every child is different. Some children may have only one episode in their lifetime.

We also know that parasomnias are not any of the following:

Not a nightmare. Sleep terrors are not nightmares. Your child is not dreaming during these events, although it may look it. Nightmares occur during REM sleep. Most of REM sleep occurs at the end of the sleep period, usually early in the morning. This means that nightmares are also more likely during the second half of the night. One of the defining characteristics of REM sleep is that you are basically paralyzed. Your eyes move, your heart pumps, and you are able to breathe, but you are not able to move. So you cannot yell, cannot sit up in bed, and definitely cannot walk. Sleepwalking, confusional arousals, and sleep terrors occur in non-REM sleep when you are not dreaming and are not paralyzed.

Not a psychological problem. Many parents become worried that sleep terrors and sleepwalking indicate that their child has some serious psychological problem. The children look terrified and frightened. It may appear to some that they are acting out some concern or problem that occurred during daytime hours, but this is not so. Many studies have been done, and the consensus is that parasomnias are not related to psychological problems. The children do not have problems with anxiety and are not depressed, and they certainly are not psychotic or having hallucinations. They are simply stuck halfway between awake and asleep.

Not possessed. Some parents say that their child looks possessed or is speaking "in tongues." Rita commented that Mark sounded as if he was speaking a language from another planet. Obviously, this can't be true. Your child just looks and acts strange during a night terror.

Distinguishing Parasomnias from Other Problems

Nightmares. It is very easy to distinguish parasomnias from nightmares if you know what to look for. The table on the next page compares the sleep disorders covered here with nightmares on several key components.

Seizures. Parasomnias can also be confused with seizures that occur during sleep. It is very unlikely that your child is having a seizure because they are quite rare, but you should be aware of what to look for. Seizures can occur at any time of the night but often happen shortly after a child falls asleep. The behavior is repetitive and stereotypic, meaning that your child will always move the same way over and over. You will not be able to arouse your child, and your child will not recall the event in the morning, similar to parasomnias. If your child is having seizures during sleep, then he may also be sleepy during the

	Parasomnias	Nightmares
Time of night	First ⅓ of night	Mid to last ⅓
Behavior	Variable	Very little motor
Level of consciousness	Unarousable or very confused if awakened	Fully awake
Memory of event	Amnesia	Vivid recall
Family history	Yes	No
Potential for injury	High	Low
Frequency	Common	Very common
Stage of sleep	Deep non-REM	REM
Daytime sleepiness	Little or none	None

day. Again, seizures in sleep are very rare compared to common parasomnias and nightmares. If you have any concern that your child is having seizures, contact your pediatrician immediately.

Causes

Just as we don't know exactly what parasomnias are, we also don't know what exactly causes them. We do know that they run in families. If a two-year-old has them, it is likely that one of his parents had them, although maybe not as severely. In some families every one of the children has them to some degree. They also appear to be a developmental phenomenon, with children most likely to have them at certain ages.

There are certain factors that cause these sleep disorders to be worse or more likely to occur.

Sleep deprivation. Not getting enough sleep is the number one reason that a child has a sleep terror or walks in his sleep. If your child doesn't get enough sleep on Wednesday night, he is more likely to have a sleep terror on Thursday night. This is because confusional arousals, sleepwalking, and sleep terrors occur during deep sleep. When deprived of sleep, the body demands more deep sleep and gets more than usual on a normal night. So the more deep sleep that your child gets, the more likely that he is going to have an episode.

Medications. Some medications can cause parasomnias. Lithium, Prolixin, and desipramine can induce or exacerbate one of these parasomnias.

Fevers or illness. A high fever or being sick can cause confusional arousals and sleep terrors. The higher the fever, the more likely an event will occur. For some children, this is the only time that they will ever have one. If you have never observed one in your child before, it can be very scary especially when your child is sick.

Strange places. Sleeping at Grandma's house, a friend's house, or any strange place can lead to a sleep terror or sleepwalking.

Stressful times. Parasomnias often occur during periods of stress. It is not the stress itself that causes the sleep problems but the sleep deprivation that often goes along with it. If you are moving or going through a divorce, or there has been a death in the family, your child may not be getting to bed as early as you would like and may not be getting enough sleep. If your child is worrying before falling asleep, he may not be getting the sleep he needs. Whenever this happens, unusual sleep behaviors are more likely to occur.

Other sleep disorders. Some children's parasomnias are made worse by another underlying sleep disrupter. For example, if your child has sleep apnea, it may be causing her to wake more frequently. This waking is causing her to have more sleep transitions. As these parasomnias occur during sleep transitions, the apnea may be triggering a sleep terror. Therefore, it is important to know whether your child is having other sleep problems. Be sure to read the other chapters in this section to learn more about other sleep disorders. If you have any concerns, contact your pediatrician or a sleep disorders center in your area.

Keep Your Child Safe

― ☾ ―

Stephanie was four years old. She would often get up during the night and sleepwalk. She usually would walk out of her room, go left, and take an immediate right into the bathroom. One night she stayed at her grandmother's house. As usual, at 10:30 at night, she got up and began sleepwalking. She walked out of the room and turned left. She then turned right, expecting to walk into the bathroom. Unfortunately, in her grandmother's house there was a stairway leading downstairs. Stephanie fell down the stairs and broke her right arm.

―✳―

Stephanie's story is typical. People can easily get injured sleepwalking when sleeping in an unfamiliar place, whether it is at a grandparent's house or at a friend's place. If your child has sleep terrors or is a known sleepwalker, be sure to use safety precautions both at home and at other places.

The most common injuries occur when a child falls out of a second-story or higher window or walks outside. Surprisingly, although your child is asleep, he can still see. This is why he doesn't bump into furniture and is unlikely to fall down the stairs. In the dark or in a strange place, however, accidents can happen. And even for children who sleepwalk regularly without incident, it is possible for their sleepwalking patterns to suddenly change. Children have been found at a neighbor's house, down the street, and in driveways. Often they walk out, go somewhere, lie down, and fall back to sleep, waking in the morning unsure of where they are.

The most important thing you can do is make sure that your child is safe. Just because your child has not sleepwalked in the past doesn't mean that she won't begin next week. It is therefore better to be safe than sorry, especially if your child has ever had a parasomnia event. Here are some things you can do to make sure that your child is safe.

Gates. Put up gates at the door of your child's bedroom and at the top of stairs. For younger children, the gates will stop them from leaving their room or going downstairs. For older children, the gate may not stop them, but perhaps it will slow them down enough for someone to hear them.

Alarms. An alarm can be very helpful in making sure that your child doesn't leave the house. An alarm is not intended to wake your child but to wake you. Any type of alarm will do, from the fancy and expensive burglar alarm to a simple and more economical option. For instance, hang a bell or other jangling item from a string in front of your child's doorway so that when the door opens it will make noise. The sound doesn't have to wake your child, but it should be loud enough to wake you. There are also inexpensive burglar alarms available that hang on doorknobs. If the doorknob gets touched or turned, a loud alarm goes off. There are even fancy electric eye systems that you can install in your child's room, even over her bed, that will trigger when your child gets up and starts moving about. A word of caution, though: If you are relying on an in-home alarm system, especially one that has motion sensors, be careful that the police don't get called simply because your child is sleepwalking.

Lock windows. Ensure that windows, especially second-story or higher, do not open enough that your child can jump out of them. There are devices available that prevent windows from opening more than a few inches. A cheaper and simpler method is to put a nail into the window jamb that limits how far the window can be opened. The nail should stick out an inch or two so that when the window is opened, it hits the nail and cannot be opened any further.

Rearrange furniture. Rearrange the furniture in your child's room so that he won't bump into anything in the dark and get hurt. A low table in the middle of the room may be perfect for drawing on during the day but can be dangerous if your child is sleepwalking in the middle of the night.

Remove things that are in the way. If your child walks in his sleep, clear away anything that he can step on or trip over during the night. Don't leave piles of blocks lying on the floor near the bedroom door, and be sure to pick up scattered toys.

Sleeping on the first floor. If your child is in real danger of going out a second-story window, consider having your child sleep on the first floor. If you live in a fifth-floor apartment, obviously you can't do this. But in other cases, this may be possible.

How to Deal with Parasomnias

Following are suggestions of things you can do to deal with your child's parasomnias:

Don't wake your child. Waking your child will not harm your child—that is an old wives' tale—but it will prolong the event.

Guide your child back to bed. Your child is asleep during these events, although he may not look it. He will eventually, and sometimes abruptly, return to normal sleep. To encourage this, guide your child gently back to bed. If he resists, let him be.

Try not to interfere too much. The normal response of parents is to try to comfort their child during a parasomnia episode. Try to resist doing this. Most children will just get more agitated; this is especially true if you try to hold a child who already appears upset. If your child is about to come to harm, though, be sure to keep her safe even if she fights you.

Increase amount of sleep. Try to increase the length of time that your child is asleep in order to avoid his becoming sleep-deprived. Parasomnias are much more likely to happen when your child is sleep-deprived. This is because confusional arousals, sleepwalking, and sleep terrors all occur during transitions from deep sleep. If your child is not getting enough sleep, he will have more deep sleep and will be more likely to have an event.

Maintain a regular sleep schedule. Parasomnias are more likely to happen on nights that your child goes to sleep at a time that is different from his usual time.

Don't discuss the event the next day. The morning after an event, don't discuss the problem with your child. Discussing the event is likely to worry him. This can lead to your child's becoming anxious about sleeping, because he is scared about what he may do. If he is anxious, he is less likely to fall asleep at night and then may become even more sleep-deprived. This, unfortunately, can lead to even more events. In addition, discussing parasomnias may lead older brothers and sisters to tease a younger child about how "weird" he was last night. Older children are also likely to ask if they acted strange during the night.

Allay your child's fears. Although this book is geared toward infants and toddlers, you may have an older child who has parasomnias. For older children, it may be helpful to discuss how common these behaviors are and to allay your child's fears or concerns that she is different or that something is wrong with her. Many older children become worried that they are crazy. Such a discussion should occur as part of everyday conversation. It is still recommended, even with older children, that you do not discuss whether such an event occurred the previous night. Again, it can make a child self-conscious and lead to avoidance of sleep.

Treatment Options

In most cases parasomnias require no treatment other than the above suggestions. After all, these events rarely indicate any serious underlying medical or psychiatric problem. Furthermore, the number of events tends to decrease in children as they get older; most children do not have them anymore after puberty. In some cases, however, medication or scheduled awakenings may be prescribed.

In severe cases, when parasomnias involve injury, violence, or disruption of the sleep of others, treatment may be necessary. This treatment may include medical intervention with prescription drugs or behavior modification techniques.

Medications

Doctors usually try to avoid giving drugs to a child who has parasomnias. However, in certain instances, when the sleep terrors are extreme or the child is in danger of hurting himself or someone else, medication may be recommended.

———————— C ————————

Kevin is five years old and has been having sleep terrors almost every night for the past eighteen months. They have gotten worse over time. Most nights he screams so loudly that he is hoarse the next day. His sleep terrors have also gotten violent. The week before he was evaluated at a sleep disorders center, he tried to throw a television set at his two-year-old sister. Now his sister is terrified of him. His mother hasn't slept in weeks because she is too worried that someone will get hurt. Kevin has become so anxious about going to sleep at night that it now takes him hours to fall asleep, and this has made his sleep terrors even worse.

In a case like Kevin's, medication is warranted. The most common types of medications given are benzodiazepines, such as Restoril or Klonopin. These drugs have a sedative effect and are often prescribed for anxiety. For parasomnias, though, they are prescribed not because of their effect on anxiety but because they suppress deep sleep—which is when sleep terrors are most likely to occur. These drugs will also help your child fall asleep, an asset if your child is scared to go to sleep. Usually a very short-acting medication is prescribed because all that is needed is to suppress deep sleep during the first few hours when sleep terrors occur. You also don't want a medication that stays in the system any longer than a few hours because you don't want your child to be groggy and feeling sluggish the next day.

Scheduled Awakenings

A treatment technique known as scheduled awakenings is available to treat parasomnias. This technique has been utilized by many with success, but there are no empirical data stating that scheduled awakenings definitively work. (While this technique can also work for confusional arousals or sleepwalking, sleep terrors will be used for ease of discussion.)

This technique involves waking your child about ten to fifteen minutes before he normally has a sleep terror. Usually you will need to repeat this procedure for about a week to ten days, and then the sleep terrors will stop. To use this intervention, your child will need to be having sleep terrors on a regular basis, at least two to three times per week, and have them at a consistent time of night. To figure out whether scheduled awakenings would be effective for your child, keep a nightly log in which you record the time that your child falls asleep and the time that he has a sleep terror (or sleepwalks, or whatever the case might be). Keep this log for at least one to two weeks, until a pattern emerges. You are looking for how often your child has sleep terrors and what time of the night they occur.

Once you have figured out the pattern of your child's sleep terror, you can begin scheduled awakenings. For the next ten days, wake your child fifteen minutes before he normally has a sleep terror. So if your child falls asleep at 8:30 every night and usually has a sleep terror at 9:45, wake him at 9:30. If your child has a sleep terror sixty-five minutes after he falls asleep, then wake him fifty minutes after he falls asleep. The exact time that you wake him will depend on what time he falls asleep on a given night. When you wake him, you don't need to totally get him up. You need only wake him to the point that he mumbles or moves or rolls over. You may need to set an alarm for yourself to remind you to wake your child. This way you won't have to watch the clock, and you won't have to worry about missing the time that you are supposed to wake him.

This technique sounds much more straightforward than it actually is. There are several things that can occur or go wrong. On a given night, your child may have a sleep terror before you get a chance to wake him. If this happens, move your scheduled awakening for the next night, and all subsequent nights, to an earlier time. If you were supposed to wake your child at 9:30 and he had a sleep terror at 9:20, then move your scheduled awakening to 9:15. Your waking him might also trigger a sleep terror. Again, if this happens, move your scheduled awakening earlier in the night. The scheduled awakenings can also move the sleep terrors back later in the night. This is the trickiest problem to deal with. What you will need to do is slowly begin moving the scheduled awakenings later in the night. If you were waking your son at 9:45, do so for about five days. Then start moving the wakings later by between fifteen and thirty minutes. So for three days, wake him at 10:15, and then for another three days, wake him at 10:45. And so on. Keep doing this until the sleep terrors end.

If the sleep terrors persist after ten days of scheduled awakenings, continue waking your child for another week. If the scheduled awakenings are effective, stop after the ten days. For many children, no more sleep terrors will occur. If they return when you stop the wakings, go back to waking your child for another week. Try stopping again. If they still continue but no sleep terrors occur on nights that you do wake your child, then go ahead and keep up the scheduled awakenings.

------------------------------ ☾ ------------------------------

Steve and Mary used scheduled awakenings with their daughter, Melissa, who was three and a half years old and had been having sleep terrors for about a year. In the beginning, when Melissa was two and a half, she would have one every few weeks. But for three months now she had been having them almost every night and often three to four times per night. Melissa would wake with a piercing scream and would cry and babble incoherently. She would shake all over as if trembling. She would appear very distressed and would climb into her parents' bed and grab hold of them with a viselike grip. The first episode would occur about seventy-five minutes after she fell asleep and the last one at about 3:00 in the morning. The increase in frequency in Melissa's sleep terrors coincided with her beginning day care and with a change in her sleep schedule because she was now going to bed a half-hour earlier and having to wake up an hour and a half earlier in the morning.

Steve and Mary began keeping track of Melissa's sleep terrors. They found that Melissa did seem to have them only during the week when she was getting less sleep. On weekends, when Melissa could sleep later on Saturday and Sunday mornings, she rarely had a sleep terror. In addition to trying to get Melissa to bed earlier in the evening, Steve and Mary started doing scheduled awakenings. Their plan was to get Melissa to bed by 7:45 and wake her nightly at 8:45. The first night all went smoothly. The second night Melissa had a sleep terror at 8:40, five minutes before they planned to wake her. From then on, Melissa's parents woke her at 8:35 every night. They woke her for the next eight days. On day 5, Melissa did have a sleep terror at 10:15 but otherwise slept soundly throughout the week. After the ten days of waking Melissa, her parents stopped the scheduled awakenings. For the next several months Melissa had only two sleep terrors. Both times they were after several days when Melissa was going to bed much later than the scheduled 7:45 bedtime.

------------------------- ✳ -------------------------

While we are not totally sure why scheduled awakenings work, there are several possible reasons for their effectiveness. Remember that sleep terrors, and other similar parasomnias, occur at the same point in the sleep cycle and happen when your child is making the transition from deep sleep to either awake or to another sleep stage. Scheduled awakenings may give your child practice in making the transition from deep sleep. That practice may allow the body's mechanism to learn how to do this effectively without getting stuck and having a sleep terror. Another reason they may work is that they are forcing the body to bypass that point in the sleep cycle when a sleep terror is likely to happen. A last reason they may work is that scheduled awakenings may lead to a new learned behavior. Rather than having a sleep terror, your child may learn to wake at that point in the sleep cycle, and thus a sleep terror doesn't have a chance of occurring. For whatever reason it works, for some children scheduled awakenings can be extremely effective in treating sleep terrors and other similar parasomnias.

Scheduled awakenings aren't for every child, however. If your child's sleep terrors are affecting others or put your child in danger of hurting himself, a more intensive intervention may be warranted. Also, if your child's sleep terrors are infrequent, then scheduled awakenings are difficult to do. They also shouldn't preclude you from instituting safety precautions. No matter what treatment you choose—including doing nothing—make sure that your child is always safe and can't hurt himself.

Reminders

- Parasomnias are unusual behaviors that occur at night.

- Confusional arousals, sleepwalking, and sleep terrors are three parasomnias that children often experience.

- Parasomnias are the result of your child's being awake and asleep at the same time. They do not indicate any type of psychological problem.

- Many things can bring on a parasomnia, including sleep deprivation, certain medications, and fevers or illness.

- There are ways to deal with parasomnias, including not waking your child and avoiding sleep deprivation.

- Other treatments for parasomnias are available, including scheduled awakenings and medication.

Chapter **12**

MUMBLING AND GRUMBLING
More Common Sleep Problems

———————————— ☾ ————————————

"All night long I hear this incredible banging from my daughter Tiffany's room."

☾

"Robert is only eight months old. Could he actually be having nightmares?"

———————————— ✳ ————————————

Many parents are concerned about head banging, nightmares, or even teeth grinding. Unfortunately, future parents very seldom hear about these behaviors, and few, if any, parenting books discuss them.

Nightmares

Nightmares are scary dreams that can wake your child, leaving him upset and in need of comfort. Many children are afraid to go back to sleep and often do not want to be left alone. Very young children do not know the difference between a dream and reality. So when they wake up, they do not understand the concept that they were only dreaming and it is now over. They may keep insisting that something scary which was about to happen in the dream is still about to occur. Your child may therefore be afraid and worried that something is still about to get him.

Many people ask whether young babies can have nightmares. We really don't know. Given that they can't tell us whether or not they dream, there is no way to know whether they are having nightmares. By the second year of life, babies definitely dream and have nightmares. It is just difficult to know whether they have them younger than that.

What do babies have nightmares about? Most young toddlers have concerns about being separated from their parents and may have a nightmare about being lost or having something happen to a parent. Nightmares are more likely to happen following some difficult event in the child's life. For example, if your child has just started day care or if you have just gone away overnight, your child is more likely to have a nightmare. For young children, nightmares may also be the reliving of a traumatic event, such as getting lost, getting a shot at the doctor's office, or being barked at by a big dog. By age two, nightmares begin to incorporate monsters and scary things that can hurt them.

How to Avoid Nightmares

Not all nightmares can be avoided. They are a part of normal development and are a sign of your child's developing imagination. There are a few things you can do, however, to help reduce the likelihood of nightmares.

Avoid scary things before bedtime. Don't read scary stories or watch scary movies immediately before bedtime. Don't play games that include your child's being chased by monsters or by the "big bad wolf." Don't play "I'm going to get you."

Assure safety. Be sure that your child understands that she is safe and that you are close at hand if she needs you. If she calls to you, be sure to respond quickly, especially following a nightmare. She will need this reassurance even more the next night after having a nightmare, so do respond to her needs.

Reduce stress. If there is something in your child's life that you know is distressing, try to take care of it and reassure your child. If she is getting bullied by a bigger kid at day care, talk to her day care providers. If she was recently bit by a dog and has become terrified of dogs, work with her to get over her fear. Read stories about dogs. Visit a puppy. If your child suddenly experiences a significant increase in nightmares, try to evaluate why. Look for recurring themes that could give you a clue as to the cause, and then work to deal with the problem.

Ensure enough sleep. After nights in which you don't get enough sleep, your body becomes sleep deprived or, more specifically, REM deprived. That is, your body needs REM sleep. When you don't get enough of it, your body will try to catch up the next night, and you will spend more time in REM sleep. Consequently, you will be dreaming more, and these dreams can often become more bizarre and scary than on other nights. So make sure that your child is getting enough sleep. This can help decrease the frequency and intensity of nightmares.

Eliminate foods prior to bedtime. High-dose vitamins taken at bedtime can disturb sleep. Vitamins should not be taken at bedtime because they, along with some foods, can cause a person's metabolism to increase and result in nightmares. (Note, too, that some medications can also bring on nightmares.)

What to Do if Your Child Has a Nightmare

The best thing that you can do if your child has a nightmare is to comfort her. For babies and young toddlers merely holding them and providing physical comfort is enough. For older toddlers and young children, verbal reassurance may also be needed. If your child is less than two years old, don't bother trying to explain the concept that "it was just a dream." She won't understand it. If your child insists on your putting a light on and leaving it on, that is okay. If you leave it on, put it on the dimmest setting possible so your child can fall back to sleep easily.

You may also have to show your child that there are no monsters under the bed or in the closet. Again, your child will have a hard time distinguishing between a dream and reality, so help your child understand that she is no longer in danger. If she insists on checking whether her sister or someone else is all right because she had a dream that that person was hurt, show her that the person is fine. (And don't be hurt if your child insists on the other parent for comfort. All children go through periods during which they want one or the other parent. This is an aspect of normal development that helps your child bond to both parents.)

Staying With Your Child

My child doesn't want to be left alone after a nightmare. Do I stay with him? Is it okay if I bring him back to our bed?

Parents often debate whether to allow their child to come into their bed and stay with them after a nightmare. This decision is a difficult one because you are trying to balance two different needs. On the one hand, you want to comfort your child, especially if he is terrified. On the other hand, you don't want to encourage him to join you in bed or give the message that it is okay to sleep with Mommy and Daddy (if it isn't okay with you).

Following most nightmares your child will be reassured by a few minutes of comfort. Stay with him in his room. Let him know that you are nearby and will make sure that he is safe and secure. Don't stay too long. Staying with him for a long time or allowing him in your bed can subtly reinforce that there really is something for your child to be afraid of. If your child is clearly terrified, though, it is fine to let him stay with you, as long as it is an infrequent occurrence. Be clear that you will stay with him or allow him into your bed only when he is sick or extremely frightened. If not, you may find that your child has decided to have a "nightmare" every night.

Nightmares Versus Night Terrors

It is important to distinguish between a nightmare and a night terror because they are two distinct entities and are dealt with differently. Nightmares usually occur in the latter part of the night, after several hours of sleep. Your child will recognize you and seek comfort from you. It may take her a while to fall back to sleep. She will also remember having the nightmare the next day. As you will recall from Chapter 11, night terrors occur within one to two hours of falling asleep. Your child will quickly return to sleep and will not remember the occurrence in the morning.

Bedtime Fears

Bedtime fears are the most common fears experienced by young children. Bedtime fears typically involve being scared of the dark. This is normal and part of normal development. Fear of the dark begins to develop as children start to understand that they can get hurt or be harmed. Once children understand this concept, it will take some time for them to understand what is likely to harm them versus what is not. Situations in which they are alone and it is dark are prime times for children to be afraid. It is important, however, for children to learn how to cope with this fear and understand that they are not in danger. This is in contrast to a situation in which a child is not likely to be afraid but could possibly be in danger. Think of all the times that your parents told you never to accept candy from strangers or take rides from someone you didn't know. This situation seems safe to children because most adults that they have had contact with are considered safe and have always been nice to them. So part of being a parent is helping your child to develop realistic fears and distinguish them from unrealistic fears. This process may take a while.

Many bedtime fears can also be learned through simple conditioning. For example, the bedroom may be a source of anxiety for some children, especially if it is the place where the child is sent as punishment. Also, if the child has a nightmare or awakens distressed in the middle of the night, a parent typically comes into the room and turns on the light. Thus, a child may associate light with comfort and associate darkness with distress or nightmares.

What to Do if Your Child Is Afraid at Bedtime

Dealing with a child who is afraid of the dark or scared to go to bed at night is like walking a tightrope. It is a fine line between wanting to reassure him and not wanting to reinforce his fears. If you ignore his fears, you feel cold and unfeeling. If you reassure him too much, you may be subtly giving the message that there is something to be afraid of. Most children outgrow their fears, but in the meantime here are some things that you may want to try.

Reassurance. It is important to reassure children. They need to be taught how to cope with fearful situations. Talk to your child about how you dealt with something that you were afraid of. Read stories about children who are afraid and conquer their fears, such as *There's a Monster in My Closet* by Maurice Sendak. (See Appendix A: Baby Bedtime Books, for suggested stories on dealing with bedtime fears.)

Monster spray. Many families have found "monster spray" a wonderful way to help a child cope with bedtime fears. Take a spray-type bottle (be sure that it has not previously had any chemicals in it such as plant food) and fill it with water. Some people add food coloring, but this can stain. Label it in large letters MONSTER SPRAY or BOGEYMAN SPRAY or whatever your child calls what he is afraid of. At bedtime, you or your child can spray the room to keep the monsters away. Keep the spray bottle next to the bed. During the night, if your child gets scared, he can spray the monsters away. This will give your child a way to cope and save you from having to come help him.

Use your imagination. Use your imagination to fight monsters. In addition to monster spray you can make up other things that will help your child. Logic isn't important. If it works, go with it. One family had a large old cat, Opus. They told their son, Jason, that Opus stayed up at night and made sure that everyone was safe. Opus also kept bogeymen away. So at bedtime they would bring Opus in, and their son would give him instructions to stay awake and guard the house. This satisfied their son. Opus, of course, would leave the room and go to sleep in his usual spot on the living room couch, but Jason felt safe believing that Opus was on patrol for bogeymen.

Set limits. At the same time that you are reassuring your child, you do need to set limits. Setting limits is necessary to prevent the behavior that your child exhibits when being scared from being reinforced. Checking closets and leaving a low nightlight on is reasonable, but allowing your child to sleep with you every night is not.

Star system. Some children receive reinforcement for being scared at night. They may be getting lots of attention or receiving special treats for being afraid. If this is the case, switch the scenario. Give your daughter lots of attention for dealing with her fears. Tell her how proud you are of her for being brave.

Set up a star system. She earns stars for being brave and sleeping on her own. After earning a certain number of stars, she can turn them in for a treat, such as watching a favorite video, going to the park, or baking chocolate chip cookies with you.

Relaxation training. You can also teach your child relaxation strategies to help her relax at bedtime and fall asleep. This will give her something else to think about while lying in bed, and it will help distract her from her fearful thoughts. Also, it is impossible to be relaxed and scared at the same time. Our bodies simply do not work that way. So being relaxed will preempt being scared.

Different relaxation strategies are presented in Chapter 7. These strategies are designed for adults but can be easily modified for children. For example, use guided imagery. Have your child develop an image of a favorite relaxing place. Young children are also very successful at learning progressive muscle relaxation. For young children, modify the progressive muscle relaxation script that is provided in Chapter 7. Rather than simply telling your child to tense certain muscles, which can be a difficult concept for a youngster, use the images described on the next page to help her tense her muscles.

Teeth Grinding

———————— ☾ ————————

Lydia is ten months old. Her mother swears that Lydia grinds her teeth. She doesn't do it every night but enough that her mother has noticed.

———————— ✳ ————————

Yes, babies do grind their teeth. That is, what teeth they have. And a large number of babies do this. About 50 percent of all babies grind their teeth before they turn one year of age. The sound of grinding teeth is unmistakable; you will know if your baby does it or not. But while the sound can be very loud and bothersome to you, there is nothing to be concerned about.

Tensing Exercises for Muscle Groups

Hands and arms—Squeeze a lemon in your hand.

Arms and shoulders—Pretend you are a furry, lazy cat who is stretching. Stretch your arms in front of you and over your head.

Legs and feet—You are walking through a big, squishy mud puddle. Squish your toes down into the mud and use your legs to help you push down to the bottom.

Stomach—Uh-oh, you are lying on the ground and a baby elephant is about to step on your stomach. Make your stomach hard so he won't crush you!

Stomach and chest—You have to squeeze through a very narrow fence, and you have to make yourself skinny. Suck in your stomach and hold your breath. Squeeze through that fence! Ah, you made it.

Shoulder and neck—Pretend you are a turtle and pull your head in tight by pushing your shoulders up to your ears. Hide your head!

Jaw—Bite down really hard on a big jawbreaker bubble gum.

Face—Try to get a pesky fly off your nose without using your hands. Wrinkle your nose and try to get him off. Oh, no. He's now on your forehead. Make lots of wrinkles and try to catch him between those wrinkles.

Adapted from: Koeppen, A. S. "Relaxation Training for Children." Elementary School Guidance and Counseling, *9 (1974): 14–21.*

Teeth grinding in medical jargon is called bruxism. Almost 95 percent of all adults have ground their teeth at least once in their life, and many do it often. It is seen just as often in children, usually after age ten. In babies, however, bruxism usually begins at about the age of ten months and occurs after the baby has her deciduous incisors (the two top front teeth and two bottom front teeth). Babies usually start to get their two bottom teeth at around six months, and by ten months have their two top teeth also. (Note, though, that it is not unusual for some babies not to have any teeth at all until they are a year old.) Babies can grind their teeth in any stage of sleep but are more likely to do it in non-REM sleep, especially stage two. This means that it is much more likely to occur in the first half of the night, although it can occur at any time. Some babies grind their teeth only sporadically, whereas others do it throughout most of the night.

While teeth grinding in adults can lead to dental problems, teeth grinding in babies is nothing to be alarmed about. It is highly unlikely that your child is doing any damage to her teeth. If you are worried, however, or see any changes in your child's teeth, be sure to see a dentist. Some babies are less likely to grind their teeth when lying on their sides, so you can try turning your baby and putting her on her side to fall asleep or once she is asleep. In any case, this behavior will eventually go away on its own.

Rocking and Rolling

Luther is twenty months old. Initially his parents were sure that Luther never slept because all throughout the night they could hear him moving around. Finally, his father sneaked into his room and discovered that Luther was moving—but he was fast asleep. What Luther was doing was rocking back and forth and banging his head against the side of his crib. They had seen him do this when he was younger.

This type of rocking and rolling is often seen in young children. It is officially called rhythmic movement disorder. Every child is different in what they do, but it is usually some type of rocking, rolling, or head banging. Oddly, children find this a soothing way to fall asleep. Your baby may do this at naptime and bedtime to put himself to sleep. And remember that babies wake frequently during the night and need to put themselves back to sleep. Your baby's head banging or rocking is his way to fall back to sleep. So don't be surprised if this behavior occurs not only at bedtime but throughout the night.

For most babies, head banging or body rolling is not problematic, but there are some children for whom it may be of concern. Some children who are developmentally disabled or autistic will rock or bang their heads, and may hurt themselves. These children may require helmets or restraints to make sure that they do not injure themselves. Some children who are blind or have some other neurological problem will also be more likely to be violent rock and rollers.

Head banging or body rolling does not mean, however, that your child has a neurological problem. If this is the only behavior that you have seen, and your child is normal and healthy otherwise, you should not be concerned. If your child has a neurological or psychiatric problem, you will be aware of it from behavior during the day.

For the baby's sake, there is nothing much that you need to do. Babies often rock or bang their heads to fall asleep. This is normal. They will eventually stop. Don't worry about having to protect your child. Even if your child is banging his head voraciously, it is unlikely that he will hurt himself, so there is no need to put extra bumpers on the crib or place pillows in strategic places. Also, it won't work. If a baby really wants to bang his head, he will do it no matter what creative tricks you try. Those children previously mentioned who require helmets are children who bang their head not as a soothing mechanism to fall asleep but as a way to injure themselves. This behavior is also exhibited during the day. This self-injurious behavior is substantially different from behavior exhibited as a way of falling asleep.

Be careful about reinforcing this behavior. If you go in to your baby every time he starts to rock or bang his head, you may be reinforcing his behavior without even realizing it. In that event he may be head banging to get your attention. If so, make sure that your child gets lots of attention from you during the day and ignore his head banging at night. You can occasionally look in on him at night, without waking him, to make sure he isn't hurting himself.

For your own sake, move the crib or the bed away from the wall if the banging or rocking is making noise and keeping the rest of the family awake. If your child is in a bed rather than a crib, be sure to put guard rails on all sides before moving the bed so that he won't roll out of bed now that the wall is not there to act as a buffer. If the moving of the crib or bed by your child is making it squeak, oil it and tighten the screws frequently.

There are other things that you can try, although they may not be very effective. Try putting a loud ticking clock or metronome in your child's room. The external rhythmic noise may help replace your child's need to bang his head or rock his body. If your child bangs his head against the side of the crib and is bruising himself, you can try to put him on a mattress on the floor. This may not always work; some children simply move closer to the wall and fall asleep there, banging away.

Sleep Starts

Most people have experienced the common "motor" sleep start—a sudden, often violent jerk of the entire body just as you fall asleep. Other forms of sleep starts also occur just as sleep begins. A "visual" sleep start is a sensation of blinding light coming from inside the eyes or inside the head. An auditory sleep start is a loud snapping noise that seems to come from inside the head. People sometimes refer to these visual and auditory sleep starts as feeling "electric." Sleep starts can be frightening, but they are perfectly normal. Many people have the sensation that they are falling and then jerk back awake.

Valerie noticed that her three-year-old son, Michael, always jerked when he was falling asleep. His entire body would seem to jump right off the bed. She used to worry that these were some type of seizure until she began to notice that her husband seemed to have them as well.

Sleep starts are caused by an intrusion of REM sleep. As you may recall from Chapter 2, REM sleep involves dreaming and paralysis of most of the body. When you fall asleep at night, your body goes into non-REM sleep. Ninety minutes later, REM sleep occurs. For some reason, though, on some nights some people will have a few seconds to a few minutes of REM sleep right when they are falling asleep at night. This is called REM intrusion because REM sleep is intruding on a time when non-REM sleep should be occurring. It doesn't mean anything other than perhaps you are really tired. Some people have these sleep starts only when they haven't gotten enough sleep. Others have them every night.

Sleep Talking

Sleep talking is formally called somniloquy. Some people talk in their sleep all the time, while others do it rarely. Sleep talking is common and normal. It does not mean that there is a medical or psychological problem. Some people talk in their sleep. Some laugh. Your child may do this fairly often. It is much more difficult to tell in babies whether they are babbling in their sleep or just half-awake. If your baby talks in her sleep, don't worry about it. Be entertained by it and otherwise leave it alone.

In older children and adults, sleep talking may occur during stressful periods, such as before the first day of school or during a stressful workweek. Don't be surprised by it and don't read too much into it. Some people believe that things spoken while sleeping come from the unconscious and are a window into the person's deepest thoughts and feelings. To date there is no empirical support for this theory.

Reminders

- Nightmares are scary dreams that can wake your child. There are ways to prevent nightmares and ways to deal with them.

- Bedtime fears are the most common fear of young children. There are ways to manage bedtime fears and teach your child to cope with these common fears.

- There are other sleep behaviors common in young children, including teeth grinding, rocking to sleep, sleep starts, and sleep talking.

Part Four

"What About Me?": Adult Sleep and Sleep Problems

✳

Chapter 13

"NOW, I CAN'T SLEEP!"
Adult Sleep

ᄃ

Sarah is five months old and is finally sleeping through the night. The first few months were difficult, but Sarah has been sleeping well for the past three weeks. However, her mother, Deborah, still cannot sleep and is feeling run-down and exhausted. She thought that once Sarah was sleeping, all would return to normal but that has not been the case. She still has difficulty falling asleep and wakes frequently throughout the night.

✳

All too often, even after the baby is finally sleeping through the night, parents continue to have sleep problems. There are also many other issues beyond babies that affect adults' sleep, including sleep deprivation, poor sleep habits, certain medications, and pregnancy.

The Basics of Sleep

"I Still Can't Sleep"

Many parents say that they still can't sleep once their baby is sleeping through the night. They often experience a delay in returning to normal sleep patterns, and it may take several months for them to finally sleep through the night.

The reason you, the parent, are having difficulty sleeping is probably that your body needs time to adjust and get back into old sleeping patterns. Also, you have learned to wake frequently through the night along with the baby. You are probably still waking up at the times your baby used to wake up. You may even be going to check on the baby to make sure that she is really still asleep. Resist this urge. If she is awake, you will hear her. Your body simply needs time to adjust and return to old sleeping habits.

If you had problems sleeping before you were pregnant or had the baby, however, you will continue to have problems even after the baby is sleeping through the night. If you did have problems, be sure to read the tips that are provided later in this chapter and read Chapter 14 to be sure that you don't have a sleep disorder that is affecting your sleep.

"I Feel Like a Zombie and I Can't Function"

As all too many parents know, not getting enough sleep has a major impact on how they are able to function as parents, on the job, and as spouses. I have done studies on this issue. The bad news is that parents are more likely to be depressed, to be more anxious, and to be less satisfied in their marriages when they have a baby who doesn't sleep. The good news is that once the baby starts to sleep, parents feel better, are happier, and are more satisfied with their marriages.

Sleep Is Important

Sleep is not negotiable. Sleep is probably the most important thing that your body needs after food and water. Surprisingly, we don't really know why people need to sleep, but we do know what happens to people when they don't sleep. After just a few hours of sleep deprivation, a person's reaction time is slower and he is more likely to forget things and to become moody. After longer periods of sleep deprivation, people begin to hallucinate—see things that are not there. You cannot be a good parent, a good employee, or a good spouse if you don't get enough sleep.

Everyone needs about eight hours of sleep per night. That is an average. Some people need nine or ten hours of sleep to feel their best. And, yes, there are some people who need only six or seven hours of sleep at night. But that is a rarity. In our sleep disorders center, we have never seen a person who gets only six hours of sleep at night who is not sleep deprived. But how can we tell that a person is sleep deprived? Careful analysis of sleep patterns reveals differences between normal sleep and the sleep of someone who is sleep deprived. For example, people dream more when they are sleep deprived, and they get different quantities of the different stages of sleep in comparison to when they get enough sleep.

But, you say, how can I get enough sleep when the baby is always crying, the laundry needs to be done, and the bills have to be paid. Well, this book has told you how to get your baby to sleep. About the other things: First, *prioritize*. Then, *delegate*.

Prioritize. This means figure out what is most important, what needs to be done, and what you can do without. Paying the bills is important; the house being spotless isn't. Dinner is important; but a full-course home-cooked meal isn't.

Delegate. You also don't have to do everything yourself. Your nine-year-old son can help by folding towels. They may not be done exactly the way you would like, but that doesn't matter as long as it is done. Delegate your spouse, a friend, or a neighbor to call in a takeout order and pick it up on the way home from work. It may be worth it for a period of six months to hire people to do things that you would normally do. Get someone to come in and clean or do the laundry. Hire a local teenager to mow the lawn, rake the leaves, or even weed the flower beds. When people ask if there is anything that they can do to help, suggest something (whether it is picking up a gallon of milk at the store while they are there or watching the baby for a couple of hours).

This is not the time to be superperson. People cannot do it all on their own. That is not realistic. Reality is that there is often too much to do and too little time to do it. So figure out what needs to be done and what is important. And remember, sleep is important.

Napping

Babies are not the only ones who nap. Adults nap, too. Napping is a universal behavior. In some cultures, napping is even the norm. Think of the Mexican siesta.

Naps are very important for parents of infants and toddlers, especially as a parent of a baby less than three months old whose nighttime sleep is almost always interrupted. Naps are essential to make up for lost sleep. The rule of thumb is to nap when the baby naps. Although this may seem the perfect time to finally get things done around the house or to make some phone calls, catching up on your sleep is probably more important.

Almost all naps occur at the same time every day, between 12 noon and 5:00 P.M. These naps occur about twelve hours after the midpoint of the sleep the night before. So, someone who slept from 11:00 P.M. until 7:00 A.M. will nap at 3:00 in the afternoon. Given this tendency for people to have what is apparently a twelve-hour rhythm, naps are likely to have a biological function. The average nap taken by adults lasts seventy minutes.

Naps can be very beneficial for daytime alertness but have two drawbacks. The first drawback is that a person can feel groggy after waking from a nap. This typically involves a few minutes of disorientation when you may not be able to think clearly. For most of us that is not a problem, but for a physician on call or anyone else who is required to function immediately upon waking, it can be a serious issue. Naps can also interfere with nighttime sleep. This usually only occurs, though, if the nap lasts longer than two hours or occurs too late in the afternoon.

Napping that occurs at times other than mid-afternoon may be a sign of a sleep problem. For people with sleep apnea or narcolepsy, frequent daytime napping is another symptom of their sleep problem. People with a sleep disorder often nap at times other than during the afternoon and can nap many times in one day. Those with narcolepsy find naps refreshing, whereas people with sleep apnea get little if any benefit from naps. Others find that naps do interfere with nighttime sleep. For this reason people with insomnia or a sleep-wake cycle disorder should avoid naps.

For others, especially parents of young children, naps are highly beneficial and may be the difference between being able to function and not being able to function.

Making Up for Lost Sleep

———————————— ☾ ————————————

Dan is the father of eight-month-old twins. During the week he usually goes to bed at midnight and has to get up for work at 6:30 A.M. If he is lucky, he sleeps the entire six and a half hours without being awakened by one of the twins. On weekends, however, he is able to sleep in and usually gets nine or ten hours of sleep. But even with all that sleep on the weekends, he is still tired.

———————————— ✳ ————————————

Dan is finding that you cannot make up for lost sleep as easily as you think. A recent study showed that it takes at least three weeks to make up for lost sleep. Sleeping in on weekends will not solve the problem of not getting enough sleep during the week. Neither will a one- or two-week vacation when you can sleep in each day. The box on the next page will help you decide if you are getting enough sleep.

The Best Way to Get a Good Night's Sleep

Here is a list of do's and don'ts for getting a good night's sleep.

1. *Maintain a regular daily schedule of activities.* Try to keep a set schedule during the day. Eat meals at the same times and plan your activities on a similar schedule.

2. *Sleep schedule.* Try to go to bed at the same time every night and wake up at the same time every morning. This will help regulate your body's inner clock. If you are having problems sleeping, avoid all naps because they can interfere with nighttime sleep.

3. *Bedtime routine.* Bedtime routines are as important for adults as they are for children. Bedtime routines help your body know it is bedtime before you even get into bed.

4. *Sleeping attire.* Wear loose-fitting, comfortable sleeping attire. Sexy lingerie may look great, but it won't help your sleep. The more comfortable you are, the better you will sleep.

5. *Exercise.* Exercise can help you sleep better. The best time to exercise is late afternoon or early evening, about five to six hours before bedtime. Avoid exercising within four hours of bedtime because it will wake you up too much.

6. *Relax.* Just prior to bedtime do something enjoyable and relaxing. Take a bath or read a good book. Don't pay your bills or choose that time to have an intense discussion with your partner.

Are You Getting Enough Sleep?

To figure out if you are getting enough sleep and func-tioning at your best, take the following test.

Considering the past month, answer true or false to the following statements.

1. When I wake up in the morning, I feel groggy.

2. I fall asleep at night in less than 5 minutes.

3. On weekends I get at least 2 more hours of sleep than I do during the week.

4. I could fall asleep at any time.

5. I have fallen asleep at a time that I shouldn't have, such as while driving or talking on the phone.

6. I often fall asleep in the evening while watching tele-vision or reading (not while in bed).

7. I nap most days.

8. I feel as if I have lost my sense of humor.

9. I become drowsy when doing repetitive tasks.

If you answered true to three or more of the above statements, you are probably not getting enough sleep.

---

7. *Light snack.* Eat a light snack prior to bedtime if you are hungry. Going to bed hungry can interrupt your sleep.

8. *Your bedroom.* Make your bedroom as quiet and comfort-able as possible. Have a good mattress and a pillow that you like. Make sure that the room is quiet. Running a fan or a "white noise maker" can help drown out sounds from the outdoors (this is not always best if it drowns out the sound of your baby). A cool bedroom is better for sleep than a warm one. Also, a dark bedroom is best. It may be worth investing in room-darkening shades or blinds if your bedroom is too light.

9. *Can't sleep?* When you get into bed, turn off the lights (and the television!), close your eyes, and try to fall asleep. If you can't sleep, try to relax and rest as much as possible. Avoid looking at the clock and worrying about being tired the next day. This will just keep you up longer. If you get frustrated, get out of bed and do something relaxing for twenty to thirty minutes and then return to bed.

10. *Sharing your bed.* If you share a bed with someone who is a snorer, a kicker, or a cover-stealer, you may want to sleep elsewhere temporarily until you reestablish a better sleep pattern. If you think your bed partner has a sleep disorder, consult a physician.

11. *Avoid caffeine.* Avoid all caffeinated beverages after lunch. Note that many sodas, including Mountain Dew and some orange sodas, contain caffeine. For example, Sunkist Orange has 42 milligrams of caffeine per 12 ounces, whereas Diet Sunkist Orange has none. Check the label.

12. *Associate your bed with sleep.* Avoid doing other activities in bed other than sleep (and sex, of course). Don't eat in bed or pay your bills. Avoid even having a television in the bedroom (although I realize that this is an idea many people won't like). Learn to associate your bed and your bedroom with sleep.

13. *Avoid all sleeping medications.* If you have to use them, then use them only on a night-to-night basis when needed. Never use them for more than two weeks in a row.

14. *Avoid alcohol.* Avoid all alcoholic beverages. These interfere with sleep. You may be able to fall asleep quicker, but they usually lead to your waking in the middle of the night.

The Effects of Drugs on Sleep

Many medications in use today may affect sleep. For example, antidepressants are a large class of drugs that are used to treat problems such as depression, anxiety, and pain. Antidepressants are also used to treat a number of sleep disorders. The more common antidepressants are amitriptyline (Elavil), imipramine (Tofranil), desipramine (Norpramin), trazodone (Desyrel), and fluoxetine (Prozac). Each antidepressant affects sleep differently. In general, most antidepressants decrease night wakings and decrease the time it takes to fall asleep. This is not true for all of them, though: Some have no effect on sleep, and others can even increase wakefulness at night. Some antidepressants can also make a person feel sluggish during the day. Because of this daytime sedating effect, many antidepressants are given as a single dose at bedtime.

Benzodiazepines are drugs that are used for insomnia, problems with anxiety, seizure control, and as a muscle relaxant. Benzodiazepines usually have positive effects on sleep, including increasing total sleep time and decreasing night wakings. Commonly used benzodiazepines are alprazolam (Xanax), chlordiazepoxide (Librium), clonazepam (Klonopin), diazepam (Valium), lorazepam (Ativan), and oxazepam (Serax). Some benzodiazepines are longer acting than others. The longer-acting ones, if taken at bedtime, can cause a feeling of grogginess in the morning. Therefore, if you are taking these types of medications for sleep problems, you may need to try different ones to find the one that works best for you at night but leaves you awake and alert during the day. In addition, some of these drugs can make some sleep disorders worse. For example, benzodiazepines make sleep apnea worse and therefore can be dangerous for the individuals who suffer from this disorder.

Other drugs that are used for anxiety, such as buspirone (BuSpar), clonidine (Catapres), hydroxyzine (Atarax, Vistaril), and propranolol (Inderal), can have variable effects on sleep. For example, buspirone can trigger restlessness. Also used to treat anxiety, as well as psychotic behavior and sleeplessness, are tranquilizers. Most tranquilizers are benzodiazepines, as discussed above. The most common tranquilizers are used for anxiety and include such drugs as Valium, Librium, and Xanax. These drugs can have some sedating effect and can help sleep. Be careful because these drugs can also be addicting.

Steroids are a common treatment for many medical problems. The most common steroid used medically is prednisone; it is known to disrupt sleep and at higher doses can lead to nightmares. Common medications for cardiac problems, such as Inderal, Lopressor, and Visken, can cause difficulty falling asleep. These drugs also increase night wakings and because of the resulting fragmented sleep often lead to an increase in the number of dreams recalled. Bronchodilators for asthma can cause sleep disturbances also. Some have no effect on sleep, whereas others increase wakefulness.

Common over-the-counter medications can also impact sleep. For example, although antihistamines often cause drowsiness during the day, they can actually increase the time it takes to fall asleep at night. Appetite suppressants, which often have a mild stimulant in them, can lead to insomnia, as you would expect. On the other hand, aspirin can be helpful for insomnia. Studies on aspirin have shown that it can increase total sleep time and decrease night wakings. Some people report that aspirin works just as well for insomnia as some sleeping pills.

Caffeine, found as an ingredient in many foods and medicines, can lead to problems falling asleep at night. For those with restless legs syndrome or periodic limb movements in sleep (see Chapter 14), caffeine will make both of these conditions worse.

Alcohol also interferes with sleep. Although you may fall asleep quicker after having a drink, it leads to middle-of-the-night wakings and earlier rising than you might prefer.

Nicotine also impacts sleep. It can cause difficulty falling asleep. Although many say that having a cigarette relaxes them, it may not help them to fall asleep at night.

Marijuana also affects sleep. Marijuana changes the amount of time in the different stages of sleep, and chronic use of the drug reduces REM sleep. After discontinuing its use, there is often REM rebound, meaning a significant increase in REM sleep to "make up" for the lost amount. This REM rebound will be experienced as a significant increase in dreaming.

Cocaine has a much more significant impact on sleep. Cocaine reduces the total amount of sleep the person obtains, especially REM sleep. Short-term withdrawal from cocaine produces significant changes in sleep, usually insomnia and fatigue.

It is important to evaluate whether any medication that you are currently taking is affecting your sleep. If you are taking any prescription medication, be sure to ask your physician or pharmacist what impact it may have on your sleep. Furthermore, it is important to stop many drugs slowly; for example, sudden withdrawal from benzodiazepines can be fatal. So be sure to ask your physician or pharmacist how to get off a drug safely if you wish to stop using it.

Sleeping Pills

Sleeping pills can often do more harm than good, especially for people whose only complaint is "I can't sleep" or "It takes me hours to fall asleep." There are a number of reasons that sleeping pills are *not* recommended:

1. Sleeping pills affect the type of sleep you get. They modify nervous system activity, which reduces REM sleep, the type of sleep when you dream. After taking sleeping pills for a while and stopping, many find that they begin to have dreams that disrupt their sleep, making them feel more tired the next day even after a full night's sleep.

2. The human body develops a tolerance to sleeping pills after their repeated use. After a while you have to take more and more to make you feel sleepy.

3. You can become psychologically dependent on sleeping pills. If you are convinced that a sleeping pill is the only way you can get a good night's sleep, you won't be able to go to sleep without them.

4. You can get rebound effects and get caught in a vicious cycle. What often happens is that people take sleeping pills for a while and then try stopping them. Usually, though, the next two nights their sleep is very poor, and so they begin to take them again, convinced that they need them. What is happening is that the body is experiencing rebound; it is actually going through withdrawal. Therefore, your sleep will be worse for several nights. So the best thing to do is to wait two weeks after being taken off them before evaluating your sleep.

5. Sleeping pills can make some sleep disorders worse. If the reason that you are having problems falling asleep at night is that you have a sleep disorder such as sleep apnea, as discussed in Chapter 14, sleeping pills can make the problem worse and even cause it to become life-threatening.

6. It is better to find out the real reason for your sleeping problem and treat it appropriately.

Melatonin

Recently there has been much in the news about melatonin and its impact on sleep. At this time melatonin is sold in health food stores under such names as Melatone. The reports state that ingestion of melatonin increases sleepiness. Some people are saying that it is the new miracle cure—a way to treat insomnia and prevent jet lag.

Melatonin is naturally produced in the pineal gland and appears to be involved in the sleep process. Melatonin production in humans is highest between 10:00 P.M. and 3:00 A.M., and drops to low levels by 8:00 A.M. Thus, as melatonin increases, the need to sleep increases. The production of melatonin is influenced by exposure to light, whether it is daylight or artificial light. Light falls on the retina, which sends a message to the pineal gland. Therefore, the argument is that if you take melatonin orally, you should get sleepy. However, there are mixed data about this phenomenon. Interestingly, people who have no functioning pineal gland, usually because of radiation treatment, continue to have good sleep patterns. That means that the pineal gland and melatonin production are only a small part of the sleep process. Sleep is much more complex.

Caution should be taken before using melatonin. First, clinical studies need to be conducted to assess its effectiveness and any potential side effects. Although some argue that melatonin is a naturally produced substance and therefore shouldn't be of any harm, many naturally produced substances can be harmful. For example, insulin is a necessary chemical in the body, but too much insulin can be fatal. Lead, a natural substance, can cause brain damage. Also, since the FDA does not regulate the manufacturing of melatonin, health food store supplies may be impure. A number of years ago L-tryptophan was the craze. L-tryptophan was supposed to help insomnia. But a batch of L-tryptophan, later believed to be contaminated, caused a serious blood disorder in a number of people. Before taking melatonin, therefore, check with your physician. Melatonin may be the answer that medicine has been looking for, but until it is a sure thing, it is better to be safe than sorry.

Should you put your child on melatonin? First, you should not give your child anything before checking with your pediatrician. Second, early studies on the effects of melatonin on baby rats showed that increased doses of melatonin can affect the development of the reproductive organs. Levels of melatonin are high in children prior to puberty. At the start of puberty, levels drop substantially. Thus, melatonin reduction may be an important aspect in the development of reproductive organs in adolescence. High doses of melatonin are also known to suppress ovulation. This knowledge is being used in Europe to develop a new birth control pill for women, where high doses of melatonin have been found to be effective. These doses of 75 milligrams per day are much higher than the doses found in Melatone or other health food store melatonin products; these are usually in doses of 1, 5, or 6 milligrams. Therefore, giving a child or adolescent melatonin may impact on sexual development. Since no studies have been done to date on the long-term effects of melatonin in children, caution should be taken before administering it to your child.

Sleep and Pregnancy

Stephanie is the mother of three-year-old twins, Ariel and Olivia. After several months of struggling, she has finally gotten the twins to go to bed by 8:30 and sleep through the night. However, Stephanie, who is now seven months pregnant, feels as though she never gets any sleep. She is up several times during the night to go to the bathroom, and at other times she is simply lying awake. She either can't find a comfortable position or is awakened when the baby starts to kick.

Each of the three trimesters of pregnancy are characterized by changes in sleep. Many women throughout their pregnancy find that their sleep is disturbed and that they are not getting a sufficient amount of sleep. This leads to feelings of fatigue and tiredness during the day. If this is your first child, you may be able to catch up by napping during the day if your schedule allows. If you already have another child at home, however, especially one who doesn't sleep, it can be very difficult to cope. The following is an overview of what to expect during pregnancy as it relates to sleep.

First Trimester

Two things contribute to the increased need for sleep in women in their first trimester. First, given that this is a time of rapid development of the unborn fetus, the woman's body is expending a great deal of energy. Second, nighttime sleep often becomes disrupted, primarily because of a need to urinate frequently. This need to urinate is caused by the fetus and enlarged uterus pressing on the bladder. These two factors result in high levels of fatigue during the day and an increasing need for sleep at night. It is very common for women to find themselves napping during the day, even if they were never a "napper" before. Pregnant women during the first trimester are also likely to increase the amount of time they sleep at night. Many pregnant women are fast asleep by 8:00 at night and sleeping until 8:00 the next morning. If your schedule allows, give in to this increased need to sleep and don't try to fight it. Your body is sending you a message as to what it needs.

Second Trimester

Sleep is much more normal during the second trimester. Development of the unborn fetus has slowed down, so less energy expenditure is required by the woman. The need to urinate at night also diminishes because the uterus has moved from the pelvic region, where it presses on the bladder, to a position higher in the abdominal cavity, above the bladder. Women often report that they feel best during the second trimester.

Third Trimester

Sleeping becomes problematic again in the third trimester. The fetus is again going through a period of rapid growth, sapping much of the woman's energy. Pregnant women also tire more easily from carrying the weight of the larger fetus. Sleep is disrupted by backaches, frequent urination, heartburn, cramping of the legs, discomfort, and shortness of breath. Some women find that the time when they are finally settling down for the night is when the baby decides to rev up. Women often complain that if the baby would just stop moving and kicking them in the ribs, they could get some sleep. The result of all of this is that women in the last trimester of pregnancy often take longer to fall asleep at night, are awake more frequently during the night, and take longer to fall back to sleep following waking.

Additionally, pregnant women are more likely to develop other sleep disorders. Studies have shown that as pregnancy progresses, women are apt to begin snoring and develop sleep apnea (see Chapter 14). After the twentieth week of pregnancy, restless legs syndrome may develop, also interfering with the ability to fall asleep at night.

Reminders

- Many adults have sleep problems.
- To combat sleep problems, make sleep a priority in your life and develop good sleep hygiene.
- Common drugs and medications can affect your sleep.
- Sleep during pregnancy can be problematic.

"I'M SO TIRED"
Common Adult Sleep Disorders

―――――――――☾――――――――

The baby is finally sleeping, but now my husband's snoring is keeping me up.

―――――――――✴――――――――

As we have seen, there is a wide array of problems that can affect the sleep of your baby. But, as all too many of us know, many of these problems persist into adulthood or even develop in adults. Whether it is your own insomnia or the snoring of your partner keeping you awake at night, you are well aware of the problems adults can have sleeping through the night.

The problem of adult sleep disorders is as common as those seen in infants and toddlers. Unfortunately, while an estimated 40 million adults suffer from chronic sleep disorders, fewer than 5 percent of these individuals have their problem diagnosed and treated. Common adult sleep disorders include sleep apnea, restless legs syndrome, periodic limb movements in sleep, narcolepsy, and insomnia.

Do You Have a Sleep Disorder?

This can be a difficult question to answer. Most people do not realize that they have a sleep disorder, or they believe that it is simply the way they are. To determine whether you have a sleep disorder, ask yourself the following questions. Do you have problems falling asleep at night or staying asleep? Are you sleepy during the day? If you answered yes to either of these two questions, you may have a sleep disorder. But first you need to be sure that you are getting enough sleep or at least trying to get enough sleep. To be sure, you need to be in bed at least eight hours at night. If you are not in bed for an adequate number of hours every night, you need to first try to get enough sleep. If you are getting enough sleep and are still having problems sleeping or are sleepy during the day, then you could possibily be suffering from a sleep disorder. The only way to really know if you have a problem is to be evaluated at a sleep disorders center. To find an accredited sleep disorders center near you, contact the American Sleep Disorders Association at (507) 287–6006.

Which Sleep Disorder Do You Have?

Again, the best way to know which sleep disorder you have is to go to a sleep disorders center and be evaluated by a trained sleep specialist. An overnight sleep study (see below for a complete explanation) may also be necessary to diagnose your problem. Without a sleep study it is not possible to identify the problem or the severity of the disorder. It would be like not having blood test results if a doctor suspects that you are anemic. You cannot know without the definitive results.

Assessment of Sleep Disorders

A thorough evaluation of a sleep disorder involves a number of steps. The first step is an extensive interview where the doctor will gather information about your sleep history. The doctor will probably ask you every possible question about your sleep:

about the time you go to bed, how long it takes you to fall asleep, whether you wake up during the night, and what time you wake up in the morning. You will be asked about any naps that you take. You will also be asked about any behaviors that occur in your sleep, such as snoring, restless sleep, and sleep talking. If the doctor suspects a specific sleep disorder, you will be asked extensively about typical symptoms experienced (these will be discussed shortly). If you share a bed with someone, that person may also be asked some questions. For example, you may not be aware that you snore or talk in your sleep.

You will also be asked a number of questions that are indirectly related to sleep. For example, you will be questioned about evening activities such as television watching and bedtime routines. You will also be asked about what occurs during a typical day, such as daytime sleepiness, meals, caffeine intake, and feelings of anxiety and depression. A complete medical history will also be taken, which will include questions about major illnesses and hospitalizations, any medications that you are currently taking, and your overall health.

The second step in the evaluation of sleep problems is to keep a sleep diary. A typical sleep diary includes information on the time you went to bed, how long it took you to fall asleep, how often and how long you were awake during the middle of the night, the time you woke up in the morning, your total sleep time, and the length and time of naps. You will likely be asked to keep sleep diaries for at least two weeks, but possibly longer. It is important that these diaries are accurate, as they help to diagnose your problem and to assess whether any prescribed treatments are working.

In cases where there is a concern about an underlying physiological problem such as sleep apnea or periodic limb movements in sleep (PLMS), the doctor is likely to schedule a polysomnography (PSG). A PSG usually involves sleeping overnight at a sleep center, although sometimes these tests are conducted at home. If you are to stay overnight at a sleep center, you will be asked to arrive two to three hours prior to your normal bedtime.

(A parent or other adult is usually allowed to stay with children or adolescents who are being tested.) A technician will tape or glue to your skin a number of sensors and monitors that will measure heart rate, breathing rate, leg movements, eye movements, and brain waves. These measurements will help evaluate when you fall asleep, the stages of sleep that you are in, and whether or not you have a sleep disorder. You will also be monitored all night by a technician, and your sleep will be recorded by an infrared video camera. "How in the world am I going to sleep?" you ask. That is a concern for everyone. Surprisingly, almost everyone sleeps, although some people feel that they do not get as much sleep as usual.

In addition to a PSG, you may be asked to have a multiple sleep latency test (MSLT). This test, which is performed the day following the overnight study, will evaluate your level of sleepiness during the day. The MSLT consists of four twenty-minute naps taken at two-hour intervals. So if you wake up in the morning at 8:00 A.M., you will be asked to lie down and try to fall asleep at 10:00 A.M., noon, 2:00 P.M., and 4:00 P.M. The test measures how long it takes you to fall asleep. If you fall asleep, you will be awakened after fifteen to twenty minutes. If you do not fall asleep, you will be asked to get out of bed after twenty minutes.

After obtaining all of the above information, a diagnosis will be made and a treatment plan developed.

Below is an overview of the most common and most disruptive sleep disorders experienced by people. You should realize, though, that there are over eighty different sleep disorders, and therefore the sleep problem you are experiencing may not be one of those discussed below.

Snoring

My husband's snoring is driving me crazy. What causes it and what can he do?

Snoring occurs only when a person is asleep. It is caused by the flapping of the airway muscles, which become relaxed during sleep. Once the muscles of the neck become relaxed, there is a tendency for the muscles of the airway to vibrate when breathing. Most snoring occurs when the person is inhaling.

Snoring can be incredibly loud. Just ask anybody who lives with a snorer. To give you some perspective, loud snoring may reach 80 decibels. Normal speech is only 40 decibels. A baby crying is about 60 decibels. Eighty decibels is similar to a large dog barking. Some people's snoring is so loud that the noise they generate exceeds government standards for noise in the workplace.

Men are twice as likely to snore as women. This may be related to a protection factor by female hormones. After menopause, when female hormone production diminishes, women are just as likely to snore as men. About 25 percent of all men snore, and the likelihood of snoring increases with age. By middle age (forty-one to sixty-five), almost 60 percent of men snore. The most likely reason that snoring becomes more prevalent as the person gets older is that there is a loss of muscle tone in the muscles of the throat.

Several factors contribute to snoring. First, someone with a small airway (caused by enlarged tonsils or a large neck) is more likely to snore. That is also the reason many overweight people snore. Obesity leads to a constriction of the airway. A second common cause is mouth breathing. People who snore almost always breathe through their mouths during sleep. Third, a number of drugs and medications can lead to snoring. Sleeping pills, alcohol, and other sedatives all can relax the muscles in the area of the throat, causing an increase in snoring. Hay fever and colds can lead to snoring since nasal congestion can force the person to breathe through his mouth.

Snoring should not be ignored. Some people believe that snoring is a sign of being a "good sleeper." This is absolutely not true. Snoring isn't normal, and people shouldn't snore. For some people snoring isn't harmful, although it can cause problems for other people in the household. Many couples sleep in separate bedrooms because one person's snoring chases the other out of the bedroom.

For others, however, snoring can actually be dangerous. Snoring can be a sign that the person has sleep apnea (which is discussed below). A way to tell if a person who snores has sleep apnea is to determine if the person has daytime sleepiness. People with sleep apnea are very sleepy during the day. A snorer who isn't very sleepy may be just a snorer.

Even if the snoring is not affecting the person's health, treatment may still be sought, especially on the encouragement of the bed partner who isn't getting any sleep. There are hundreds of devices available that claim to stop snoring. Most try to keep the mouth closed or open the nasal airway. Such devices include bandages that go over the nose (such as Breathe Right) or prongs that widen the nose. Other devices try to keep the sleeper off his or her back, since many people snore only when on their back. An easier and cheaper method is simply to sew a pocket onto the back of a pajama top or T-shirt and place a tennis ball in it. Other more elaborate and expensive methods include alarms that go off when the person rolls over onto his or her back.

There are some excellent dental devices available that also help with snoring. Be careful about substituting an athletic mouth guard for a proper dental device because there can be problems with difficulty breathing. For some, snoring is so bad that they opt for surgery. The two most common surgical techniques include the removal of the tonsils and adenoids or a uvulopalatopharyngoplasty (UPPP), which removes much of the tissue in the airway.

Sleep Apnea

———————— C ————————

Steve is forty-four years old and has been snoring for ten years. His snoring has gotten much worse over the past two years, and now many nights his wife ends up sleeping in the guest room because his snoring is so loud. His wife says that many times throughout the night Steve seems to stop breathing. In the morning he often wakes up with a headache, which goes away after a few hours. And even after getting eight hours of sleep at night, Steve still feels terrible during the day. He is always sleepy and feels lethargic. He often naps during his lunch hour.

Steve is a classic example of someone who has sleep apnea, a disorder in which a person has repetitive episodes of upper airway obstruction during sleep. This means that numerous times throughout the night a person stops breathing because his airway closes. These events cause frequent arousals and awakenings during the night. To receive a diagnosis of sleep apnea, someone must stop breathing at least 5 times per hour. However, most stop breathing many more times than that. For example, there are some people who stop breathing over 150 times per hour. Basically, these people can't sleep and breathe at the same time.

The concern many people have about apnea is that they are going to die in their sleep. This will not happen. The body is incredible. Immediately after the person stops breathing, the brain will tell the body to wake up, and breathing will resume. The more immediate concern is the excessive sleepiness that occurs during the day and the dangers that can go along with it, such as falling asleep while driving. A more long-term concern is that the individual is at much greater risk for heart disease and early death. Basically, the body does not react well to repeated lapses in breathing.

The typical person with sleep apnea is an overweight, middle-aged man, but many others do get sleep apnea. Women get sleep apnea but are much more at risk for it after menopause. Thin people also get sleep apnea. But even though weight is often a determining factor, the heaviest person may not have sleep apnea whereas the skinniest person may.

Symptoms of Sleep Apnea

Some people will have all of the symptoms listed below, whereas someone else will have only a few. Most people with sleep apnea don't even know that they have a problem. Usually it is the bed partner who suspects a problem or is so bothered by it that he or she forces the person to seek help.

- *Snoring.* Most adults with sleep apnea snore. Not all snorers, though, have sleep apnea. Snoring is caused when the muscles of the airway relax during sleep. When the muscles become relaxed they have a tendency to flap (like a sail not pulled taut in the wind). Snoring is the sound of the muscles flapping. Most people with sleep apnea snore every night and throughout the night. Snoring is more likely to occur when lying on your back, but can occur in any sleep position. Many people are not even aware that they snore unless others tell them (including the neighbors). Other snore so loud that they even wake themselves.

- *Breathing pauses.* Sleep apnea is characterized by breathing pauses. A person will stop breathing anywhere from just a few seconds to, at the most, forty-five seconds. To start breathing again the person must first wake up.

- *Daytime sleepiness.* The one symptom that is almost universal to sleep apnea, and the only one these individuals are often aware of, is daytime sleepiness. The daytime sleepiness is caused by the numerous arousals throughout the night. It is almost like being awakened by your baby every five minutes throughout the entire night. People with sleep apnea may be so sleepy that they fall asleep during sex, while driving, and even in the midst of conversations.

- *Coughing and choking during sleep.* Some people with sleep apnea find that they wake up during the night coughing and choking.

- *Dry mouth.* Many people with sleep apnea wake up with a dry mouth. This is because they are breathing and snoring with their mouth open.

- *Morning headaches.* Another common symptom of sleep apnea is a headache in the morning. This is caused by the decrease in oxygen to the brain throughout the night. Usually by mid-morning the headache has gone away.

- *Restless sleep.* Because of the frequent arousals throughout the night, a person with sleep apnea often appears to be a restless sleeper. With each arousal the person may move his legs or turn over. In addition, the person may find his bedcovers are all over the bed when he wakes in the morning.

  Other common symptoms include:

- *Insomnia.* Surprisingly, some people with sleep apnea complain of insomnia. Although they are extremely sleepy and tired, they are unable to fall asleep at night. This is because they stop breathing as they are falling asleep. When the breathing pause occurs, they have an arousal and wake up. The "insomnia" is, thus, caused by the breathing problems.

- *Impotence.* Impotence has been found to be related to sleep apnea in some men. Once the apnea is treated, the impotence problems often go away.

- *Daytime problems.* Another common complaint of people with sleep apnea is that they don't feel that they function well during the day. They may become forgetful. They may feel irritable, anxious, or depressed.

Treatment of Sleep Apnea

There are a number of treatment options available. The best treatment for you will depend on the severity of your sleep apnea, what is contributing to your symptoms, and what will work best for you. Some of these treatments are similar to those mentioned above for snoring.

Continuous positive airway pressure (CPAP). For most people with sleep apnea, CPAP is the treatment of choice. CPAP is a machine that has a mask attached to it. There are two types of masks, one that is worn over the nose and one with pillows that are placed in the nose. The purpose of CPAP is to keep the airway open so that normal breathing can occur. The CPAP machine generates air pressure, and this air pressure is forced down the nose, causing the airway to stay open. CPAP machines can be set at different pressures. An overnight test will need to be conducted at a sleep center to find a pressure that is optimal for you, one that gets rid of snoring, decreases apnea, and does not interfere with your sleep. A typical CPAP machine costs between $1,000 and $1,500, and many insurance companies will pay for it as part of your medical coverage.

Surgery. There are a number of surgical options available to treat sleep apnea. In a tracheotomy, the only treatment option known up to ten years ago, an incision is made into the airway through the neck, and a breathing tube is inserted. By bypassing the back of the mouth and upper portions of the throat, breathing can occur normally through the tube. Although tracheotomies are very effective, they are rarely performed for sleep apnea anymore because other, less invasive treatments have become available for this disorder.

In some instances the removal of the tonsils and/or adenoids can be effective. This surgery is usually done on children with sleep apnea and is the treatment of choice for them. In adults, this procedure is performed if it is clear that the person's tonsils or adenoids are enlarged and are obviously contributing to the problem. It is generally effective if the person has very mild apnea, but it may also benefit some cases of moderate to severe apnea. An ENT (ear, nose, and throat) specialist will evaluate you for this type of surgery.

For some individuals sleep apnea is caused by a severely deviated septum (that is, the wall that divides the nasal passages is crooked), and surgery to correct this abnormality can solve the problem. An ENT doctor will provide expertise in this area.

A surgery that is becoming more common in the treatment of sleep apnea is called a uvulopalatopharyngoplasty, otherwise known as a UPPP. This surgery, typically done by laser but also done surgically, removes excess tissue in the airway, including the tonsils. This widens the opening of the airway so that no obstructions occur, and the person can breathe normally while sleeping. This surgery can be conducted on an outpatient basis, but it does not work for everyone. It works best for those with mild to moderate sleep apnea and is effective in about 50 to 70 percent of individuals.

Dental appliance. As in the treatment for snoring, some people with mild to moderate sleep apnea benefit from a dental appliance. Similar to that used for people who grind their teeth in their sleep, this appliance is worn at night, and it moves the lower jaw slightly forward. Moving the jaw forward helps keep the airway open and will decrease both snoring and sleep apnea. The use of a dental appliance on a nightly basis does not cause any jaw problems, which is a common concern. A dentist or orthodontist usually fits this device, which can be expensive, costing anywhere from $300 to $1,500. Unfortunately, most medical insurance will not cover the cost.

Weight loss. Weight is often a contributor to sleep apnea. For some people a difference of even five pounds can increase or decrease sleep apnea. Five pounds less, and the sleep apnea goes away. Five pounds more, and it comes back. For these people simple weight loss can solve the problem. For people who are more overweight, weight loss will help decrease apnea, and enough weight loss can also treat the problem. In the meantime, however, additional treatments are recommended.

Sleep position. For those people who snore and have apnea only when sleeping on their backs, sleeping in any other position will often treat the problem. There are many devices on the market that are geared toward preventing people from sleeping on their backs. The easiest solution, however, as previously mentioned, is to sew a pocket onto the back of a pajama top or T-shirt and place a tennis ball in it. Then, when you roll onto your back and get jabbed by the tennis ball, you will roll back over onto your side or stomach. This easy solution can solve the problem for some people.

Tongue retaining device (TRD). This unpleasant sounding device pulls the tongue forward using suction. The device looks like a mouth guard with a space for the tongue to be pulled forward. When sleeping on your back, the tongue relaxes back into the airway. Pulling the tongue forward keeps the airway open. As you might expect, wearing such a device is not very comfortable, but it may be worth a try.

Medication. Some people can be helped by a medication that stimulates breathing. The most commonly prescribed drug of this type is protriptyline. This drug keeps the person in lighter stages of sleep, in which apnea is least likely to be troublesome. Although these drugs are beneficial for treating sleep apnea, they do affect sleep.

If allergies or nasal congestion cause your sleep apnea, drugs that reduce these symptoms can help you sleep. Although over-the-counter medications can help, it is best to discuss these problems with your doctor.

What Not to Do

First of all, sleep apnea is a serious problem that should not be ignored. Unfortunately, many people do ignore it because they don't know they have it or discount it since they think "everyone snores." However, it is important to avoid certain courses of action.

- *Don't take sleeping pills.* If you are having a difficult time falling asleep, you may be inclined to take a sleeping pill. This could backfire on you. Sleeping pills can make sleep apnea significantly worse because they will relax the muscles that you use to breathe even more. The more relaxed the muscles, the worse sleep apnea will be. Therefore, sleeping pills can be dangerous and can cause you even more sleeping problems.

- *Exercise caution when using any form of sedative, tranquilizer, antihistamine, or painkiller.* If you think that you have sleep apnea and are taking these types of medication for anxiety, allergies, or pain, be sure to discuss this with your doctor. These medications may make your sleep apnea worse.

- *Avoid alcohol.* Alcohol is sedating and makes sleep apnea worse. Not only does alcohol increase sleep apnea, but it also interferes with sleep. Although alcohol may help a person fall asleep faster, it can lead to waking in the middle of the night and early morning rising. It also makes a person sleep lighter, getting less deep sleep than is needed.

- *Reduce caffeine intake.* Caffeine is a stimulant that can interfere with falling asleep. However, for many people, caffeine becomes part of a vicious cycle. These people are sleep deprived from the sleep apnea, leading to daily sleepiness. They take caffeine to stay awake, which makes it more difficult to fall asleep the next night. The cycle then continues the next day and the next. In the long run, if the sleep apnea is treated, the sleepiness and need for caffeine will be reduced.

Restless Legs Syndrome and Periodic Limb Movements in Sleep

Two sleep disorders that are often related are restless legs syndrome (RLS), which interferes with falling asleep, and periodic limb movements in sleep (PLMS), which can also interfere with going to sleep but primarily leads to frequent wakings during the night.

Restless Legs Syndrome

RLS is characterized by an uncomfortable "crawling" feeling in the legs, usually below the knee, when the person lies down to go to sleep. This uncomfortable feeling is alleviated by moving the legs while still in bed or leaving the bed to walk or pace. Unfortunately, the symptoms return when you stop moving. The result is difficulty falling asleep and insomnia. This feeling is often difficult to describe, but some people say that it is like "worms crawling" or that it is "creepy-crawly," or they use words like "prickling," "tickling," and "itching." In addition, RLS symptoms can occur at any time of the day, resulting in problems when sitting for long periods or driving. No one knows what exactly causes RLS, although in some people it is related to a deficiency of iron or low levels of folic acid. It is also not known why some people have RLS symptoms one night and not another.

RLS is relatively common, affecting about 5 to 15 percent of adults. RLS is more common in women than men and can be associated with pregnancy (11 percent of pregnant women have RLS, which usually appears after the twentieth week). And many people with RLS also suffer from PLMS (although the opposite is not always true).

Periodic Limb Movements in Sleep

PLMS is a condition in which a person's limbs, usually the legs, repetitively jerk or kick during sleep. If you have this disorder, you may complain that your legs often jerk, and anyone who shares your bed will report that you kick in your sleep. People with PLMS often find that they are restless sleepers, and their bed is often a mess in the morning. These people typically complain of insomnia, either because they can't fall asleep or because they wake frequently. PLMS is similar to apnea in that people with these disorders often are unaware of their problem, other than the resulting daytime sleepiness and/or insomnia that may result. As with RLS, PLMS may be related to an iron deficiency or low levels of folic acid. But for most people there is no clear reason for the sleep disorder.

In contrast to RLS, an equal number of men and women get PLMS. Although we don't know exactly how many people have PLMS, we do know that the prevalence increases with age. For example, 34 percent of individuals over the age of sixty experience PLMS.

Treatment

For those people whose RLS or PLMS is related to an iron deficiency (anemia) or low levels of folic acid (which can be detected with a simple blood test), the treatment is simply taking iron or folic acid supplements. For most people, however, medications are prescribed, such as clonazepam (Klonopin), clonidine (Catapres), and temazepam (Restoril). In addition, it is known that caffeine makes RLS and PLMS much worse. Therefore, cutting back or eliminating caffeine may help. Finally, getting adequate sleep will also help, because sleep deprivation will make these problems worse.

One unusual and disturbing situation associated with RLS and PLMS is that the medications for these disorders often make other sleep disorders worse. In turn, the treatments for many other sleep disorders often make RLS or PLMS worse. For example, Klonopin, while it may solve the RLS or PLMS problem, will make sleep apnea worse. Likewise, if an antidepressant is prescribed to alleviate narcolepsy, it can make PLMS worse. It is therefore important that a person recognize all of their sleep disorders and that the proper combination of treatments be utilized.

Narcolepsy

———— ✷ ————

David is thirty-eight years old. He is always sleepy. Even as far back as the ninth grade he remembers falling asleep in class on a regular basis. He is afraid to drive because he has already had one near accident from falling asleep at the wheel. His wife and his boss are frustrated with him because he keeps falling asleep. The other day he even fell asleep in the middle of an important meeting with a new client.

———— ✷ ————

David has narcolepsy, a relatively rare disorder that can significantly interfere with a person's ability to function. Although there is no "cure" for narcolepsy, it can be treated, and people with this disorder can lead normal lives.

Narcolepsy usually begins during adolescence, although there have been a few documented cases of its occurring before puberty. Symptoms can appear all at once or can develop slowly over years. Narcolepsy is often referred to as "sleeping sickness," although the way it is often portrayed on television, with someone constantly falling asleep whether standing up, sitting down, or even while playing baseball, is not correct.

Symptoms of Narcolepsy

There are four major symptoms of narcolepsy, although not everyone with narcolepsy has all of these symptoms.

1. *Excessive daytime sleepiness.* This is usually the first symptom, and for some people the only symptom, of narcolepsy. People with narcolepsy may feel sleepy all the time or just frequently throughout the day. They may feel sleepy at times that other people feel sleepy, such as after a heavy meal or during a boring lecture, but they also feel sleepy at those times when normal people wouldn't, such

as during an exciting movie, while talking on the tele-phone, or while driving. If a person with narcolepsy takes a short nap when feeling sleepy, he usually feels refreshed afterward.

2. *Cataplexy.* Cataplexy refers to brief episodes of sudden loss of muscle control. The feeling can be mild with just weakness in the knees, or it can be severe with complete loss of muscle control leading to a fall. Cataplexy is trig-gered by a strong emotion, such as laughter, surprise, anger, or anxiety. Some people just simply have to think about an emotional event, and they will have cataplexy. Cataplexy only occurs with narcolepsy; that is, if someone has cataplexy, then he definitely has narcolepsy. Cataplexy can be the first symptom of narcolepsy or may develop years later, or not at all.

3. *Sleep paralysis.* This occurs when a person is waking up or falling asleep. It is a feeling that the person is unable to move or speak. Sleep paralysis usually lasts for only a few moments, but to the affected person it can feel endless. If the person is touched by another, the sleep paralysis will disappear. Some people refer to sleep paralysis as "witch riding," the belief that a witch is sitting on the person's chest. And while it may be associated with narcolepsy, many people who do not have narcolepsy experience sleep paralysis.

4. *Hypnagogic hallucinations.* These also occur when a per-son is waking up or falling asleep. These are dreamlike events that are difficult to distinguish from reality. The person is awake but seeing or hearing images or sounds. Often these dreams are mistaken for the hallucinations of someone who is schizophrenic. People other than those with narcolepsy experience this phenomenon, especially when sleep deprived.

In addition to these four major symptoms, individuals with narcolepsy may also experience other symptoms.

1. *Automatic behavior.* This is the performance of routine tasks without the person's being aware of doing it. These activities can include such simple things as folding laundry or having a conversation. They can occur at times that are potentially dangerous, such as when driving a car or cooking. Sometimes the person does something inappropriate, such as putting dishes into the washing machine rather than the dishwasher. The person has no recollection of doing these automatic behaviors.

2. *Disturbed nighttime sleep.* Surprisingly, although individuals with narcolepsy may feel sleepy all day and even have difficulty staying awake, their nighttime sleep may be disturbed. People with narcolepsy can wake frequently during the night, adding to the problem of their daytime sleepiness.

3. *Dreaming during naps.* Most people do not dream when taking a short nap, less than thirty minutes. Individuals with narcolepsy typically will dream. In addition, someone with narcolepsy finds a short nap refreshing, whereas others may feel groggy upon waking up.

4. *Impaired functioning.* Because of the excessive daytime sleepiness, many individuals with narcolepsy have impaired functioning; that is, they may feel lethargic all the time, are unable to concentrate at school or at work, and even have memory problems. Narcolepsy can definitely interfere with school or work performance, and it usually takes a toll on marriages and families if not diagnosed and treated.

What Causes Narcolepsy?

The exact cause of narcolepsy is still not known. What is known is that it tends to run in families, indicating a potential genetic link. If someone is diagnosed with narcolepsy, there is often a parent, grandparent, or aunt or uncle with the same problems, although not always. Keep in mind that narcolepsy is not always diagnosed.

The symptoms of narcolepsy apparently involve the regions of the central nervous system that control sleeping and waking. Many of these symptoms are caused by what is called "REM intrusion." As you may recall from Chapter 2, there are two major stages of sleep, non-REM and REM. REM sleep is characterized by dreaming and muscle paralysis. People with narcolepsy keep moving into REM, as if their body doesn't get enough of it and needs more of it or because the central nervous system switch is unable to suppress REM.

Treatment

As mentioned above, there is no known cure for narcolepsy. Instead, the treatment of narcolepsy focuses on managing the disorder in the following ways.

Medication. Many people with narcolepsy try to treat themselves, often without realizing it, by ingesting large quantities of caffeine. There are some who will drink twelve cups of coffee, two liters of caffeinated coke, and a gallon of iced tea in one day. Others will take over-the-counter medications such as No-Doz. This system does not work well and can interfere with nighttime sleep, which doesn't help the daytime sleepiness. A better method is developing a medication regimen with a physician. Medications can be given to decrease daytime sleepiness and to help control cataplexy. Two medications that are commonly prescribed for daytime sleepiness are Cylert and Ritalin. Drugs used to control cataplexy are often antidepressants, including imipramine or desipramine; they are prescribed not because the person is depressed but because they suppress REM, the cause of cataplexy.

Lifestyle management. There are some changes in lifestyle that can help individuals with narcolepsy control their disorder. The following suggestions are often extremely helpful:

- Get a good night's sleep. This includes having a good sleep schedule. Go to bed and get up at the same time every day.

- Nap on a schedule. Take one to two short naps every day to help feel alert and refreshed.

- Avoid tasks or jobs that are repetitive or boring. The more physical and active the job the better.

- Avoid driving or other dangerous activities, such as swimming or riding a bicycle, when sleepy.

Provide information and educate. It is very important that your family, friends, and coworkers know and understand your narcolepsy. Do not try to hide it because others will notice. Rather than attribute your sleepiness to a sleep disorder, they will often believe that you are lazy, bored, insolent, or depressed. Some will even think that you have a psychiatric or psychological problem. So be sure to inform people. If your adolescent has narcolepsy, make sure that all teachers are informed and educated.

Seek support from a support group. There are many others out there who also have narcolepsy. A list is provided in the back of this book that will help you find a local support group in your area. If there isn't one available, start one.

Insomnia

———————————— ☾ ————————————

For the past few years Stephanie has been having problems falling asleep at night. Every night she gets into bed at 11:00. She then tosses and turns until about 12:30 when she finally gets frustrated and goes downstairs to watch television. She usually returns to bed at about 1:00, finally falling asleep between 2:00 and 3:00. When her alarm goes off at 7:15, she feels as if she could sleep for another few hours. She says that she walks around like a zombie all day, both looking forward to and dreading going to bed again that night.

---✱---

Insomnia usually begins during a person's late twenties or early thirties. Many people go for years before ever seeking help, and many simply treat themselves by using drugs or alcohol to help them sleep at night and by drinking a great deal of caffeine during the day to combat their sleepiness.

Symptoms

There are two primary symptoms of insomnia.

1. **Difficulty sleeping.** People with insomnia have problems sleeping, whether that is falling asleep at night, waking in the middle of the night, or waking up too early in the morning and not being able to return to sleep.

2. **Daytime fatigue.** The result of not getting a good night's sleep is being tired during the day. This can lead to a significant impact on daytime functioning at home, on the job, and socially. Although people with insomnia often feel fatigued, they usually are not excessively sleepy.

Other symptoms include:

· **Effects on mood.** Many people with insomnia feel depressed or anxious. They may be irritable and have little energy.

· **Decreased attention and concentration.** As a result of the sleep deprivation caused by insomnia, some people will have problems with concentration at work or at school, especially when listening to a lecture or in a meeting.

What Causes Insomnia?

Insomnia can have many different causes. It is different from the other sleep disorders discussed because it can be the result of many things. Again, it is important to understand that not all people who have problems sleeping actually have insomnia. Many other sleep disorders, such as sleep apnea and restless legs syndrome, interfere with a person's ability to fall asleep and thus are experienced as insomnia. For those who do have insomnia that is not the result of another sleep disorder, it can be the result of many factors. For example, some people have insomnia as the result of anxiety or depression. However, most people's insomnia is learned. Something happens that interferes with a person's sleep, whether it is the birth of a baby, illness, pain, or shift work. Once the sleep becomes disturbed, it continues to be problematic because there is a continued association between sleeplessness and situations and behaviors that are associated with sleep, such as lying in bed. Then lying in bed where you just spent several sleepless nights will cause conditioned arousal. This arousal will continue the problem of having difficulty sleeping. Once the pattern is established it can continue for months or years.

An additional problem for some is an exaggerated concern with the inability to sleep. This is experienced by many insomniacs and also leads to a vicious cycle: The more you try to sleep, the more agitated you will become and the less likely you will be able to fall asleep. Trying too hard to fall asleep can simply add to the problem.

Treatment

The best treatment for insomnia depends on what is causing the problem. For example, if the problem is a result of depression or anxiety, then the best treatment is psychotherapy or medication, such as an antidepressant or antianxiety drug. In addition, it is important to find out whether another sleep disorder, such as sleep apnea or restless legs syndrome, is causing you to have problems falling asleep. What will feel like insomnia to you may actually be another problem. If this is the case, treating the actual sleep disorder will cure the problem.

If your insomnia is not caused by depression, anxiety, or another sleep disorder but involves some other disturbance of your normal sleep routine, a number of options may be considered:

Medication. Many people try medication for insomnia. Some of the more common ones are Halcion, Restoril, and Ambien. The best choices are short-acting drugs that do not interfere with your daytime functioning. Drugs to help you sleep at night are not good long-term solutions, however. They should be phased out after a maximum of two to three weeks (see Chapter 13 for why drugs are not always the answer).

Relaxation. Research has shown that relaxation training is effective in 45 percent of cases. You can learn to relax using a number of different techniques, including progressive muscle relaxation, guided imagery, and meditation. Several methods are covered in Chapter 8. There are also several good books available to teach you ways to relax.

Hot bath. A twenty-minute hot bath taken two hours before bedtime can often help you to sleep. The hot bath affects body temperature, which makes you tired and helps to prolong deeper natural sleep. Be careful about hot baths if you have any circulatory disorders. If this is the case, consult your physician first.

Keep a strict sleep schedule. It is best to maintain a strict sleep schedule in which you go to bed at the same time every night and wake up at the same time every morning.

Don't stay in bed too long. One problem that people often have is staying in bed too long. Don't stay in bed nine or ten hours if you need only eight hours of sleep. It is better to be in bed only the exact number of hours that you need sleep. This is called sleep restriction. It will consolidate your sleep, especially if you have long periods of being awake in the middle of the night or wake too early in the morning. To do this, you will need to keep a sleep diary to determine how much you actually sleep. Many people believe that they sleep less than they actually do. By keeping a sleep diary for two weeks you can figure out the average amount of time you sleep per night. Then for the first five to seven days limit the time you are in bed to the average number of hours that you actually slept for the past two weeks. Once you are sleeping the entire time that you are in bed, gradually increase the amount of time that you allow yourself to sleep. Increase this time by small amounts, anywhere from fifteen to thirty minutes. This method will help consolidate your sleep and will help you associate your bed with sleep. This process can take a few days to several months to accomplish. The one side effect that you need to be aware of is that you may be sleepy during the day from the initial sleep deprivation.

Don's sleep diaries showed that he was going to bed at 11:00 every night but not falling asleep until 12:30. He would then wake at 7:00 every morning. He averaged six and a half hours of sleep every night. To start sleep restriction, he limited himself to being in bed only six and a half hours a night for one week. By the end of that week he was sleeping the entire time that he was in bed. He then gradually increased the amount of time that he was in bed, starting with six hours and forty-five minutes and adding fifteen minutes every few nights. It took him several weeks to get to the eight hours that he believed he needed, but he found that he was now falling asleep quickly and sleeping the entire time that he was in bed.

Stimulus control. If you are not asleep within twenty minutes, it is best to get out of bed and do something relaxing out of the bedroom (if you have a separate bedroom). Read a book, watch television, or do something else relaxing, then go back to bed. Again, if you are not asleep within twenty minutes, get up. Keep repeating this cycle until you fall asleep.

Reduce alcohol and drug use. Alcohol and drugs interfere with sleep. For someone with a drug or alcohol problem, withdrawal can occur in the middle of the night, causing the person to wake. Reducing or eliminating alcohol and drug use is beneficial to combating insomnia.

Watch the clock and stay up as long as possible. Some people get caught in a vicious cycle of trying to fall asleep and then becoming frantic. Being frantic does not help falling asleep. If this is true for you, simply watching the clock and trying to stay awake as long as possible will break this pattern. Do this for a few nights in a row, and you will learn that you can still function the next day with less sleep than you would want. You will also decrease the worry when you can't fall asleep on other nights. This suggestion, while it seems to counter all the other advice provided in this book, can be helpful for some, but it may not work for all.

Sleep hygiene. Keep good sleep hygiene. Chapter 13 provides a list of the best do's and don'ts for getting a good night's sleep.

Reminders

- Sleep disorders are experienced by 25 percent to 30 percent of all adults.

- A thorough assessment of sleep disorders will include an extensive interview concerning sleep patterns, the maintenance of a sleep diary, and possibly an overnight polysomnography.

- Snoring is a common sleep disorder that can disrupt your sleep and the sleep of others.

- Sleep apnea involves repetitive pauses in breathing during sleep and can be dangerous to your health.

- Restless legs syndrome and periodic limb movements in sleep can interfere with going to sleep and can lead to frequent wakings throughout the night.

- Narcolepsy, a rare disorder, involves excessive daytime sleepiness and other unusual symptoms.

- Insomnia involves difficulty falling asleep or maintaining sleep. It can have many different causes but is highly treatable.

- There are more than eighty diagnosed sleep disorders, with the most common ones discussed here. Don't allow a sleep problem suffered by you or someone in your family to go undiagnosed and untreated. Seek help and get treatment so that everyone gets a good night's sleep.

BABY BEDTIME BOOKS

Books for Infants

A Child's Good Night Book, Margaret Wise Brown
In this award-winning story, sheep, kangaroos, bunnies, and children all close their eyes and go to sleep.

The Going to Bed Book, Sandra Boynton
A silly book about animals going to bed on a boat. Very enjoyable.

Good Night, Baby, Clara Vulliamy
A lullaby book about bedtime for a baby.

Good Night Gorilla, Peggy Rathmann
A gorilla and all the other animals sneak out of the zoo at bedtime to all get in bed with the zookeeper's wife.

Goodnight Moon, Margaret Wise Brown
Goodnight Moon is the all-time classic book for bedtime. Many a parent says that this is the first book they ever read to their baby at bedtime.

Night, Night, Mark Burgess
A rhyming book about a bear's getting ready for bed.

Ten Bears in a Bed, John Richardson
A classic counting rhyme about ten bears in a bed, based on the children's song "Roll Over." This edition is a delightful pop-up book.

Books for Toddlers

Bedtime, Everybody, Mordicai Gerstein
A little girl, Daisy, tries to get her stuffed animals to go to bed.

Bedtime for Frances, Russell Hoban
Frances, the beloved bear, uses well-known stalling tactics at bedtime.

Dr. Seuss's Sleep Book, Dr. Seuss
Another favorite Dr. Seuss story about sleep, where everyone is yawning.

Five Little Monkeys Jumping on the Bed, Eileen Christelow
Five little monkeys get ready for bed. This book is a remake of the classic children's song.

In the Night Kitchen, Maurice Sendak
A boy has a dream about a kitchen where bakers make cakes for the morning.

Sleep Well, Little Bear, Quint Buchholz
A little bear who can't fall asleep thinks about his day and makes plans for the next, until he is ready to go to sleep.

The Napping House, Audrey Wood

A story in cumulative rhyme about a house where everyone is sleeping, including a snoozing cat, a dozing dog, and a dreaming child.

Time for Bed, Mem Fox

This book says good night to all the animals.

Time for Bed, Ruth Huddleston and Wendy Madgwick

Your child will enjoy tucking in each of the animals who fall asleep after Benny Bear's birthday party.

Wind Says Goodnight, Katy Rydell

The wind and all the animals help a little girl fall asleep.

Books for Dealing with Bedtime Fears

Go Away Big Green Monster, Ed Emberley

This award-winning book helps children deal with their nighttime fears.

My Mama Says There Aren't Any Zombies, Ghosts, Vampires, Creatures, Demons, Monsters, Fiends, Goblins, or Things, Judith Viorst

Although a little boy's mother insists that none of these things exist, he is not so sure.

There's an Alligator Under My Bed, Mercer Mayer

A boy bravely confronts the alligator that lives under his bed, one that no one else can see.

There's a Nightmare in My Closet, Mercer Mayer

A little boy discovers that the nightmare in his closet is just as scared as he is.

We're Going on a Bear Hunt, Michael Rosen and Helen Oxenbury

This children's classic is about a family going on a bear hunt insisting that "we're not scared," only to return to the safety of their bed.

Where the Wild Things Are, Maurice Sendak

A boy confronts the scary things that appear in his dreams.

Appendix B

RESOURCES FOR PARENTS

Products

Crib tent. A crib tent will keep your baby in the crib and will not allow him to climb out. It also keeps pets out. It attaches to any standard-size crib.

Side sleepers. A number of products are available to keep your baby sleeping on his side. The American Academy of Pediatrics recommends that babies should sleep on their sides or back to decrease the risk of SIDS. You can buy one of these products at almost any baby supply store, and they are also available through catalogs.

Crib sheets. Crib sheets that attach to the bars of the crib with Velcro make sheet changing much easier. Many stores that specialize in baby items carry these sheets. They are also available by catalog.

Catalogs

The following catalogs carry the above products:

Right Start Catalog
   (800) 548–8531

One Step Ahead
   (800) 274–8440

Organizations and Associations

General Sleep

American Sleep Disorders Association
   1610 14th Street, N.W., Suite 300
   Rochester, MN 55901
   (507) 287–6006
   The American Sleep Disorders Association can help you find
an accredited sleep center in your area. It also has a number of
educational materials available.

National Sleep Foundation
   1367 Connecticut Avenue, N.W.
   Suite 200
   Washington, DC 20036
   (202) 785–2300
   The National Sleep Foundation is a clearinghouse for information about sleep and sleep disorders.

Sleep Apnea

American Sleep Apnea Association
   P.O. Box 66
   Belmont, MA 02178
   (617) 489–4441
   Fax: (617) 489–4761

This organization has self-help groups throughout the United States. In addition, they publish a newsletter every two months called "WAKE UP CALL: The Wellness Letter for Snoring and Apnea." Patient education videos are also available.

National Association of Apnea Professionals (NAAP)
P.O. Box 4031
Waianae, HI 96792
(602) 239–4740
Provides information on sleep apnea in children and provides referrals.

Restless Legs

Restless Legs Syndrome Foundation, Inc.
514 Daniels Street
Box 314
Raleigh, NC 27605–1317

Narcolepsy

American Narcolepsy Association
1139 Bush Street, Suite D
San Carlos, CA 94070–2477
(415) 591–7979

SIDS

SIDS Clearinghouse
2070 Chain Bridge Road
Suite 450
Vienna, VA 22182
(703) 821–8955

SIDS Alliance
10500 Little Patuxent Parkway
Suite 420
Columbia, MD 21044
(800) 638–7437

Twins and More Groups

Mainly Multiples
(800) 388-TWIN
Distributes a catalog of products available for twins.

National Organization of Mothers of Twins Clubs (NOMOTC)
P.O. Box 23188
Albuquerque, NM 87192
(505) 275–0955
A nationwide network of parents of multiples clubs that share information and advice.

Mothers of Supertwins
P.O. Box 951
Brentwood, NY 11717
(516) 434-MOST
A support and information network for parents of triplets.

Center for Study of Multiple Birth
333 East Superior St.
Room 464
Chicago, IL 60611
Send a self-addressed, stamped envelope for a free list of resources.

Breast-feeding

Breast-feeding Support Network
330S Eagle Street
Oshkosh, WI
(414) 231–1171

La Leche League International
9616 Minneapolis Avenue
P.O. Box 1209
Franklin Park, IL 60131
(708) 455–7730
(800) 525–3243
Provides counseling, information, and referrals to local groups nationwide. Also provides information on where to rent breast pumps.

Premature Babies

Parenting Premies
P.O. Box 530
Stevens Point, WI 54481

Parents of Prematures
P.O. Box 3046
Kirkland, WA 98003
(206) 283–7466

$\mathcal{I}$ndex

active sleep. *See* REM sleep
adenoidectomy, 193
adenoids, 188, 189, 193, 201,
    256, 260
adult sleep. *See* sleep, adult
adult sleep disorders. *See* sleep
    disorders, adult
age, sleep analysis by, 22–25
alcohol, 243, 245, 263, 275
allergies, 194
American Academy of Pediatrics,
    197
American Sleep Disorders
    Association, 190, 252, 282
antidepressants, 243, 265, 272
antihistamines, 244, 263
apartment living, 134–35
aspirin, 244
attention-seeking, 81–82, 109

baby-sitters, 134, 159, 170–71
basic bedtime method, 86–90, 109
bed, 118–20, 135
    See also crib
bedroom, 35, 77–78, 120–21
    sharing a, 5, 74–75, 78,
        132–33
bed sharing, 5, 75–77, 78, 242
bedtime, establishing, 26, 63–65,
    78, 130–31

bedtime fears, 25, 82, 224–27, 233
bedtime feedings, 94–97
bedtime routines, 68–71, 78
bedtime rules, 164
bedtime snacks, 241
bedtime struggles, 79–82
bedtime transition, 71–72
behavior management, 8, 27–45,
    81–82, 100–2
benzodiazepines, 215, 243
biological disposition, and sleep
    problems, 3–4
birth of sibling, 159, 162–64
body rolling, 230
books, bedtime, 277–280
bottles, 94–96
breast-feeding, 6, 111, 285
    at bedtime, 94, 96–97
    and SIDS, 198
    and sleep, 51, 60, 121–23, 135
breathing difficulties,
    sleeping, 184, 201
breathing pauses, 184, 188, 201,
    258
bruxism. *See* teeth grinding

caffeine, 242, 245, 263, 265
cataplexy, 267, 269
central nervous system, and nar-
    colepsy, 269

choices, and behavior management, 31, 45
colic, 5, 55–58, 62
confusional arousals, 203, 219
consistency, and behavior management, 39, 41–43, 45, 100, 119
continuous positive airway pressure (CPAP), 194, 260
coping
  with difficult situations, 111–34
  with sleep disturbances, 136–57
co-sleeping, 5, 75–77, 78, 242
crib, 113–16, 159, 160
  See also bed
crib death. See Sudden Infant Death Syndrome
crib products, 116, 281
crib-to-bed transition, 159-62, 181
crying, 52–55, 61, 104–5, 134–35

daytime sleepiness, 258, 266–67, 271
death in family, 6, 179–81
deep sleep, 12
dental appliance, 256, 261
depression, 271, 272–73
developmental changes, 6
deviated nasal septum, 194, 261
diaphragmatic breathing, 154–55, 157
diet, 6, 106
diurnal sleep pattern, 16, 22
divorce, 159, 177–79, 181
dreaming. See REM sleep
drugs. See medications

ear infections, 5, 172
early risers, 127–30
ear, nose and throat (ENT) specialist, 193, 260–61
emotional aspects of sleep, 139–41
ENT specialist. See ear, nose and throat specialist
environment
  bedroom, 8, 77–78, 241–42
  change of, 8, 209
exercise, 240

falling out of bed, 161–62
fears
  bedtime, 224–27, 233
  and parasomnias, 213–14
fetal sleep patterns, 14, 26, 51
folic acid deficiency, 264, 265

gender, 5, 255, 264, 265
genetics, and narcolepsy, 268–69
getting out of bed, 118–20, 135
gradual parent removal, 103, 109
guided imagery, 155–56, 157, 273
guilt, parental, 134, 137–39, 200

head banging, 220, 230
hypnagogic hallucinations, 267

ignoring inappropriate behavior, 36–37, 45
illness, 6, 159, 172–73, 181
  See also under specific illnesses
  and childhood sleep apnea, 189
  and parasomnias, 209, 219
  and snoring, 255
inappropriate behavior, 33–41
infants, 48–62
injuries. See safety
insomnia, 239, 251, 259, 270–75, 276
iron deficiency (anemia), 264, 265

jumping out of crib, 114–16, 135

leaving the bedroom, 120–21
limits, setting, 81, 125–26, 137, 226

medications
  and children, 105–6, 110
  effects on sleep, 243–48, 250
  and insomnia, 273, 275
  and narcolepsy, 269
  and nightmares, 222
  and parasomnias, 209, 214–15, 219
  and periodic limb movements in sleep, 265
  and restless legs syndrome, 265

and sleep apnea, 262, 263
and snoring, 255
and teething, 124
meditation, 156, 273
melatonin, 247–48
menopause, 255, 256
methods
  basic bedtime, 86–90, 109
  behavior management, 28–32
  for resolving sleeping problems,
    90–106
  to stop snoring, 256
milk intolerance, 6
mouth breathing, 184, 201
multiple sleep latency test (MSLT),
  254

naps, 17–19, 23–25, 26, 100
  adult, 238–39
narcolepsy, 239, 251, 266–70,
  276, 283
nightclothes, 77–78
night feeding, 23
nightmares, 181, 185, 220–24,
  233
  versus sleep terrors, 205, 206,
    207, 208, 224
night owls, 49–51, 130–31
night terrors. *See* sleep terrors
night wakings, 16, 19–20, 26,
  79–80, 85–86, 109
  and sleep apnea, 185
  handling, 90–94, 97–100
non-REM sleep (quiet sleep),
  11–13, 14–15, 16, 17, 26
  and parasomnias, 206
  and teeth grinding, 229
nursing. *See* breast-feeding

obesity, 194, 255, 257, 261
obstacles to sleep, 158–81
organizations and associations,
  282–285
overnights, 159, 168–69

pacifiers, 53, 85, 117
painkillers, 263

parasomnias
  causes of, 208–10, 219
  dealing with, 212–14, 219
  definition, 202, 219
  features of, 205–8
  and safety, 210–11
  treatment options, 214–19
  types of, 202–5, 219
parental separation, 158–59,
  177–79, 181
parenting
  conflicting styles of, 142–43
  and guilt, 134, 137–39, 200
  single, 133–34, 135
  and sleep problems, 4–5, 17–18,
    236
  and stress, 157
periodic limb movements in sleep
  (PLMS), 251, 253, 263–64,
  264–65, 276
pillows, 24
polyphasic sleep periods, 16
polysomnography (PSG), 253–54,
  275
praise, 29
pregnancy, 248–50, 264
products, bedtime, 281–282
progressive muscle relaxation
  (PMR), 149–54, 157, 273
psychological problems
  and bedtime problems, 139
  and parasomnias, 207, 219
punishment, 33–35, 45

quality time, 29–30
questions
  and behavior management, 31,
    45
  often asked by parents,
    138–39
quiet sleep. *See* non-REM sleep

rapid-eye-movement sleep. *See*
  REM sleep
reinforcement, and behavior management, 28–31, 43–44, 119,
  226–27

relaxation, 227, 240, 273
  strategies, 149–57, 228
REM intrusion, 12, 232, 269
REM sleep (active sleep), 11, 13,
    14–15, 16, 17, 26
  and medications, 245
  and narcolepsy, 269
  and nightmares, 206, 222
  and sleep starts, 232
resource guide, 281–85
restless legs syndrome (RLS), 251,
    263–64, 265, 272, 276, 283
returning to work, 6, 174–77
rhythmic movement disorder,
    229–31, 233
rolling over in crib, 113, 135
routines
  bedtime, 68–71, 78
  daily, 65–68
rules, and behavior management,
    31–33, 45

safety
  and co-sleeping, 76
  crib, 78, 114, 115–16
  parasomnias and, 204, 161–62,
    210–12
  and rhythmic body movement,
    230–31
  saying no, 35–36
scheduled awakenings, 104, 109,
    215–19
seasonal changes, 173–74
sedatives, 263
self-soothers, 20, 26
setting limits, 81, 125–26, 137, 226
sharing a bedroom, 5, 74–75, 78,
    132–33
sibling birth, 159, 162–64
SIDS. See Sudden Infant Death
    Syndrome
signalers, 20, 26
single parenting, 133–34, 135
sleep, adult
  basics of, 236–40
  cycles, 13
  determining adequacy of, 241

effects of medication on,
    243–48, 250
  patterns, 16
  and pregnancy, 248–50
  requirements, 237
  structure, 14–15
  suggestions, 240–43
sleep, childhood,
  basics of, 11–26
  benefits of, 9, 17–18
  and chronological age, 22–25
  cycles of, 13–14
  emotional aspects of, 139–41
  function of, 2–3
  importance of, 26
  noisy, 15
  overview of, 1–10
  patterns of, 16–17, 26
  requirements, 21, 26
  stages of, 11–13, 26
  structure of, 14–16
sleep apnea, adult, 251, 253,
    256–57, 276
  and insomnia, 272
  organizations, 282–83
  symptoms of, 239, 258–59
  treatment of, 244, 259–63
sleep apnea, childhood
  assessment of, 190–93, 201
  and breathing pauses, 188
  causes of, 188, 201
  and co-sleeping, 76
  definition of, 183–84, 201
  and family history, 190
  getting help for, 190
  and night wakings, 7–8
  organizations, 282–83
  and parasomnias, 210
  prevalence of, 189–90
  risk factors for, 189
  and SIDS, 196
  symptoms of, 91, 184–187, 201
  treatment for, 193–94
sleep associations, 51, 82–85
  negative, 84–85, 94, 106, 109,
    117, 135
  positive, 84, 109, 117, 135

sleep deprivation, 138, 219, 237, 265, 271
  and nightmares, 222
  and parasomnias, 209
sleep diary, 253, 274, 275
sleep disorders, adult
  assessment of, 252–54
  prevalence of, 2, 251, 275
  specific disorders, 254–76
sleep disorders (problems), childhood
  causes of, 3–4
  determining, 6–8
  family impact, 9
  prevalence of, 2, 3, 8
  predictors of, 4–6
  specific disorders, 183–233
sleep disorders center, 193, 201, 252
sleep habits, establishing, 3, 47–181
sleeping pills, 245–46, 263
sleeping through the night, 9, 22
sleep loss, coping with, 148–49
sleep paralysis, 267
sleep position, 185, 197–98, 262
sleep starts, 231–32, 233
sleep talking (somniloquy), 232–33
sleep terrors (night terrors), 16, 185, 202, 203, 204–5, 219
  versus nightmares, 205, 206, 207, 208, 224
sleepwalking (somnambulism), 16, 203–204, 210–12, 219
snoring, 184, 201, 254–56, 258, 276
somnambulism. See sleepwalking
somniloquy. See sleep talking
soothing strategies, 60–61
spanking, 34
special occasions, 159, 171–72
stalling bedtime, 25, 125–26, 135
standing up in crib, 113–14
staying up later, 81, 109
stress
  and nightmares, 222

  and parasomnias, 209
  parental, 157
Sudden Infant Death Syndrome (SIDS), 5, 188
  causes of, 196–97
  and co-sleeping, 76
  definition, 195
  family impact, 199–200
  organizations, 283–84
  prevalence of, 195
  prevention, 194, 197–99
  risk factors, 78, 196
surgery
  for sleep apnea, 260–61
  for snoring, 256
sweating, 12, 185

teeth grinding (bruxism), 220, 227–29, 233
teething, 124
temperature, bedroom, 77
time changes, 173–74
time-out, 37–41, 45
toilet training, 124–25, 135, 160
tongue retaining device (TRD), 262
tonsillectomy, 193
tonsils, 188, 189, 193, 201, 255, 256, 260
tracheotomy, 260
tranquilizers, 244, 263
transition
  to bedtime, 71–72
  crib-to-bed, 159–62, 181
transitional objects, 73–74, 78
treats, and behavior management, 30
twins, 131–32, 135, 284

undressing in crib, 117–18
uvulopalatopharyngoplasty (UPPP), 256, 261

vacations, 158, 159, 164–67, 181
vomiting, 111, 112

weaning, 95–97, 122–23